MOMENTS IN *Time*

AMIT SARKAR

iUniverse LLC
Bloomington

MOMENTS IN TIME

Copyright © 2013 Amit Sarkar.

All rights reserved. No part of this book may be used or reproduced by any means, graphic, electronic, or mechanical, including photocopying, recording, taping or by any information storage retrieval system without the written permission of the publisher except in the case of brief quotations embodied in critical articles and reviews.

iUniverse books may be ordered through booksellers or by contacting:

iUniverse
1663 Liberty Drive
Bloomington, IN 47403
www.iuniverse.com
1-800-Authors (1-800-288-4677)

Because of the dynamic nature of the Internet, any web addresses or links contained in this book may have changed since publication and may no longer be valid. The views expressed in this work are solely those of the author and do not necessarily reflect the views of the publisher, and the publisher hereby disclaims any responsibility for them.

Any people depicted in stock imagery provided by Thinkstock are models, and such images are being used for illustrative purposes only.
Certain stock imagery © Thinkstock.

ISBN: 978-1-4917-1258-0 (sc)
ISBN: 978-1-4917-1259-7 (hc)
ISBN: 978-1-4917-1260-3 (e)

Library of Congress Control Number: 2013918996

Printed in the United States of America.

iUniverse rev. date: 12/19/2013

To my wife, Reba

An Introduction

India today is one of the fastest-growing countries. The narratives in this work, however, relate to preindependence India. Although mostly based on episodes of real life, this work may not be grouped in the genres of autobiography or memoir. Some of the chapters may even be akin to belles lettres. In telling these stories, I have strayed into the realms of history, social customs, philosophy, ethics, and even aesthetics to validate my views.

Every story has a message relevant to the time and place. I hope readers will find interest in the episodes describing the status of women in early twentieth-century India vis-à-vis social perceptions, traditions, and customs of the time. I have also discussed the secular perceptions of Sufism and the Baul sect.

Space is devoted to the concept of Viraha-Bhakti, literally meaning pangs of separation from the loved one, leading to devotion in the aspect of the ultimate love. The concept of unconditional love was first propagated and popularized by the Alavar or Alwar satint poets of Tamil country in southern India during the sixth to ninth centuries AD. Later, the concept was immortalized in the verses of Jaydeva's *Geeta Govinda* in the twelfth century AD. The Viraha-Bhakti concept formed the basis of all forms of art and culture in India. Even during the Mogul regime, Viraha-Bhakti continued to inspire and develop as the principal perception of various forms of art and culture all over India. For further reading on Viraha-Bhakti, interested readers may refer to Friedhelm Hardy's *Viraha-Bakti: The Early History of Krasna Devotion in South India* (1983) Oxford.

I have recounted my childhood experiences of World War II in my hometown. The war almost ubiquitously affected normal life and activities. In later life, I studied the sociopolitical and economic ramification of the war on India. Historically, the Indian Rebellion (Sepoy Mutiny) of 1857 shattered British rule in India. For almost a full year, Hindus and Muslims jointly rebelled to successfully inactivate British rule. They enthroned Mogul emperor Bahadur shah Zafar to revive the Mogul rule in India. Rani Lakshmi Bai of Jhansi lost her life fighting with the British during the rebellion.

The British authorities in India decided not to rely on their India-raised forces. They imported British soldiers from Britain to replace their Indian forces. The strategy adopted by the British was to create a wide rift between the Hindus and Muslims in India.

M. A. Jinnah, a successful barrister, was not really interested in politics, not to speak of leading the Muslim League for the creation of Pakistan. He joined the Home Rule movement with Annie Besant and others, and joined the Indian National Congress in 1904. He was in the moderate group and advocated Hindu-Muslim unity.

The *Swadeshi* or Self-Rule movement, also a joint movement of the Hindus and Muslims, was initiated in Bengal in the early nineteenth century. Many renowned leaders, including poet Rabindranath Tagore, took part in the movement. Gandhi was not in India at that time.

With a view to crash the movement, the British government partitioned Bengal in 1905 to isolate the Muslims from the Hindus, creating Muslim-majority East Bengal and Hindu-majority West Bengal. The Muslim League was created the next year, 1906, in Dhaka.

Nonetheless, the movement could not be quelled. Bengal had to be reunited in 1911, and the British authorities decided to shift their capital from Calcutta to Delhi. Jinnah continued to be a member of the Indian National Congress until 1920, when Gandhi took over the party's leadership with his manifesto of Ramrajya, Ramdhun, and village-based pyramid structure for the economy. Jinnah could not accept the Gandhian ideology and took over the leadership of the Muslim League at the request of the leaders of the League.

The two-nation theory was introduced by poet Sir Muhammad Iqbal. The Pakistan Resolution was moved by Choudhury Rahamat Ali in 1933 in Lahore. Jinnah, however, was firm in his belief about Hindu-Muslim unity.

In this context, it is relevant to quote Mahatma Gandhi's statement on the two-nation theory, as cited in D. G. Tendulkar's *Mahatma: Life of Mohandas Karamchand Gandhi* (1988): "The 'two-nation' theory is an untruth. The vast majority of Muslims in India are converts to I's slam or are descendants of converts. They did not become a separate nation, as soon as they became converts."

In 1942, Gandhi gave his Quit India call. Japanese forces occupied the Indian Ocean islands and were proceeding toward mainland India. Gandhi made a statement that the Japanese must be fought nonviolently. British intelligence reports interpreted the statement to mean that Gandhi and the entire Congress favored the Japanese advance. The entire leadership of Congress, including Gandhi and Pandit Jawaharlal Nehru, were arrested and kept in a high-security prison for a period of three years. Gandhi, however, was released early on grounds of health. That was the time when the Muslim League had the freedom to popularize their demand for Pakistan.

Atom bombs were dropped on Japanese cities, and the war ended abruptly. Radical national leader Subhas Chandra Bose, who organized the Indian National Army (INA) with Japanese POWs of Royal Indian armed forces and declared war against the British in India, was lost. The INA members were brought to India under arrest and were charged with treason. All political parties in India, including the Muslim League and the Hindu Mahasabha, protested against the trial and harsh punishment of the INA members. Men of the Royal Indian Navy in the ports of Karachi, Bombay, and Visakhapatnam rose in protest against the trials. Approximately 1,700 men of the Royal Indian Navy lost their lives in police action. Thousands of workers in mills in Bombay went on strike.

All these events created a cumulative effect, leading to nationwide violent and nonviolent struggle. British Prime Minister Clement Attlee felt that his administration could no longer rely on the Royal Indian forces. The British decided to quit India and grant independence to India.

A question remains unanswered. The Indian independence movement was initiated as a movement for self-determination by the Hindus and Muslims of India even before the Indian Rebellion of 1857. The British Cabinet Mission probably had no moral or legal right to decide the partition of India into India and Pakistan without a plebiscite to ascertain whether all Muslims of India wanted to separate from their Hindu brethren.

While the Indian National Congress and Gandhi called for the British to quit India, Gandhi is believed to have been opposed to the partition during independence and suggested an agreement that would have required the Congress and Muslim League to cooperate and attain independence under a provisional government. Thereafter, the question of partition could be resolved by a plebiscite in the districts with Muslim majority.

This proposal was similar to the British Cabinet Mission's first proposal, agreed upon by both the leaders of Congress and the Muslim League. But Pandit Jawaharlal Nehru, as the Congress president, declared in Bombay in a press conference that Congress had not accepted the mission's proposal of a federal India. It only accepted creation of a constituent assembly to draft a constitution. This statement triggered violence when Jinnah gave a direct action call, resulting in the historic Calcutta killing.

In his work *Nehru: The Making of India* (2006), M. J. Akbar commented that while the people of India could unite for a cause regardless of their faith, culture, or religion, the leaders could not. Was it the struggle for leadership that divided India? Akbar wrote that Jinnah on his deathbed told his sister Fatima and his personal physician Iiahi Box "the creation of Pakistan was my life's greatest blunder."

Another viewpoint is that in 1947, Joseph Stalin was the de facto leader of Soviet Russia behind the iron curtain. The Western Allies probably needed a foothold to fight a possible Russian advance in Afghanistan and further. In that context, it is interesting to cite British Field Marshal Sir Auchinleck, who satirically suggested that if Pakistan became a reality, it would need a British garrison to defend it against Afghan and maybe Russian encroachment.

Amit Sarkar
September 21, 2013

1

I vividly recall the day I got into the train to go to Calcutta for higher education, my first long-distance journey all by myself. My parents, my sisters, and my little brother all came to my hometown railway station and gave me a hearty send-off.

The signal bell rang. I took leave of my parents, hugged my sisters and my little brother, and then got into the train. My mother wiped her tears. Father gave me a smile, and my sister Anita pressed my hand and said, "Best of luck, Dada; do write letters."

The railway guard waved his green flag and blew the whistle. The locomotive hissed a volley of steam, giving a gentle pull and a clang, and the train started moving slowly. Through the window I waved to my family as long as they were visible standing on the receding platform. The train turned a corner after the distant signal, and suddenly the platform was no longer visible. The train now ran parallel to the interstate highway by the side of marshy bed of the Gadadhar River. Tall trees lined up on both sides of the railway track and the road.

Slowly, the sun slanted down the western sky. After a short run, the train came to a halt at a makeshift railway junction. It was already dark. Until the partition of the country, this particular post was a cicada-shrilling, glowworm-gleaming forest gate by the through railway line connecting Assam to the rest of the country. In fact it was a railway yard for goods trains. Railway lines brunched out up to the forest gate. Trained elephants hauled logs from the forest for loading on the railway wagons. Railway men, mahouts with their elephants, and laborers worked here only during the day. The stationmaster and his staff worked from the station house that looked like a forest bungalow.

Long-distance passenger trains did not stop here. Only local shuttle trains stopped here for the convenience of nearby villagers who wanted to commute to the bazaar in a nearby town. A lone tea-stall keeper offered travelers boiled milk-tea made in a large aluminum kettle on his indigenous bucket-stove and served in small glass tumblers called *singles*. Besides tea, he vended boiled eggs and sweet buns kept in typical glass jars. Near the tea stall, another vender offered betel nuts and *paan* leaves for chewing, bidis—smoking tobacco wrapped in *sal* leaves—and cheap cigarettes from his specially made wooden box. It had a drawer for keeping coins and currency bills. A thin rope with a smoldering light at its loose end hung from a nearby guava tree. Smokers used it to light bidis and cigarettes. As the last shuttle train moved out before sundown, the stall keepers closed up their stalls and hurried to their homes in the nearby forest village.

When high-speed mail or express trains approached the station at night, the stationmaster held out a green flag, and the signalman stood nearby with a flaming torch as the all-clear signal. Indian Railways had this arrangement for the wayside forest stations probably to scare away inquisitive black bears. After the night train passed, the forest station plunged into the quiet of darkness, except for the howling of jackals.

At the partition of India, the broad-gauge railway line from Siliguri to Calcutta was cut off because a part of the track fell in East Pakistan. Rail communication between Assam and the rest of India was completely severed. A meter-gauge line was laid to realign Assam with the rest of the country. But the line laid over the floodplains of the Teesta River valley was washed away during the next monsoon flood. Once again railway link to Assam was snapped. Thereafter, the meter-gauge line was relaid with transshipment to the existing broad-gauge line to Sealdah station in Calcutta. The new route was circuitous and time-consuming, using a river ferry to cross the Meghna River.

Consequently, the station at the forest gate became a railway junction for passengers from Western Assam to change over to the mail train to Calcutta. A new railway junction, with necessary arrangements, was nearing completion. Outside the station sprouted a country piazza offering inexpensive meals.

As the train from my hometown station arrived at the new junction, all passengers alighted from the train. The platform came alive with passengers, porters, and railway men. The electricity-lit station no longer had the creepy look of a logging yard.

During World War II, many extra and special trains ran, carrying armaments, provisions, and the allied troops to the fight against Japanese forces advancing toward the northeastern border of India. These wartime special trains disrupted normal operation of passenger and goods trains all over the railway network. Even the mail trains ran erratically, often several hours behind schedule. The war ended, but the chronic syndrome of the late-running of trains did not. The late running of trains thus became taken for granted.

On that particular evening, however, the Siliguri-bound mail train arrived at the new junction only a few hours behind time. All passengers hurriedly embarked on the train, which was already filled with travelers from Northern Assam. My porter helped me to find a place to sit in the only interclass coach of the train.

As the train resumed its run, I, like all other waiting passengers, felt a great sense of relief. I sat at the end of a berth in the longish compartment. Indian Railways, in all mail and express trains, had first class for the bosses and aristocrats, second class for the midlevel bureaucrats and small-business executives, and third class for the great multitude of common men. M. K. Gandhi traveled by third class, thereby putting a patriotic stamp on third-class travel.

Interclass was perhaps introduced as a compromise between the second and the third classes of travel and to provide some comfort to the educated middle class. These coaches had two tiers of lightly padded berths, two bathrooms at the two ends of the compartment, and electric fans. But there was no provision for reservation of seats. Spreading one's bed to sleep by night on the upper berths was on first-come, first-served basis. When I entered the compartment, all available room on the upper berths was already occupied by travelers. I managed to sit in a corner of a lower berth. After some time, I found enough space to sit comfortably.

In my compartment, everybody was cooperative and there was no inconvenience of any type. The train left the junction and gradually gained speed. Nothing outside was visible except the darkness of night. Fleeting lights of passing signal posts and lampposts of wayside railway stations appeared as the train passed these stations without stopping. From the characteristic clanking and passing shadows of truss girders, I could make out when the train was crossing bridges over rivers and ravines. Northeastern and Eastern India was full of rivers, mountain streams, and brooks. High railway bridges, many with fairly long spans, were built over the flood-prone streams running down the hills through thick rainforests. The swinging rhythm of the train and the thought that I was traveling to Calcutta animated me. I did not want to sleep. I wanted to enjoy every moment of my journey.

Slowly the day dawned. I was amazed to observe the mud-brown waters of a wayside pool shining like a sheet of tainted glass. Shadowy reflections of tall grasses rising from the marsh looked like scrawls of crayon. The train entered a dense forest. Fleeting nuances of light and shadow created intriguing arboreal patterns. From Kaziranga and Manas in Assam to Jaldapara in northern West Bengal was an extensive belt of the most spectacular range of forests that stretched up to Bhutan and East Pakistan. During the monsoon rains, swelling streams deluged the rich habitat, forcing animals to take refuge in the highlands. These rainforests had an incredible variety of trees, vines, and shrubs. The jungles also abounded in orchids, wildflowers, and birds.

The sun rose, spraying light over the forests. After a while the train crossed the forest and ran over a wide area of grassland with a silvery-blue backdrop of faraway mountain peaks. A village appeared on the scene—green paddy fields with thin borders of earthen ridges defining various geometrical patterns. In some fields, peasants cultivated their lands with plows dragged by water buffalo.

The train passed the village and entered a long cantilever bridge set on high piers. Below the bridge, a wide stream of brick-red water flowed. Fast-spinning whirlpools were visible from the train. The panorama looked awesome and wild in the pristine morning light.

The train passed spans of arched girders. I was looking to the river below. Suddenly, my eyes fell on a full-size clay image of the Hindu goddess Kali on the sandy edge of the river. She was heavily worn by rain. Yet she stood firm on legs fixed to a wooden stand. Her head was bald and the colors of her eyes and protruding tongue had been washed away. Only her earthen body had a pale bluish tint. She looked like a corpse standing on its feet. The icon had probably been immersed in the river somewhere upstream. Currents had floated her to the point below the bridge. As the water level shrank, she became stuck in the sand. But how did she end up standing on her legs? Once again I realized that nature is fantastic.

After crossing the bridge, the railway line branched into several lines. Signal posts, signal boxes with stretched cables, old and unserviceable passenger coaches, goods wagons, and railway implements on sidings suggested that we were approaching Siliguri junction. At Siliguri railway station, the train stopped for some time. The sun was now a blazing dot on the forehead of the morning sky.

Siliguri was an important station in the Darjeeling district of West Bengal. From here one could take the toy train, as the narrow-gauge train was called, or a cab or a bus and go to the picturesque hill station of Darjeeling—the queen of the Himalayas, seven thousand feet above sea level.

From Siliguri one could also go to Kalingpong, another exclusive hill resort near Darjeeling. Siliguri was the access point for those going to Doers and its many tea gardens at the foothills of Bhutan. One could hire a jeep to drive up to Pheuntsholing and then to Thimpu, capital of Bhutan. Siliguri was the gateway to Gangtok, capital of Sikkim, and to Katmandu, capital of Nepal.

But nothing was more awesome than the Teesta River. As the train moved out from Siliguri junction, I could view the river quietly flowing by a thickly wooded mountain, thawing out from the baffling heights of the Himalayan foothills. The deep green of alpine woods on lesser mountains stood by the left bank of the Teesta. Silvery rocks and pebbles lined up on the river's edge. The river looked like a two-toned sheet of satin. One part of the stream reflected the shadows of the mountain range in surreal copper blue, and the other part reflected the silvery blue of the sky. As the train curved like a caterpillar on the edge of a bend, I had a distant glimpse of the Coronation Bridge, also called the Sevak Bridge—a slender line corniced into the mountain cliffs above a bottomless gorge.

As I turned my eyes from the view outside, I had glimpses of my fellow passengers. A self-absorbed man was looking through the window, carefully adjusting his elbow on the backrest, his chin resting on his palm. I could not make out whether he was enjoying the passing panorama or was immersed in thoughts.

Another passenger stooped, his head and shoulders like a question mark. He appeared lost in meditation. He could have been a crook, thinking how to swindle his business partner, how to deceive his kin and grab the joint family property, or how to set fire to his wife's sari when she was all alone in the kitchen. Who knew? Bride burning and dowry deaths were notorious problems of the time. Then I thought, *Why should I imagine things about a person I don't even know? Why should such bad thoughts occur to my mind?* It could have been that he had no sleep the previous night, or he could have been tired or sick. Maybe he had a bad headache? I thought that I mustn't assess a person without knowing him.

Next my eyes fell on a young couple. They looked like newlyweds. The parting of the woman's hair was thickly dabbed with vermilion. Her feet were bordered with red *alta*—a dye used for adorning the feet of Indian women, especially those of young brides. They were whispering to one another, smiling. Now and then the woman blushed. She arranged the *anchal*, the upper end of her sari, like a veil on her head. Every time she raised her arm to keep the veil in place, brand-new gold bangles on her wrist sparkled. I was sure that they were newlyweds. But how come they were traveling alone, without the groom's party? Did they fall in love and get married without the participation of elders and family members? *Love-marriage* was the common Bengali name for such marriages, as opposed to what was known as negotiated marriage. Calcutta was modern; Calcutta was a trendsetter in social changes. They must have been going to Calcutta after their wedding.

On the opposite berth, a baby was suckling at the rubber nipple of its bottle, holding the bottle like a squirrel holds a nut. It was throwing its legs toward its proud watching mother. The baby looked cute. A few senior students, perhaps returning to college after vacation, placed a leather suitcase over a steel trunk to improvise a table. They were absorbed in playing cards.

As I looked to the farthest end of the compartment, I caught sight of a woman. She wore a white sari and sat in the opposite corner of the coach. She lowered her eyes, pretending to tidy the gathers of her sari. I hadn't realized she was watching me. She looked smart in the simple white cloth with thin black borders. She was wearing a pair of lenses. Seemingly she concentrated on reading an English paperback. She had spoken to no one throughout the journey. She kept her eyes fixed to the book.

I now had a full view of the woman. She was in her late twenties, I guessed. She had no ornaments on her neck or wrists. She wore only a wristwatch with a black leather band. I remembered my hometown lady doctor, who was from Calcutta. She dressed exactly like the lady in my coach. *She could be a lady doctor,* I thought. She had no vermilion mark on the parting of her hair. She could have been a spinster or a widow. She could have been a Christian or a Muslim woman, who do not use vermilion. She had no veil either. She looked lonely. I thought it might be interesting to know her.

By sheer coincidence, our eyes met. She gave me a polite smile. I reciprocated. She cast down her eyes to her book and didn't look at me again. I wondered what the message was in her smile. Did she mean hello? Did she mean to signal her disapproval of my glance? Did she mean to imply that I was too young to be interested in her?

I played it safe. I averted my eyes and resumed viewing the scenes passing beyond the window.

The train slowed down, stopping or moving very slowly at the waving of flag-signals by railway men on the ground. The train was on a temporary track laid on the sandy riverbank. We were approaching the steamer crossing over the Meghna, a river that combines the streams of the Ganges, Padma, and Dhaleswari Rivers. The thought that I would cross over the river and board the broad-gauge train to Calcutta excited me.

Railway porters, some in red shirts, some in other colors, and some bare-bodied, all wearing turbans on their heads, stood precariously on the footboards of the compartments, holding the door handles. As the train approached the riverside, they hastily entered the compartments. Without asking anyone, they started pulling out passengers' luggage to transfer to the ferry. As the train finally stopped, they ordered the passengers to follow them as if they were in full control of the passengers and luggage.

The question-mark man tried to prevent a porter from touching his luggage. In broken Hindi, he rebuked a bare-bodied porter for pulling a steel trunk from under the berth without his permission. There were commotion and confusion as the porters raided the compartment. Passengers bargained with the porters, who were unrelenting in their efforts to get as much as they could. The question-mark man, who had looked so quiet before, took the lead in haggling with the porters. He called them coolies. I never knew a frail-looking man could have so much lung power.

The young porter who took my suitcase and bedroll assured me that he wouldn't charge anything more than whatever I was happy to pay him. He said that he would safely take my luggage to the steamer, find the best available place for it, and locate a good seat for me. He asked me to ignore the *jhanjhat*, meaning the confrontation and haggling kicked up by the other passengers and porters. He asked me to follow him.

I had never before experienced such a confusing situation. I wanted to get out of the situation. I followed my porter. He was barefooted and walked very fast on the long stretch of sandy riverbank. With my shoes on, it was difficult for me to keep pace with him. Snaking through the stream of passengers and porters carrying luggage as head-loads, my porter vanished like a grain of camphor. Despite my best efforts to walk fast, I lost track of him in the muddle.

I was very worried. Totally disheartened, I joined the procession of passengers trekking down the sandy bank. At the end of the track were the boarding planks to the steamboat. A ticket checker in a black suit was punching tickets as passengers rushed to the steamer, each porter trying to go ahead of the others. I thought I could report to the ticket checker about the loss of my luggage. But, before I could open my mouth, he mechanically punched my ticket and waved at me to make room for the next passenger.

I got a hard push from behind that placed me well past the check-in point. I floated in the melee up the stairway to the top deck of the steamer. Suddenly, to my surprise and great relief, I found my lost porter waving at me and smiling from ear to ear. I waved back to acknowledge his greeting.

"Come, sahib, come; I have kept the best seat for you!" he shouted exuberantly.

Once again, I thought, I had been too hasty in judging people. The porter was an honest man; he did not run away with my luggage. On the contrary, he brought my luggage very fast, and in spite of the crowd, he managed to keep an exclusive place for me. He was a nice fellow. I decided to give him a good tip.

My porter had neatly kept my suitcase and the bedroll at the front end of the deck. He was sitting on a chair fixed to the deck, saving the seat for me. The deck was already crowded with passengers and their luggage. As I came near him, he stood up and offered the chair to me, saying, "Sit down, sahib, and don't leave the seat. Everybody is after the front row of seats. If you leave it, you won't get it back." He added, "I have done my job as I promised you. Now it is up to you to give me whatever you think just."

Happily, I asked him how much he wanted. He insisted that he wouldn't tell me anything. It was entirely up to me, he said. I didn't know how much I should pay him. I offered him two one-rupee notes. He didn't touch the money and grumbled, "Sahib, you're offering me only this much for all that I did for you? I don't know what to tell a *sariff* [high-minded] person like you. Please do justice to this poor man. What else can I tell you, sahib?"

He had put me in a fix. I didn't know how much I should offer him. I took out two more one-rupee bills from my wallet and offered them to him.

Suddenly, someone from behind grasped my hand. I looked back and found a roly-poly middle-aged man standing behind me. He gave me a smile and said, "What are you doing, young man? Is this your first journey in this line?"

Nonplussed, I gave him a vacant look that only confirmed his assumption. He took all the one-rupee bills from my hand and, holding them before me, said, "Put them back into your wallet. Let me tackle this coolie guy. He is trying to take advantage of your goodness and is extorting you."

The porter murmured to the intruder, "What's that to you, sahib? I am a poor man. If someone gives to me out of compassion, it shouldn't matter to you. I am not asking anything from you. Sahib, please don't deprive me of my honestly earned money."

"You shut up," scolded the intruder, adding, "One more word and you will be handed over to the inspector. You're trying to cheat an innocent passenger."

I thought we were heading toward unnecessary wrangling. In fact, I felt annoyed at the manner in which the intruder shouted at the porter. I thought the porter would respond in kind. But to my surprise, his reaction was altogether different. Most submissively, he told the intruder to have mercy on him. The intruder then asked the porter, "Show me your license. You don't look like a registered porter. You're not in a railway porter's work shirt. Where is your armband?"

"Sahib, I have applied, but I have not yet been registered. I am a poor man working very hard for survival. Please don't be unkind to me." The porter folded his hands.

The intruder then said, "The rate here is six annas per *maund* (a local measure of weight) of luggage carried. The luggage that you carried is less than a maund; isn't that correct?"

The porter meekly nodded in affirmation. The intruder took some coins from of his purse and counted out six annas, which was little more than one-third of a rupee. He gave the coins to the porter, and to my astonishment, the porter accepted the payment. Then the porter saluted him and begged for some baksheesh.

"Okay. I don't mind giving you some baksheesh too," replied the intruder. He gave the porter a few more small coins and scornfully commanded, "Now, go away and get lost."

The porter quietly left, totally ignoring my presence. Before I could understand the fast sequence of events, the intruder extended his hand to me. "I am called Kasturilal Kak. I am a man from Jammu, but I live in Kalkatta," he said, giving the name of Calcutta in Urduized

Hindi. "I deal in fresh fruits and nuts. My shop is in the Burra bazaar in Kalkatta. I could guess that you were a new traveler and the coolie fellow was trying to swindle you. I thought I must come forward and help you. These guys are an awful lot."

Like a bemused creature, I put my hand on his and uttered my name. Before I could say anything more, Kasturilal asked me, "Are you visiting Kalkatta for the first time?"

I nodded in the affirmative.

"Are you going to visit some *ristadar*—relative?"

By then, I had regained my poise and replied in normal tone, "Thank you, Mr. Kasturilal. I am a student, going to Calcutta for education."

"Oh, wonderful. Please do come to my humble store anytime you like."

He took a business card from his pocket and gave it to me. The card was printed in red with an image of the elephant-headed Ganesha, god of prosperity, as a logo. He was the owner of a store named *Adarsh Bhandar*—Ideal Store. "I will consider it a great privilege to receive you in my store," he added.

I thanked him and wanted to reimburse him for the coins he had given to the porter.

"Oh, please, don't put me to shame. You don't have to return those few coins. By the grace of God, I am free from want." A flash of contentment glittered on his glossy cheeks. A solid gold chain with a locket was visible through the unbuttoned neck of his silken shirt.

Kasturilal persistently refused to accept my coins. He continued speaking about Calcutta and life in the city as both of us stood, holding the railing around the steamer deck. I watched the spectacular panorama of the rolling waves reflecting the last rays of sunlight. Fishermen on their boats were throwing and drawing back nets, collecting floundering fish that sparkled like silver. Dolphins popped up and plunged back into the wide waters. Plying between the lines of buoys indicating safe passage, the steamer took more than half an hour to cross the river and enter the railway jetty on the other bank. Station sheds, passenger cars, and freight wagons came into view. Following Kasturilal's advice, I stood close to my luggage.

Even before the gangway planks were fully laid, porters rushed to the steamer deck. Without asking me anything, Kasturilal made arrangements with a porter who, after some bargaining, agreed to carry all of Kasturilal's and my luggage in one go. Kasturilal instructed the porter to spread our beds on the upper berths in the interclass coach of the Calcutta-bound train. We followed the red-shirted man with the mountain of luggage on his head through the thick crowd of passengers.

The distance from the riverbank to the railway platform was not as long on this side as it had been on the other bank. We boarded the train. In spite of all sorts of shoving and jostling, the porter and Kasturilal could not find enough space to unroll two bedrolls on the upper berth of the coach. After an exchange of repeated courtesies between us, Kasturilal yielded to my request that his bed be spread on the available space and my bedroll kept rolled up. We sat on the lower berth.

The porter claimed extra tips for his promptness and skill in finding enough space to spread Kasturilal's bed. I was keen to repay my debt to Kasturilal. But, unyielding, Kasturilal insisted that I sit quietly. After some bickering, the porter accepted fourteen annas from Kasturilal—the price that had been settled on the steamer deck.

Kasturilal postured as though he had won a battle. He proudly told me, "Now, you might give him a tip if you like."

I felt somewhat relieved. I offered two one-rupee bills to the porter. Out of habit, the porter demanded more. Kasturilal angrily raised his finger and ordered the porter to get out at once or else Kasturilal would call the inspector. The porter grumbled but left the coach.

Annoyed, Kasturilal looked at me and groused, "My friend, you're going to Kalkatta. You must be shrewd in dealing with people. If you are too generous, you will be cheated at every step. Please don't misunderstand me; I only wish you good luck."

Kasturilal's bossy and meddlesome behavior was getting on my nerves. I didn't know how to get rid of him. I tried to divert my attention to something else. I opened my attaché case, keeping its cover upright to create a symbolic barrier between Kasturilal and me. Inside, I found the book I had been reading before leaving home. I tried to concentrate on that. Kasturilal kept quiet.

The train took its own time to steam off from the station. The compartment in the broad-gauge car was larger and the berths broader compared to a meter-gauge train. It was filled with passengers of both sexes and of various ages and appearances. As the heavier train gained speed, its sound and swinging rhythm were also different from the meter-gauge train.

The train stopped at a busy station. Platform peddlers hawked food, tea, soda, fruits, bidis, cigarettes, and other items a passenger might need, all in their typical tone. I put the bookmark on the page and closed the attaché case. The big, old station house and the platform were brightly lit and crowded with people busy on their errands. Some passengers debarked from the train and others got in.

Railway waiters brought trays of food for passengers who had earlier placed orders for dinner. I looked at my wristwatch and found that the time was 7:30 p.m. I realized that I should have ordered my dinner at the station where we embarked. Kasturilal had contributed to my confusion, and I forgot to order dinner.

I asked a waiter if he could get me dinner. He replied that they could only serve dinners ordered in advance. He suggested that I go down to the platform and buy a packaged dinner from the railway restaurant. But, he told me I must hurry up, as there were only a few minutes before the train would leave the station.

I was not sure if I could find dinner in the perplexing environment of the busy station. Passengers who got their dinners served could take their time eating because their trays would be collected at the next stop.

An older passenger sitting next to me understood my problem. He, in chaste Bengali, offered to share his dinner. "I won't be eating so much food," he said. "If you have no objection, please share my dinner. It will be my pleasure to share with you."

Suddenly, someone tapped me from behind. I looked back and found a beaming Kasturilal sitting behind me. In his Urduized Hindi, he said, "Please don't worry, my friend. As long as Kasturilal is here, you wouldn't have to starve. I always carry food for at least three or four people. You never know who your fellow passengers will be or what situation they will be in. You can never be sure of anything on a train journey."

With another complacent smile, he pointed out the magnum-size dinner basket under the berth and said, "There's everything in it." He named some delicious items of North Indian food and added, "If you like to sweeten your mouth after dinner, you may even have *halwa* [a nut-butter dessert], all homemade. Can you get such items from the railway restaurants?"

The train steamed off. Before giving me a chance to say anything, Kasturilal drew out his dinner basket. All eyes were now on him. From the first tier of the basket, he took out paper plates and extended one to me. Helplessly, I looked to the older man sitting next to me. He nodded his approval in a fatherly manner. Hesitantly, I took the plate from Kasturilal's hand. Heedless of all others, Kasturilal took out two heavy *parathas* [buttered flatbread] and put them on my plate. He added some lamb curry and said, "Start with this, and I will give you more. Please don't feel shy. Eat to your heart's content."

Embarrassed, I told him that I wouldn't need any more. He emphatically replied, "My friend, there is nothing to feel shy about. Just start and I will forthwith join you. Eating good food is one of the most pleasurable experiences of life; we all work hard to have good food."

Looking to the older passenger, he added, "Sir, don't you think so?"

The senior gentleman nodded his approval. He commented with a smile, "You have, indeed, realized the most vital truth of life!"

Most others in the compartment burst out in laughter. I felt all the more embarrassed holding the plate of food in my hand. To my surprise, Kasturilal appeared to have taken the comment and the laughter as a compliment. He too joined the laughter.

As a matter of courtesy, I thanked him for the food. Kasturilal replied, "Your satisfaction is my pleasure."

After dinner, he bade me good night and climbed up to his bed on the upper berth. I gained more space on the lower berth to stretch myself comfortably.

In the rocking rhythm of the train, I too sank into slumber. When I woke up, it was already morning. The train was passing by a village. It was not like the villages of Assam and North Bengal. The village was full of mud-plastered cottages with gabled roofs of dried palm leaves. A few houses had terracotta tiles. There were scanty trees here and there, ponds and tanks full of algae and weeds, old temples, naked children playing in small courtyards and winding lanes. Occasionally there were old single- and double-storied buildings with mortared roofs of lime and brick dust. There were stray dogs running, rickety cows grazing on sparse patches of grass, domestic pigeons, crows and sparrows on the rooftops, and doves and common Indian mynahs perching on the power cables.

At the end of the village stood a timeworn, two-story building with a few tall trees within its partly broken brick wall. Worn-out steps led to a nearby tank in front. The water in the tank looked thick and green. Three damsels sitting on the steps of the tank were scouring pots and pans with grassroots and mud. The house looked haunted. Out of a crack in its wall sprouted a lustrous green stem rising toward the sky. Its fresh leaves held out, as it were, the victory flag of the new over the old. The youthful faces of the giggling damsels watching the passing train had a similar sheen. Youth, I thought, had its natural glow everywhere despite grimy water, malaria, malnutrition, and maltreatment.

The scene changed as the train moved out from the village. I resumed my silent survey of the passing landscape. The setting changed from rural to urban. There were roads, brick and cement houses, buses, trucks, bicycles, and rickshaws. Men and women moved, spoke, worked, and thronged the bazaars.

We passed a marshy area and a small railway station. After that was a road junction with a milepost inscribed, "Murshidabad 167 miles, Plassy 171 miles."

I recalled that Murshidabad had been the capital of Bengal in the early eighteenth century when Murshid Quli Khan, nabob of Bengal, shifted his capital from Dhaka and named the city after himself. Mughal Sultan Aurangzeb was then emperor of India. Murshidabad continued to be the capital of Bengal until the last part of the century.

I also recalled that it was in a village named Plassy in Murshidabad district that Nabob Siraj-ud-Dawlah had been assassinated in a camp. This occurred during the historic Battle of Plassy fought between the forces of the nawab of Bengal and those of the British East India Company, led by General Robert Clive.

The train ran through the urbanized areas on the outskirts of the city. Roads over viaducts, overpasses, congested towns, industrial sheds, suburban markets, storehouses, filth, and squalor were in glaring contrast to the natural landscapes of Assam and North Bengal. I never imagined that the approach to the historic city would be so full of congestion and pollution. The train ran on a raised pair of tracks running side by side. A metal road zigzagged far from, then close to the railway track.

The train slowed down miles before entering Sealdah railway terminus. It ran alongside passenger and goods trains traveling in the opposite direction. It passed through small stations in the industrial areas outside the metropolis: railway yards and workshops where stationary locomotives hibernated, breathing out steam, some gushing out clouds of vapor, dark with coal particles.

The train passed through a portion of the track that was darkened by shadows of old brick buildings. Perhaps this side of suburban Calcutta had neither space nor time. People here were too busy punching time cards in a desperate attempt to make ends meet. On both sides of the track were posters: old and new, handwritten and printed, English and Bengali. They were stuck to the walls of railway sheds, and on damaged wagons on abandoned tracks. These posters announced the employment demands of the railway men. They symbolized the growing class struggle in West Bengal and the rise of the so-called Left Front.

I counted the moments until I saw my dream city, Calcutta.

2

My train entered its destination, the huge interior of the Sealdah railway terminus. The very thought that I had arrived in Calcutta tremendously excited me. Railway porters swarmed into the passenger cars, shouting, "*Cooli hai, coolih . . .*" One of them took my luggage and carried it as a head load, effortlessly putting my bedroll over my suitcase, and asked me to follow him.

The din and bustle that began well before the train came to a stop continued even after the passengers had made arrangements with porters and alighted from the train. My porter and I joined the human stream eager to check out. We inched toward the waist-high gate to get to the atrium. Every passenger had to show his or her ticket to the ticket collector at the exit gate and then cross the turnstile to pass through the large foyer of the terminus.

Passengers like me, who were new to Calcutta and nurtured many expectations about the historic city, joined the crowd with an ardent urge to be done with the journey. We anticipated the discovery of all that the great city held in store. The rest of the travelers had come to Calcutta on business or as students returning to schools after vacation. The rush and the noise were nothing unusual to those familiar with the milieu. A family waited beyond the platform gate to receive with great ceremony a pair of newlyweds. Others, including chauffeurs, employees, and business agents, waited with bouquets of flowers to welcome their valued guests. Yet others were waiting with paperboards inscribed with the names of unmet but important passengers.

My porter had already passed through the gate and was waiting for me in the overcrowded lobby. As I joined him, the first thing that attracted my attention was nothing of glamour or glory, but the shocking scenes of human misery. Right before me was a large convergence of the destitute masses of refugees from East Bengal, recently and suddenly turned into East Pakistan.

These brave and hardy souls had survived the communal massacre during the partition of the nation into India and Pakistan. They had desperately endured their odyssey from East Pakistan to West Bengal. They were a large cluster of men, women, and children who had lost their loved ones among the two hundred thousand slain. They were the victims of political decisions made by the leaders of India and Britain. They were a large swath of humanity that had been denied their basic human rights.

In fact, neither the national government nor the state government of West Bengal knew what to do with the multitude of refugees. Seemingly, the partition of India was decided without regard for the probable consequences, so there was no plan to rehabilitate the refugees who bore the brunt of the partition. The entire process of the transfer of power from the British Empire to the political leaders of India and Pakistan was done in an undue hurry. It even gave rise to the suspicion that India's political leaders wanted the partition because they did not like to share power.

The fact that the so-called "two-nation theory" was opposed to Indian history and tradition was proved by the simple fact that thirty million Muslims refused to leave their homes in India to migrate to Pakistan. Their progeny now comprise thirteen percent of India's total population, as detailed in the census report of 2010–2011.

The entire process of partition was completed in less than three months. The last British viceroy of India, Lord Louis Mountbatten, took over on June 3, 1947. He had already been given instructions to divide the nation into India and Pakistan. The British Parliament passed the Indian Independence Act on July 15, 1947, and the ceremonial transfer of power in Delhi took place at midnight on August 15, 1947.

Cyril Radcliffe, an English barrister turned judge, was appointed chairman of the boundary commission. The commission came to India to demarcate the boundaries of India and Pakistan, and separately for Bengal and Punjub. The commission had to entertain a lot of representations from people likely to be affected. The commission submitted what were known as "Radcliffe Lines" on August 17—that is, two days after partition. The records also show that the leaders of India and Pakistan only got a couple of hours to review the boundary lines. According to another source, boundary demarcation was done on August 16. Whatever the truth, Radcliffe's lines scratched on the map of India arbitrary boundaries that cut across thickly populated villages, causing horrendous bloodshed on a massive scale, not to mention unchecked looting and rape.

Before leaving India, Radcliffe destroyed all his records.

Most refugees from East Bengal were peasants who had lived in villages in fertile river valleys. They grew rice and jute, rowed country boats, and sang *Bhatiali* songs—a type of boatmen's songs. Most lived below the poverty line. Their sense of deprivation always had the potential to be explosive if they were pushed beyond the brink. Already overpopulated West Bengal was still reeling from the shock of the great famine of 1943 and the prepartition communal massacre of 1946. Therefore, it was not difficult for the British administration and communal leaders to ignite the fury of Hindu-Muslim antagonism, which led to rioting. In fact, the partition of India formalized the communalism that dominates electoral politics in the world's largest democracy even today.

Bulldozed by the partition, these peasants were uprooted like chunks of grass pulled from the ground. They lost everything they had. Hunger and thirst, death and dishonor haunted them as they crossed the border of the divided nation. Unknown numbers of victims breathed their last in the aimless odyssey. Survivors took shelter wherever they could. The largest cluster of East Bengal refugees entering Calcutta took shelter in Sealdah railway station.

The elderly and the sick among them lay in relatively obscure corners of the building. Young women and girls, in their efforts to hide their shame from so many prying eyes, stayed behind curtains of saris and bedspreads draped over ropes tied to the building's pillars. During the day, refugees on the platform were comprised only of women, infants, the elderly, and the sick. There was no medical aid available. Able-bodied men and hungry children were all out in search of food. The little ones went begging; the adults went in search of jobs in a city covered in "No Vacancy" posters. Half of the children never returned. Unprotected girls, lured by thugs, were lost forever. The plight of the refugees epitomized the utmost state of human misery.

The hurriedly established Relief and Rehabilitation Department of the government of India hardly had any concrete and feasible plans to rehabilitate the refugees. Only a few resourceful immigrant families managed to register themselves as refugees and got unduly large financial benefits. These well-to-do families from East Bengal crossed over to Calcutta in their imported cars before or during the communal riots.

According to historians, the partition of India was one of the ten greatest tragedies in human history. It is believed that the two-nation theory sprouted in 1923. Radical leader and author Vinayak Damodar Savarkar, in a pamphlet titled "*Hindutva*," meaning Hinduness or Hindu nationality, argued that Hinduism was a social and political tradition. He contended that it had been a national identity since ancient times, distinctly different from Hinduism practiced as a religion. He pleaded for the reestablishment of Hindutva by reconverting Hindus, who, during the Muslim rule in India, were converted to Islam. Savarkar founded the Free India Society in London and was arrested in Marseilles and in London. His trial raised international controversy. He was sentenced to life imprisonment in the outrageous Cellular Jail of the Andaman Islands.

Years before Muhammad Ali Jinnah came to the forefront as a Muslim League leader, nationalist Lala Lajpat Rai defined four Muslim majority areas in India and proposed separation of those areas from India by amicable settlement. Syyed Jamaluddin Afghani, leader of the Pan-Islamic movement, visited India in 1838 before the Indian Rebellion, and again in 1869. The British Raj in India welcomed him. Later he preached against the dismemberment of the Ottoman Empire and pleaded for the retention of the *caliphate,* or the Islamic empire of the caliph. It is well known that M. K. Gandhi in India supported the Pan-Islamic Khilafat (Caliphate) movement during the First World War and built up the Khilafat movement in India, supported by some of his followers. Gandhiji's Khilafat movement was a desperate move to bring the Indian Muslims into Congress even though the move was opposed to the secular principles to which the Indian National Congress Party was committed.

Poet-lawyer Sir Muhammad Iqbal, in his presidential address on December 29, 1930, in the Lahore session of the Muslim League, expressed his vision of creating, within or outside the British Empire, a Muslim state comprised of the Muslim-majority northwestern region of India. In his scheme, there was no plan for central administration.

Muhammad Ali Jinnah reacted against the proponents of Hindutva when Pandit Madam Mohan Malviya and Lala Lajpat Rai supported that concept. Malviya and Rai actually broke away from Congress during the midtwenties. Analyzing the political situation in India before independence, Professor K. M. Panikar, in a memorandum of October 10, 1945, stated that no constituent assembly could succeed except on the basis of a Congress-League accord. He contended that the two political parties must formulate a procedure to bring the parties together on some minimally acceptable basis before the constituent assembly met.

In 1939, during the course of discussions with the viceroy, Lord Linlithgow, Jinnah demanded a plebiscite and territorial divisions that supposedly would create a Hindu-Muslim balance. Almost simultaneously, the premier of Punjab, Sir Sikander Hayat Khan, proposed the division of India into autonomous zones within a federal structure. In fact, according to M. A. Jinnah's version of the situation, several plans were put forth as alternatives, but none of them matured.

On September 11, 1939, Viceroy Lord Linlithgow announced suspension of the federal part of the Government of India Act of 1935. This, by implication, has been interpreted as the first British step to divide India based on the two-nation theory. In an article dated January 19, 1940, in the *Time and Tide* of London, Jinnah asserted that there were two nations in India, both of which had to share the governance of their motherland. According to some, this clearly implied an amicable partition between the two religious communities within a united government. On February 6, 1940, Jinnah and the Muslim League passed the Pakistan Resolution.

The resolution contained five points, including the provisos that no constitutional plan would be workable or acceptable to the Muslims unless geographically contiguous areas were demarcated into regions, which should be constituted with such territorial adjustments as necessary. Considering that the areas in which Muslims were numerically in the majority were in the northwestern and eastern regions of India, it was determined that they should be grouped into independent states in which the constituent units would be autonomous and sovereign. The resolution further stated that adequate, effective, and mandatory safeguards for minorities should be specifically provided in the federal constitution, including protection of religious, cultural, economic, political, and administrative rights.

The League's historic session met in Lahore on March 21, 1940. The session discussed the preliminary points of the resolution and provided in clause (e) that the regions could delegate to a central agency, designated the Grand Council of the United Dominions of India, and on such terms as may be agreed upon, provided that such functions would be administered through a committee on which all religions, dominions, and interests would be duly represented. Actual administration would be entrusted to the units.

Clause (f) stated that no decision of the central agency would be effective or operative unless at least a two-thirds majority carried it. Clause (g) provided that in the absence of agreement with regard to the constitution, functions, and scope of the Grand Council of the United Dominions of India, (h) the regions (dominions) would have the right to refrain from or refuse to participate in the proposed central structure, and (i) the peacetime composition of the Indian Army would continue on the same basis as existed on April 1, 1937.

Subsequently, Mr. Jinnah changed the resolution and removed clauses (f) and (g).

These facts reveal the history and the backdrop of the partition of India. It appears that Jinnah and the Muslim League were not sure as to whether their demands would be acceptable to other Indian leaders.

Perhaps the League and Mr. Jinnah were prepared to make allowances, because nowhere does the resolution mention the partition of the nation or the creation of Pakistan.

Nonetheless, the Lahore Resolution, also known as the Pakistan Resolution, laid down the basic principles for the Muslim majority areas of India. The resolution entrusted the Muslim League Working Committee to *finally* provide for all powers, such as defense, external affairs, communications, customs, and other such matters. Dr. B. R. Ambedkar, in his *Pakistan or The Partition of India*, wrote that he asked Gandhi in their meeting in 1944 what the word *finally* meant, as it occurred in the last paragraph of the Lahore Resolution. Probably, the question was too delicate to answer. Probably the only answer could have been the partition of the nation. Did the League contemplate a transition period during which Pakistan would not be an independent and sovereign state? Dr. Ambedkar raised the question of the Lahore Resolution in the context of a Gandhi-Jinnah meeting in Bombay in 1944 and the Rajagopalachari formula (CR formula) that proposed a referendum on the partition of India and provided for a peaceful solution of the question of division. Many Congress members, however, opposed the proposal.

Professor Ayesha Jalal, in her book *The Sole Spokesman: Jinnah, the Muslim League and the Demand for Pakistan,* contended that by apparently repudiating the need for a center and keeping quiet about its shape, Jinnah calculated that when eventually the time came to discuss an all-India federation, the British government and Congress alike would be forced to negotiate with organized Muslim opinion. At that stage, they would be ready to make substantial concessions to create or retain the center. She held that the Lahore Resolution should therefore be seen as a bargaining counter, which had the merits of being acceptable (on the face of it) to the Muslim majority provinces and of being totally unacceptable to the Congress and, in the last resort, to the British also. This, in turn, provided the best insurance that the League would not get what it was apparently asking for and which Jinnah, in fact, did not really want.

The above opinion finds support in certain other documents relating to Jinnah and the Muslim League. Organized Muslims of India were worried about the safety of Muslims who chose to remain outside after the groupings were complete. The majority of Muslim opinion was to retain an organic link with the center so that they could retain control of the center. But Congress was not interested in sharing power. With Maulana Abul Kalam Azad, Saifudin Kitchlew, and Khan Abdul Gaffar Khan at his side, Gandhiji was complacent that Indian Muslims would resist grouping or partition, even though the 1937 election proved otherwise.

Pandit Nehru had a different view. In his jail diary dated December 28, 1943, he recorded that instinctively he thought it was better to have Pakistan or almost nothing, if only to keep Jinnah far away and not allow his continued, muddled, and arrogant interference in India's progress. He also wrote that he couldn't help thinking that ultimately the Muslims of India would suffer the most.

Some leaders of the League did not endorse Jinnah's contentions. They thought it proper to make a deal with Congress. Of them, Chaudhury Khaliquzzaman and the Nawab of Chhatari particularly feature in the records.

The British Cabinet Mission's first plan was to group the Muslim and Hindu majority provinces and knit those together in a sort of loose federation until the constituent assembly could make the future constitution of independent India. In a letter dated March 19, 1947, addressed to Frederick Pethick-Lawrence, the British secretary of state for India, Viceroy Lord Wavell, wrote just three months before partition that Jinnah gave an impression to Colin Reid, a correspondent of the *Daily Telegraph* in London, that he might accept the Cabinet Mission's first plan of independence for an undivided India, if Congress accepted it on unequivocal terms.

But the All India Congress Committee, on April 2, 1942, resolved that they were opposed to compelling the people of any territorial unit to remain in the Indian union against their will. Although Congress was committed to national integration in its election manifesto of May 2, 1942, the party declared liberty for any component state or territorial unit that chose to secede. The core principle of C. Rajagopalachari's formula of March 1944 was that Congress should offer Pakistan to the

Muslim League based on a plebiscite of all the people in the areas where Muslims were in absolute majority.

On September 24, 1944, Gandhi offered Jinnah his plan for two independent states. After the Labour Party came to power in Britain, Prime Minister Clement Attlee sent Lord Mountbatten with a definite brief to partition India into India and Pakistan within three months.

In 1984, the Ram Janam Bhumi-Babri Masjid in Ayodhya became the foremost political issue, thereby proving that the partition of India did not solve the Hindu-Muslim rivalry. It only opened up opportunities for interested powers to take advantage of the traditional bellicosity of the two religious communities of divided India. Individually, Hindus and Muslims of India are amicable and peace-loving people. Communally and politically, they are rivals.

To consent to the proposal to divide the nation was a matter of political decision, but it was an overwhelming challenge to offer relief and rehabilitation to the uprooted multitude. The national government of the newly liberated India hardly had the resources and infrastructure. It was far beyond the capacity of the West Bengal state government and charitable nongovernmental organizations (NGOs). Leftist political parties took the opportunity to organize protest rallies and processions, encouraging refugees to rebel against the government.

* * *

Within a couple of years of my coming to Calcutta, the scenario in the city had undergone phenomenal change. It was most unfortunate that the original inhabitants of Calcutta looked upon the refugees as intruders into their city. They characterized the refugees as disorderly, obstinate, and stiff-necked troublemakers—a source of disturbance. Thus, instead of sympathy, the refugees were treated with contempt.

One and a half million refugees took shelter in various public places. Many of them were educated and skilled middle-class professionals. When no help was forthcoming and they were only hated and despised, they turned into rebels. Circumstances made them deviants from the traditional Indian ethos; they decided to go the radical way. They took to the squatter movement, which in Bengali was called *jabardakhal.* They adopted a drastic *modus operandi.* In the dark of night, batches of refugees occupied land by force in the comparatively open and less crowded areas of the city's outskirts. They acted with lightning speed and overnight erected shanties of bamboo and clay, roofed with thatches of tall *hogla* grass.

The Communist Party and other left parties supported the refugees. It is said that many in the Relief and Rehabilitation Ministry of the Indian national government regarded the movement as a blessing in disguise. The victims of partition undertook to solve their problem themselves. In no time, they built self-contained colonies in areas they named according to their own choice. These colonies had schools, temples, shopping areas, bazaars, and medical clinics, all comprised of shanties built overnight. In South Calcutta, such colonies were built around Dhakuria Lake and Tollygunj. An open area of trees and grassy lawns off Tollygunj, where one of my aunts and her husband and children lived, became one such refugee colony named Azadgarh. Refugee stalls selling clothes and items of everyday use sprung up in Gariahata and Rash Behari Avenue. Within a short period, the refugee stalls in Rash Behari Avenue turned into a fashionable shopping plaza for the middle-class Bengalis. Intellectuals and social leaders took the initiative in establishing schools, colleges, hospitals, and universities. Jadavpur Engineering College was made into Jadavpur University in 1955.

In the years from 1964 to 1971, more refugees migrated to Calcutta and other parts of West Bengal because of the civil war in East Pakistan that gave birth to Bangladesh. The pouring in of further streams of refugees completely changed the demographic complexion of Calcutta. Even before partition, Calcutta-born residents constituted less than one third of the city's total population. The rest were from other states. After the refugees increased the city's population by a third, the Calcutta way of life underwent a total change. Later, the leftist government recognized these colonies.

From 1977, the Left Front governed West Bengal for the next thirty-four years, led by the Communist Party (Marxist), abbreviated as CPM. In due course, CPM became one of the members of the United Progressive Alliance (UPA) that formed the central ministry in the government of India.

The question of relief and rehabilitation of the refugees in West Bengal and neighboring states was no longer an outstanding problem by this time, except in political questions of ethnicity and language in northeast India. The end of CPM rule in West Bengal came in 2011. Trinamul Congress, in coalition with the Socialist Unity Center and the Indian National Congress Party, formed a government in West Bengal with Mamata Bannerjee as the chief minister.

3

I was the eldest child of my parents, firstborn in the third generation of an English-educated, middle-class Bengali Hindu family permanently settled in the headquarters of a district in the southwestern region of Assam in British India. The picturesque district town was on the bank of the mighty river Brahmaputra. The river rushed by incessantly and during the monsoon rains caused relentless flooding.

My grandfather, a qualified lawyer, emigrated from East Bengal sometime before the transfer of the district in 1876 from the Bengal Presidency to Assam. He joined the district bar as a practicing lawyer. My father, eldest son of my grandparents, was born in the town, as were his two brothers and two sisters. Although they were Assamese by birth, they were Bengali by culture and tradition.

There being no university in Assam until 1948, they obtained their higher education at Calcutta University. In fact, the sizable Bengali Hindu community of the town looked upon Calcutta as the hub of culture and advancement.

My grandfather was a learned and respectable man, unwaveringly firm in the conformist principles he believed. He was equally well versed in Sanskrit, mathematics, and English grammar. Occasionally, he helped me with my homework, teaching me English grammar from J. C. Nesfield's *Outline of English Grammar* and Sanskrit grammar from Baladeva Vidyabhusana's *Vyakarana Kaumudi*. He knew Hindu scriptures and texts so well that priests and pundits looked upon him with trepidation. A highly religious man, every evening he walked to the local Shiva temple, leaning on his walking stick for support. He was the *karta*—the patriarch of the Hindu joint family.

My paternal grandmother, a traditional Hindu wife, dutifully abstained from questioning her husband's wisdom. She had an endless stock of myths and legends she often narrated to me in her inimitable way. She could also chant a few Sanskrit verses from memory. She believed in devotion more than in rites. She was the prima donna of our home. Everyone acknowledged her exclusive position in the family. Womenfolk of the neighborhood looked upon her as their mentor. Those in need of advice on family matters or occasional financial help visited her during the quiet afternoons. She helped them in whatever way she could and never asked for anything in return.

As I grew up, I discovered that behind her modest disposition, Grandma had a distinct personality. Although she had no formal education, she was a poet by instinct. Her self-acquired knowledge and education made her reasonably conversant with Bengali literature. She regularly glanced through the Bengali daily newspaper to keep track of current events. Everyone in the family happily accepted her authority over domestic affairs. She maintained the family balance.

My father, a brilliant scholar throughout his career as a student, had to abruptly discontinue his research in physics and take up law because my grandpa wanted his eldest son to succeed him in the legal profession and retain the clientele he had built up over a lifetime. My father had to give up his academic career, and he joined the law college when he was already a married man. Weimar University in Germany published his incomplete thesis on the refraction of light in a scientific journal. Three years later, my father came home with a first-class degree in law and a gold medal he had won in a poetry competition presided over by the poet Rabindranath Tagore, who handed the medal to him. He joined the district bar as a practicing lawyer.

My mother was the youngest daughter of a *zamindar,* or landholder, in another town in the province. Her grandfather had migrated from East Bengal to Assam and obtained settlement of an estate granted by the British government. The British also decorated him with the honorary title of *rai bahadur*. My maternal grandfather succeeded his father as a zamindar. He had the title of *rai sahib*. He was an honorary magistrate, a position of high appellation, conferred on him because of his impeccable loyalty to the British crown. My mother knew excellent Bengali. She could recite many verses of the poet Rabindranath Tagore from memory.

My aunt Amrita—my father's first sister, married to a Calcutta-based covenanted executive of an English firm—was a university graduate. My father's second and youngest sister, Renuka, a high school graduate, was virtually my second mother. My sister Anita and I called her *Pishi*, a Bengali name meaning "father's sister." My father had two younger brothers, who joined the civil service in the British administration as an executive magistrate and an assistant civil surgeon respectively.

My sister Anita, younger than I by just a year, was my playmate and companion.

Traditional Hindu values, conveniently customized to suit the prevailing social situation, represented our family ethos. Conservative Hindu mores and contemporary reforms, often inconsistent with one another, strangely coexisted without any apparent discord. Nonetheless, many middle-class Bengali Hindus of the town looked upon our family as a paradigm of the ideal Hindu joint family.

* * *

One afternoon Anita and I returned from school together. When we entered our home, we sensed that the home atmosphere was unusually calm. The first family member we encountered was Pishi, our loving aunt. Although she greeted us with a smile, she appeared disturbed, but she didn't tell us anything. Her oddly empty and expressionless smile surprised us.

It was even more unusual to find Grandma sitting on a wicker stool in the courtyard, facing a long-unused bedroom at the end of the main dwelling house. The door of the room was closed. Saudamini, the housemaid, was standing near Grandma. As usual, Grandma greeted us with a smile. She too looked different. An expression of concern was conspicuous on her face. The strange air of suspense all around the home environment confused us. We asked Grandma why she was sitting there at that hour of the day.

Perhaps our question assuaged her tension a bit, because her expression relaxed and she looked much more normal. She said in her typical style that she was sitting there for a very, very special reason. When we asked her to tell us the special reason, she replied that if she told us immediately, there would be no more suspense left. She attempted another smile and asked us to wait patiently for the great event. We looked at each other, wondering what event could be so great. We kept begging her to tell us what it was. It became more mysterious for us when she said that she too did not know who would emerge from that room. She asked us again to be patient until the special event occurred.

We assumed that our mother was inside the room. We had not seen her anywhere. We asked Grandma about our mother. Pointing to the room, Grandma replied that our mother was doing fine. She added that Mother was awaiting the arrival of our new brother or sister, whose auspicious emergence was imminent.

We already knew that our mother was expecting her third child. We also knew how a baby is born. But we never thought that Mother would be inside the unused bedroom to give birth to her third child.

We were about to climb the steps and go into the room when Grandma jumped up from her stool and dragged us away from the door. She strictly forbade us from entering the room. Grandma said, "Let the newborn arrive from heaven. You will see the baby when the time comes. No one must go inside the room now. This is the rule, which no one must break." We knew that she was deliberately dramatizing the process of childbirth, but we had to pretend ignorance to conform to the conventional etiquette of the time.

She told us rather firmly that we should go and have our tiffin; she said that she would call us when it was time to see our newborn sibling. Her unusually firm manner surprised us and made us more anxious about our mother. Before we could ask her anything more, the closed door opened slightly and an unfamiliar woman's face appeared. The face whispered something to Grandma and then disappeared inside the room. She closed the door again.

Grandma, in turn, gestured at Saudamini, who quietly brought a bowl of hot water. She knocked at the door. The stranger came out through a heavy curtain and stood before the threshold, blocking the view inside the room. We had a glimpse of the stranger as she carefully lifted the bowl and took it inside. She closed the door immediately, not allowing even a peek of what was transpiring inside.

She was a middle-aged woman dressed in a tight white sari with border designs. She looked professional and serious. Her quiet but hurried movement intensified our anxiety. We had no idea whatsoever of what was going on inside that room. No one other than Grandma and Saudamini, not even Pishi, was allowed anywhere near.

We hovered anxiously, not really knowing what we should do even though Grandma had told us to leave. In our instinctive anxiety for our mother, Anita and I stood near Grandma like adjutant storks standing on the edge of a puddle. Worry weighed heavily on our patience.

I mustered some courage and asked Grandma, "Who is that woman, Grandma? What is she doing with hot water? What happened to Mother?"

"Well, the woman is a *dhai*. She will do whatever is necessary to bring the newborn from heaven. Your mother is doing fine," replied Grandma.

"What is a dhai, Grandma?" Anita asked impatiently.

Grandma hesitated for a moment and then whispered, "Well, she is a *sudra* woman. She knows how to bring babies from heaven."

"What is a sudra woman, Grandma?" was Anita's next question.

Lest Anita blurt out any further questions, I pressed her hand, hinting that she should keep quiet. Then with as much humility as I could command, I suggested to Grandma, "Dhai must be a very pious person. She has access to heaven where the gods and goddesses live; she can even bring babies. Isn't that correct, Grandma?"

"No," hissed Grandma rather sternly. She added, "Sudras are untouchable. Even their shadows could pollute a caste Hindu. Never go anywhere near her."

It roused Grandma's annoyance further as I exclaimed, "My God, we might have already had her shadows on us!"

Almost simultaneously, Anita asked, "Why is the sudra untouchable, Grandma?"

Just to stop our incessant questions and comments, Grandma said hastily, "Sudras are untouchable because of their lowly *varna*." Then she waved her hand backward in a gesture of dismissal as if shooing away a fly.

"What is varna, Grandma?" Anita asked impulsively.

Grandma heaved a sigh of exasperation. "Please don't ask me any more questions. I am tired of answering them. I am busy. Go away from here. I will call you when you may see the newborn." She turned her face away to show us that she was annoyed with us.

That was the first time Grandma behaved so irritably with us.

Many fears flashed through my mind. The only thing that consoled me a little was my conviction that Grandma never lied. When she said that Mother was doing well, she must have known for sure that Mother was doing well. I winked at Anita to follow me.

Anita and I moved away to the other end of the courtyard.

Despite Grandma's censure, we managed to stay put at a point from which we could see the closed-door room and Grandma's long gray hair on her sari-covered back as she sat on the wicker stool.

We could not control our anxiety for too long. After a while, both of us went back to Grandma. I politely pleaded, "Only one more question, Grandma, and we will go away."

Grandma looked at me with annoyance in her eyes, but I needed to ask her the question because it seemed very logical to me. "If dhai is untouchable, when she touches Mother and the newborn, won't they be untouchable too?"

Visibly annoyed, Grandma replied, "Varna is caste. Caste is hereditary and cannot be lost unless one does some prohibited thing. Neither your mother nor any of us has done anything prohibited. All sudras are progeny of the firstborn sudra. All sudras are low caste and hence untouchable. High-caste men, women, and children, if touched by an untouchable, can always get themselves purified by performing the *samskara*—the purifying rites."

Grandma had answered my question with such patience that I felt emboldened to ask her another.

"Why should this untouchable be here in our house at all?"

Perhaps Grandma had no answer to my question. She suppressed her embarrassment and annoyance. Her face contorted. For a moment, she fumbled for a suitable answer. In a hushed tone, she said, "Ancient texts enjoin that untouchable sudra women are most proficient in the social duty of midwifery. Traditionally, therefore, they touch high-caste expectant mothers and their newborn babies. After the baby is born, your mother and the newborn, like all high-caste mothers and their newborns, will be freed from impurity by performing samskara. Do you understand now? Are you satisfied?"

Grandma again turned her face away. I never knew what was in her mind by the way she spoke. Her tone was affected by her loose teeth and the way she used her tongue to form her words. Besides, I was not sure if she really believed in the ancient texts or if she was constrained to abide by the traditional Brahminical interpretation. There was no ostensible reason for her to be so agitated. Until then she had always been friendly to us. She had always been our loving Grandma.

It was difficult for Anita and me to bear the suspense. Both of us felt angry with our father for making our mother suffer in this way. Father was a highly educated man, a successful attorney, and a man of distinction. He loved our mother. We could see no reason for his passive acceptance of such an arrangement for welcoming his third child. Why didn't a qualified midwife attend our mother? Why should the so-called dhai handle the delivery of a child? Why did he not send our mother to the hospital?

This was especially difficult to understand because there was a state hospital in our town with qualified doctors and midwives in attendance. There were a couple of qualified private medical practitioners as well. Many of our friends' baby brothers and sisters had been born in the hospital. It made no sense to leave our mother to the quackery of a rustic woman such as the untouchable dhai. I had a feeling it didn't make sense to Grandma, either, even though she would never speak her mind.

Anita and I were very angry, so we searched out our father to confront him about this. He was sitting on an easy chair in his home office near the shelves that contained law books and morocco-bound volumes of law journals. Perhaps he had come back from the court early; perhaps he had never gone to the court that day. We weren't sure, but he certainly looked relaxed and comfortable. He was reading a book, his legs stretched over the long arms of the easy chair.

When we stood near him without saying a word, he put the open book on a nearby table, lowered his legs, and sat up straight. He said nothing and attempted a smile. He extended his arms and drew both of us close to him, but Anita and I resisted. Before he could say anything, I pulled out of his grasp and blurted, "Why is Mother inside the empty room under the care of that impostor woman? Why wasn't she sent to the hospital? Why was that woman called in at all?"

Father stood up. With his arms on our shoulders, he slowly led us to the window overlooking the Gadadhar River, a tributary of the Brahmaputra, flowing by the side of the road near our home. He said in a deep voice, "I understand your concern. I agree with you that the hospital would have been the best place for her. But don't worry; she will be all right. Your grandma is overseeing everything. She has been sitting right near the room."

He gathered both of us in a hug and added, "Your mother will surely be moved to the hospital if need be. Let's hope that there will be no such necessity; let's hope everything will be fine."

"Why not move her to the hospital anyway? You could take her right now!"

He answered my question with a question of his own. "*Papa*," as he used to call me, "would you like to go against your father? Would you like to fight with him?"

I replied, "No, I wouldn't; I will never fight with you, ever."

He nodded. "Right, and similarly, I too cannot go against my *baba*; I cannot fight with him," he said, obviously referring to Grandpa. "Everything is done in the way he desires, and so we must bear all this, however hard it might be. You know how loving your grandpa is. He must have had some good reason to make this arrangement to receive his new grandchild."

Perhaps Father suppressed his anguish, lest we lose our respect for our grandfather. He planted kisses on our heads. His manner of speaking made me feel that he too must have had similar concerns as ours, but he had to put up with the conventional Hindu tradition because his father so desired.

Fathers always knew more than their sons did. Some conformist Hindus of the time held the notion that it was the duty of a virtuous son to honor his father's wishes unquestioningly, even when such wishes were unreasonable or harsh. I, however, did not know if they also believed in the ancient Hindu proverb that if a woman or a son was lost, a man would have no dearth of women to marry, and the new wife would beget new sons. But a disobedient son might lose his father, never to get him back again. Therefore, a father was the faith, a father was heaven, and a father was the first god for adoration before any other god. Although my grandfather and my father were both loving fathers, on that day, I had a feeling that my father strenuously suppressed his resentment at having to follow the old traditions.

Mother stayed inside the closed room and Anita and I continued to be in a state of anxiety. We went back to where Grandma was supervising dhai's activities. The very thought that, inside the closed room, our mother was suffering like a helpless bird in a cage was agonizing. All sorts of frightening thoughts gathered in my mind.

Dhai again opened the door slightly and whispered something to Grandma. Grandma asked Saudamini to wash her hands with soap and water and then go into the room to help. She cautioned Saudamini, "Don't do anything unless dhai asks you to do so."

Saudamini nodded obediently, washed her hands, and went into the room. The door closed again and Grandma continued to sit on her stool.

Saudamini was just about twenty years old. She was not a low-caste housemaid. She came from a very poor caste Hindu family. She had been married in her childhood, and soon thereafter, she became a widow. Luckily, she was not encumbered with a child, so she could escape from the family home of her deceased husband's brothers, where her in-laws would have compelled her to a life of slavery. She lived on the outskirts of the town with her widowed mother and a younger brother.

Soon after returning to her mother, Saudamini took the job in our home. She wore her waist-length hair hanging loosely down her back, and she did not dress as a widow or practice the traditional austerities of a Hindu widow. No one in our home spoke to her about the sensitive topic of her marriage and widowhood. She was soft-spoken and good-natured. Everyone in the house liked her.

I had no idea how much her wages were. She stayed in our home and took her food from our home kitchen. She got saris and other essential things from our family. On special occasions, such as Durga Puja and the Bengali New Year's Day, she received new saris. Saudamini took good care of everything and everyone in our home. She was practically a member of our family.

After a while, Grandma's normal, happy mood returned. Perhaps she guessed our feelings of anxiety and wanted to calm us. Addressing me, she said, "There's nothing to worry about, honey. You, too, were born in this way, three years after your parents were married, and Anita a year after you."

I asked her, "Were we born at home? Were there dhais at our births?"

"Very much so," replied Grandma. "Both of you were born at home and there were dhais to welcome you. This is the rule, and righteous Hindus follow the rule."

She lifted our faces by our chins, using the fingertips of both her hands, and said in a lighter vein, "How else would we have been blessed with such beautiful grandchildren? May *Bhagavan* (God) bless you."

She kissed her own fingertips in a typical gesture of affection. We felt abashed and lowered our faces.

After Saudamini went inside the closed room, it became difficult for us to wait patiently. Anita blurted out, "What is dhai doing to Mother? Is dhai a witch, Grandma?"

Grandma put her forefinger on her lips, hinting that Anita should be quiet. She whispered, "No, she is not a witch. She is a dhai, a midwife, as I told you. She is looking after your mother. Everything is fine," she added in a normal tone.

After a while, Grandma, perhaps realizing that we were impatient, said again, "Don't you worry, honey. Everything will be fine. I'm sure you'll have a lovely baby brother or sister very soon. Both of you are growing well, by the grace of Lord *Narayana* (Vishnu), and your mother too is doing fine. So why worry? Have patience for a little while more."

"Why wasn't Mother sent to the hospital, Grandma?" I asked.

"Well," replied Grandma after a pause, "the hospital is for people who cannot afford to hire the services of dhais. Since, by the grace of Lord Narayana, we could hire an experienced dhai, your mother is comfortable at home, and she can take her food and get everything she needs here. God forbid, if any necessity arises, we will call a doctor at once to come and attend to her. She could even be moved to the hospital."

I didn't ask her anything more because she had answered my question without involving Grandpa. I already knew from Father that it had been Grandpa's decision.

Grandma didn't give us any more chances to ask her questions. She continued her monologue. "Whenever a child is born, the mother suffers much pain, but she forgets the pain the moment she sees the newborn's face. That is why mothers are mothers; there is no substitute for mothers. They are like the Great Goddess, the mother of all creation, preservation, and dissolution."

We hardly understood what she said and looked at her with curiosity. She continued, "The Great Mother gives birth to plants, animals, and human beings. She provides every living being with food, drink, and shelter. Nobody knows when she created the world. She is also called *Jagāt Jananī*, Mother of the World, and *Jagaddhatri*, the One Who Holds the World. She is the *Maha Devi,* the Great Goddess whose presence can be felt everywhere, and yet she is not visible. This is why she is also called the *Mahamaya*, the Great Illusion and the Supreme Power."

Grandma looked absorbed in her thought, and then she said, "I know what we can do to help you not be apprehensive about your mother's health as we wait for the new baby. Come; let us sing together the glory of the Great Mother."

She folded her hands, closed her eyes, and recited in mantra rhythm and in a low tone the Sanskrit verses in praise of the Great Mother. We copied her pose and joined her in praying for the welfare of our mother in our own silent way. Never before had we heard the verses chanted by Grandma. The set of Sanskrit verses rendered into English would read,

> Thou create the universe and sustain it too.
> Thou protect thy creations ever since and forever.
> O Goddess, thou consume thy creations at the end of time.
> Thou art the power that preserves everything.
> Thou wield dissolution of the universes.
> Thou art the cosmos and the cosmos is thine,
> Thou art the embodiment of supreme knowledge.
> Thou art the personification of the ultimate power.
> Thou art the matchless mind and the mighty memory.
> Thou art the endless illusion and the infinite valor.
> O Devi, thou art the greatest of all that are great.

Grandma concluded her prayer and said, "Are you getting the feeling of peace? The Great Goddess is reassuring us. She is ordaining that we must seek her grace, and everything will be fine."

We kept quiet, hardly understanding anything. We had always admired Grandma for her knowledge and accomplishments, as we loved her deeply.

For a while, she closed her eyes again and prayed quietly.

As if in response to Grandma's recitation, we heard the sudden cry of a newborn from inside the closed-door room.

The whole household came out to the courtyard, including the *thakur*, the bare-bodied Brahmin cook, who wore his sacred thread, and the *jhuli*, the old manservant who attended Grandpa in addition to other household duties. They all stood near the veranda. Pishi came out and stood on the veranda. Only my father and grandpa were conspicuously absent.

From outside, Grandma asked dhai whether the baby was a boy or a girl.

"A beautiful girl. Please keep sweets ready for me," she gleefully announced. It was customary to distribute sweets to everyone to celebrate happy and auspicious occasions, including childbirth.

Grandma sat again on the stool and asked dhai, "How is the mother doing?"

"Oh, she is doing fine; don't worry," replied dhai, adding confidently, "She is admiring her baby."

Now old Grandpa, who could walk only with the aid of a cane, came out to the courtyard. He gave us a smile. He too anxiously waited to see the newborn.

After we held on breathlessly for a time, the door opened. Dhai showed up at the door holding the tiny newborn thoroughly swaddled. She came down to the courtyard so that everyone could have a glimpse. The baby's face looked chubby and cute. Her eyes were closed, unable to bear the first glare of earthly light.

Pishi exclaimed merrily, "What a lovely little thing! Look at her!"

A happy Grandma drew Anita and me into a close hug, and Pishi joined in too.

4

Myths are an unreal rendition of social situations of the past. They are like potent fantasies that lend credence to absurdity. These narratives, intimately blended with local culture, traditionally determine the social ethos.

Myths made the Brahmaputra River a mystic phenomenon. According to a Tibetan legend, the Brahmaputra, called the Tsangpo in Tibet, was born out of a snow horse's mouth. It therefore had the stallion's power to traverse rugged hills and deep ravines. Originating from the bewildering heights of Xizang, the plateau of ethnocultural Tibet in China, the river gushes through the Himalayan mountain range and enters India at Tezu in Arunachal Pradesh at the northeast extremity of India, five thousand feet above sea level. Here the name of the river is Lohit, or the Red River. The river flows over a vast and variegated topography, covering eighteen hundred miles. Sweeping the bustling plains of Assam and Bangladesh, it joins the Ganges and then exhausts itself in the Bay of Bengal.

The *Kalika Purana*, written sometime around 1000 AD, narrates the legend of the birth of the Brahmaputra as the son of Lord Brahma, the Puranic god of creation. The text asserts that rivers and mountains have opposite natures. Rivers are streams of waters, and mountains are static obelisks. Human beings do not know that rivers and mountains have distinct bodies and discrete souls. Just as living beings exist within the seemingly lifeless shells of mollusks and conches, the spirits of the rivers and mountains live unknowable and unseen by human beings. Rivers and mountains could take any form at will if they chose to do so.

The *Kalika Purana* describes the Brahmaputra as *Maha Bahu*, or the One with Great Arms. The river frequently changes its course, spreading its long streams in different directions. During the rainy season, it swells up in overflowing floods, deluging and devastating human habitats and large tracts of rainforest that are home to myriad species of wildlife. Again, the benign Brahmaputra of winter and spring grants amazing boons of new river islands with freshly set up villages of lush paddy fields. In bright sunlight, these islands shine like emeralds set amid the vast expanse of silvery waters.

In Assamese folklore and folk songs, the river assumes the roles of the icons of splendor, prosperity, and devastation, all at the same time. In Assamese the river is called the *Luit*, a derivative of Lohit. As in the valleys of the Nile in Egypt, the Volga in Russia, and the Huang Ho in China, the life and culture of the inhabitants on the banks of the Brahmaputra are intimately associated with the river. The Brahmaputra bordered three sides of my hometown.

In the ancient epics, the Ramayana and the Mahabharata, the Brahmaputra has been sometimes called the *Lauhitya*, the Red River, and sometimes the *Lauhitya Sagara*, the Red Sea. In a passage in the "*Kiskindha Parvan*" of the Ramayana, the Lauhitya or Lauhitya Sagara features in the context of Hanuman's conquests. Hanuman, son of the Wind, was a warrior and devotee of Lord Rama. In the original translation from Valmiki's Ramayan, the relevant passage relates:

> Then having triumphed over various lands and after taking treasures there from, the mighty son of the Wind went to the river Lauhitya. He had all the chiefs of the barbarians who lived on the Sea Islands bringing tribute and treasures of all kinds—sandalwood, aloe and textiles, priceless gems and pearls, gold and silver, diamonds, and precious coral.

In Veda Vyasa's Mahabharata, the great epic of the Bharata dynasty, "*Duryodhana*" describes the native kings who lived on the banks of the Lauhitya River:

> They were the mountain kings who lived beyond the Himalaya of the Sunrise Mountain on the banks of the Vārisenā and the Lauhitya; they sustained on fruits and roots, and were clad in hides. They brought lots of sandalwood, aloe wood and agallochum, piles of hides, lots of gems, gold and perfumes, and numerous slave girls, exotic birds and animals, all from the mountains and stood at the gate. They were denied admittance.

The Lauhitya is full of blood-red waters, as described in the chapter "*Conquest of the World*" in the Mahabharata:

> Then having crossed the frightful Lohitya Sea, full of blood-red waters, you would see a mountain overgrown with massive Salmali trees. The palace of Garuda adorned with precious gems like palaces in the Kailasa designed and built by Visvakarma the architect of gods, would greet your eyes. You will find Rakshasas, called Mandeha of the dark and dreadful look, dangling from the mountain peaks.

My grandma once told me the story of Parasurama, an incarnation of Lord Vishnu, who was the son of a Brahman named Jamadagni and his wife Renuka. To fulfill his enraged father's wishes, Parasurama slew his mother with his ax. Because this was such a grave sin, the bloodstained ax stuck to Parasurama's hand and he could not remove it. In spite of years of penance and prayers, Parasurama could not expiate his sin.

At last, he went to the Brahmakunda, the sacred cavern filled with Brahmaputra waters at Tezu in the foothills of the Himalayas. He offered oblations and chanted propitious mantras. The Brahmaputra was pleased at his devotion. As soon as Parasurama took a dip into the holy waters, the bloodstained ax was detached from his hand. Waters of the Brahmakunda and the Brahmaputra mixed with the matricidal blood from Parasurama's ax and became red. Since then, the Brahmaputra has been the Red River.

During the *Makar Sankranti*, the Indian festival of harvest, Hindus take dips in the Brahmakunda to wash away their sins. Local people keep alive the Parasurama story and refer to Brahmakunda as *Parasu Kuther*, meaning the Ax of Parasurama.

The greatest legendary feature of my hometown, however, was *Netai Dhopanir Ghat*, where the mythical washerwoman Netai washed clothes. Nobody, however, knew at what age of human history she had washed those clothes.

During the winter months, the water level of the Brahmaputra receded and the bank-to-bank span of the river became shorter. The natural configuration of rocks on the riverbed emerged above the water level, obstructing the rushing stream, so the water constantly bubbled and frothed around the rocky projections.

On one of the rocks near the bank, there was an imprint resembling a giant human foot. It appeared as though an immense human being had stood on the rock, impressing it with a giant toe mark. People said that on the opposite bank of the river, an identical imprint existed. On a third rock in the middle of the river, there was a rectangular slab of stone resembling a giant washing board. It balanced on the rocks as if someone had carefully placed it on the tips of the submerged hills. It was the popular belief that Netai Dhopani had stood with her feet planted on either side of the river, five miles apart, thrashing her laundry against the gigantic slab. Nobody knew what the sizes of the clothes were or who her patrons were. Nonetheless, the existence of Netai, the washerwoman, was borne out by rock-strong evidence.

Once I asked my grandma if she knew about Netai Dhopanir Ghat. She replied assertively, "Oh yes. Netai Dhopani was not an ordinary woman. She had spiritual powers. Had there been no Netai Dhopani, Behula would never have got her husband back."

Astounded, I looked at her with curiosity. I wondered who Behula was, but before I could ask her, Grandma said, "Netai Dhopani was washerwoman of the gods and goddesses in the heaven. She used to wash their heavenly attire in the holy waters of the Brahmaputra in her ghat."

I asked, "How did Netai Dhopani look? Did anyone see her? Who was Behula?"

Grandma had become used to my inquisitive nature and answered, "These are matters of the *Satya Yuga*—the eon of truth, when only truth prevailed. Netai Dhopani was a woman of the Satya Yuga. Nobody knows how huge Netai Dhopani was. One may only guess her size from the impression on the rock bearing her footprint."

I nodded solemnly, trying to imagine such a giant standing astride the river, but I was still curious about Behula. Before I opened my mouth to ask again, Grandma continued, "Behula was another great woman of the time, daughter of Chand Sawdagar. She was the embodiment of forbearance and faith. She proved the power of a *sati*—a devoted wife. By her sacrifices, she proved that absolute devotion to a god or goddess could work wonders. I'll tell you all I know about Netai Dhopani and Behula."

In my eagerness to listen to her stories, I sat close to her on her bed. Slowly she began telling me the story.

"In the good old days of the Satya Yuga, when Netai Dhopani used to wash the clothes of the gods and goddesses in the holy waters of the Brahmaputra, a fabulously rich merchant named Chand Sawdagar lived in his palatial mansion in a distant town on the riverbank. He had an exquisitely beautiful daughter named Behula.

"A pious ascetic once told Chand Sawdagar that he, Chand Sawdagar, could amass much wealth and never lose any of it if he worshipped *Monosa*, goddess of the serpents, who would then bless him by having her watchful snakes guard Sawdagar's treasures. The ascetic advised Chand Sawdagar that as a mark of gratitude to the goddess, Sawdagar must offer a proper *puja*, an act of worship, to the serpent goddess. But Chand Sawdagar was too proud to follow the ascetic's advice. He scornfully replied, 'I have greater gods and goddesses to worship than the snake goddess. I am not going to offer any worship to Monosa.'"

My eyes grew wide at the thought of all the snakes guarding the treasure, hissing away anyone or anything that tried to snatch it away.

Grandma continued, "The goddess Monosa heard the proud statement of Chand Sawdagar. The multihooded serpent goddess was so angry that all her hoods inflated in wrath against Chand Sawdagar. Nonetheless, she could not take revenge on Chand Sawdagar because he was a devotee of Lord Siva, the greatest of the great gods."

Grandma raised her folded hands to her forehead in adoration to the greatest god, and perhaps to the goddess Monosa, and then she resumed her story.

"Because the angry snake goddess was unable to do anything to Chand Sawdagar, she pronounced her curse against his daughter. She cursed that Behula's groom would die of snakebite on their nuptial night.

"In the course of meditation, the ascetic came to know about the curse and told Chand Sawdagar about it. Yet Chand Sawdagar did not offer any puja to appease Monosa. Instead, he prayed to Lord Siva, as he always did.

"In due course, Behula's wedding was arranged with an accomplished groom named Lakhindar. Chand Sawdagar built a new castle for his daughter and her groom, and he made sure that the nuptial chamber had no windows, no cracks, no openings, and not even the tiniest fissure anywhere for a snake to enter."

"How would they breathe in such an airtight chamber?" I asked.

"Nothing is known as to how they breathed inside the chamber," Grandma replied hastily, adding, "Just listen. Behula was duly wedded to Lakhindar with pomp and grandeur and in the presence of many eminent guests. Under tight security and strict vigilance, the newlyweds entered the snakeproof nuptial chamber.

"Meanwhile, in heaven, Monosa was determined to effectuate the curse, so she asked her trusted lieutenant, the deadliest serpent *Kalnag*, to get into the nuptial chamber of Behula and Lakhindar and bite Lakhindar so that he would die on their nuptial night. Kalnag lowered his hood, bowed to the goddess, and said, 'As you wish, my goddess.'

"Kalnag had an abominable appearance like Yama, the god of death. His entire body was full of deadly venom. He had the power to change his shape and form at will. Kalnag used this to his advantage and slithered into a florist's shop, where he changed his shape to that of a fine thread and hid amid a clump of threads used to tie bunches of flowers together. When a wedding guest bought a bunch of flowers to present to the newlyweds, the florist tied the bouquet of fresh flowers using Kalnag as the tying thread. The guards at the check gate of Behula and Lakhindar's nuptial chamber allowed the bunch of flowers in as a harmless gift. And that was how Kalnag gained his entry into the nuptial chamber. The deadly snake waited quietly for the opportune moment.

"In the middle of the night, when the bride and groom were fast asleep, Kalnag detached himself from the bunch of flowers and assumed his real form. The baneful serpent bit sleeping Lakhindar on his forehead and infused into Lakhindar's brain all the venom he had. Lakhindar died instantly. Thus the snake goddess Monosa won the battle of wits against Chand Sawdagar."

Grandma once again touched her forehead with folded hands.

I asked, "Are you doing *pranam* (a gesture of reverence) to the serpent goddess, Grandma? Don't you think she is too mean to be worshipped?"

"You cannot utter or even think such things about a goddess," Grandma warned me. "Whenever you narrate or listen to any miracle of the gods and goddesses, you must show your respect to them. The goddess Monosa, in particular, can cause great harm to any human being. If she feels offended, she will do the worst possible harm through any of her kin, who are in abundance everywhere in our town."

She insisted that I too offer pranam to Monosa, and so I did.

"But that was not the end of the miracle," continued Grandma. "Bodies of the snake-bitten dead are placed on rafts made with the trunks of the banana plant and then floated on a river. The banana raft with the dead body floats from place to place. The idea is that some *ojha*—an exorcist or a snake charmer—might find the floating dead body somewhere, sometime. It is a traditional social obligation that whenever an exorcist or a snake charmer finds a snake-bitten dead body, he must, as a matter of duty, use his special powers to revive the dead. If he does not perform his duty, he will lose all his magical powers.

"Lakhindar's dead body was placed on a banana raft and left to float in the waters of the Brahmaputra. As a faithful and devoted wife, Behula sat on the raft by the side of her husband's dead body. She took a vow that by suffering the most rigorous penance and by her most dedicated prayers to the goddess Monosa, she would see her dead husband revived, or else she too would die to be with her husband in their next lives.

"The raft with Lakhindar's dead body floated from town to town and village to village for many days and nights and for many weeks and months, with Behula sitting by her dead husband's side. In the scorching sun and drenching rain, in winter chill and summer heat, steadfast Behula underwent incredible suffering and continuously prayed to Monosa for the revival of her dead husband. Birds and fishes ate up Lakhindar's skin and flesh. Only the skeleton remained. By meditation and devotion, Behula overcame her hunger and thirst. She remained steadfast to her vow."

"How could she remain without eating and drinking all the time the raft was floating with the rotting dead body?" I asked Grandma.

"By the sheer power of devotion," replied Grandma. "One can work wonders with devotion." After a pause she added, "This is the teaching of the legend.

"At last, the banana raft got stuck in the rocks of Netai Dhopanir Ghat in our town. Netai Dhopani took compassion on the wretched state of Behula and appreciated her abiding virtues as a sati and her profound devotion to Monosa. She washed Lakhindar's skeleton in the holy waters of the Brahmaputra to purify it."

"What happened then?" I asked doubtfully, certain that Grandma was going to tell me something miraculous, but not certain that I would believe it.

Grandma replied, "Netai Dhopani took Behula, carrying her husband's skeleton, to the goddess Monosa in heaven."

"How could she go to heaven?" I asked incredulously.

"I have already told you that Netai used to wash the holy apparel of the gods and goddesses. Monosa was one of them. She, naturally, had access to all the gods and goddesses in heaven as her customers."

"Oh," I said simply, not knowing what else to say.

Grandma went on, "Netai Dhopani led Behula, still carrying her husband's skeleton, to the luxurious palace of the serpent goddess Monosa. The deadly venomous snakes guarding the palace knew Netai Dhopani and admitted her. On Netai Dhopani's assurance, Behula too got into the palace with her husband's skeleton. Monosa was holding court with her husband, Sage Jaratkaru. Her serpent courtiers, including Kalnag, attended them. Behula most fervently prayed to the goddess to restore her husband to life. Netai Dhopani too pleaded for Behula.

"Monosa was already pleased with Behula's sacrifices and devotion. When Netai Dhopani also pleaded for Behula, the goddess ordered Kalnag to take his venom back from the skull and bones of Lakhindar. Obedient Kalnag sucked out the venom from Lakhindar's skeleton. At once, Lakhindar came back to life! Thus, by the grace of the goddess Monosa, Lakhindar came back to life as a young man with Behula still by his side as his young wife. They lived happily ever after."

* * *

Later, as I grew up, I learned that the Behula-Lakhindar story is from "Monosa Mangal Kavya," an ode from the Mongal kavyas of medieval Bengal believed to have originated during the fifteenth to eighteenth centuries. According to others, the kavya form originated in the seventh and eighth centuries. These odes, dedicated to folk deities of non-Aryan origin, were born out of human fear of fierce animals, reptiles, and deadly epidemic diseases. The story signifies how the concept of sati or suti was popularized during the time when Hinduism degenerated and the oppression of women was common.

5

Panch Pīrer Darga, the shrine of five saints, stood amid the rows of residences of the top officials of district admiration. The tarmac road in front of the Darga ran parallel to the Brahmaputra. The shrine existed long before the British annexed the country and raised the official residences. The pīrs (spiritual guides), whose bodies lay in their tombs in eternal rest, were Islamic saints. Both Hindus and Muslims considered the shrine sacred. People came to the shrine with their entire families, including small children. They lit earthen lamps and candles, placed offerings of milk, sweets, and money, and prayed for fulfillment of their wishes—recovery for the ailing, marriage for an unwed daughter, victory in a court case, success in a business deal, good grades on an exam, and anything else that worried them.

Panch Pīrer Darga, although a holy shrine of five Islamic saints, was strikingly different from the famous Darga Sharif of Ajmer in Rajasthan, both in terms of history and popularity. Ajmer was conquered by the twelfth-century Muslim invaders from Afghanistan. Islamic evangelist Khawjah Mu'īnud-Din Chistī came from Persia. He set up his retreat in Ajmer in Rajasthan to popularize the Sufi creed of Islam in India. It is believed that in the 114th year of his life, he locked himself up in a room in his retreat. After seven days, his lifeless body was found lying in the room as his holy soul migrated to heaven.

Abū Ishāq founded the Sufi order of Islam in Chistī, a Syrian village in western Asia. In the later part of the twelfth century, the Sufi saint Muīn-ud-Din Chistī established the order in Ajmer in India, where he lived the rest of his life. Sufism gained popularity throughout the Indian subcontinent. The doctrine of the unity of all beings and the oneness of God is the heart of Sufi doctrine. Pacifist Chistī principles were essentially based on policies of amity and assimilation rather than bellicosity and retribution toward so-called *kāfirs,* or infidels.

The Chistī saints in India adopted many Hindu and Buddhist practices. Their lifestyles were comparable to those of Hindu ascetics and gurus who believed in tolerance. They were thus highly successful in converting large numbers of Hindus and Buddhists to the Islamic faith.

The thirteenth-century Persian poet Amir Khusrau, a follower of Muhammad Nizām-ud-Din Awliyā of the Chistī dervish order of Delhi, expressed religious tolerance and the need to show reciprocal respect between the two religious communities of India as the fundamental principle of pacifism. The poet proclaimed that one must not sneer at the idolatry of the Hindus but learn from them the depth of devotion. He said that although Hindus did not profess the same religion, they believed in the same things as the faithful.

Ajmer was the capital of the eleventh-century Rajput ruler Ajayadeva. Some archeologists and historians believe that the Chistī saints' darga was originally a Hindu temple of Brahma or a Jain temple converted to an Islamic shrine. This inference is drawn from the ornate ceiling of the saints' memorial. It bears carvings of lotus motifs, symbol of Lord Brahma in Hinduism and transcendental wisdom in Jainism. The design of the white marble spire on the shrine further corroborates the inference.

The Chishtīyah, or the period of the Sufi saints, had its highest impact in India between circa 200 and 1356 AD. Of the monarchs of the fifteenth-century Khilji dynasty, Sultan Mahamūd Khilji visited Ajmer in 1455. According to others, Sultan Ghiyās al-dīn Khilji (1469–1500) made the tomb. Sher Shāh (1540–57) of the Sur dynasty of northern India also visited the darga in Ajmer. The Mughal emperor Akbar took a lot of interest in Sufi doctrine and the saints' tomb, also known as Hazarat Kawaja Garib Nawaz Darga in Ajmer.

Over time, the mystic order split into various branches and sects and took root in fourteenth-century monasteries all over India. The Ṣābirīyah branch of the fifteenth century was established at Rudawli in the Barabanki district of Uttar Pradesh. The Nizāmīyah in Delhi was revived by Shā Kalim Allāh Jahānābādī in the eighteenth century.

The particular sector of Delhi in which the tomb exists is known as Nizamuddin.

There was no such authentic historical background for the origin and identity of Panch Pīrer Darga of my hometown. According to the history told in the region, sometime around 1658, the Mughal governor of Bengal, Mir Jumlah, sent his general, Rashid Khan, to fight back the intruding Shan tribe—the Ahoms, who ruled Assam up to the north bank of the Brahmaputra. The Hindu king Prān Nārāyan ruled the south bank of the river. Rashid Khan's army fought the Ahoms back to the Arakan range in Burma.

Under the terms of the subsequent truce, the Ahom king Jayadhvaj resumed his rule over the northern part of Assam beyond the Manas River. During the period of his occupation, which included my home district, Rashid Khan built a mosque and dug a deep well at a point called Panbari, twenty-two miles north of my hometown. The mosque was known as Mir Jumlah's mosque. However, there appears to be no distinct historical link between Rashid Khan's occupation and the origin of Panch Pīrer Darga.

In 1675, the Mughal emperor Aurangzeb sent an army under the command of Raja Ram Singh to crush the revolt of the Ahom king Chakradhvaj. Five Sufi pīrs accompanied the raja on his expedition. In all probability, Panch Pīrer Darga is the tomb of those five pīrs. Nothing more, however, is known about the history of the shrine. Since people of both the Hindu and Muslim communities consider the shrine holy, it is most probable that the darga is of Sufi saints. Between the twelfth and the fifteenth centuries, Sufism spread all over India, including Bengal. Southern Assam being close to Bengal and linked to the rest of India by land and water routes through the Brahmaputra and its connecting streams, it may be presumed that Sufism spread to the area.

Unlike the darga in Ajmer, the vicinity of the darga in my hometown was never crammed with hundreds of thousands of pilgrims and tourists of all faiths and cultures. There were no narrow lanes and alleyways leading to the shrine and no congestion of shops and stalls. There were no eateries, no camel-carts, no horse-drawn coaches creeping through the suffocating crowd on the narrow roads. There were no peddlers selling rose petals and sweets as offerings, no crowd of beggars, no nerve-wracking hubbub, and no baton-wielding policemen to clear the road for the VIP pilgrims visiting the shrine to seek blessings.

In sharp contrast to the Darga Sharif at Ajmer, Panch Pīrer Darga was located in a serene environment refreshed by the bracing breeze off the Brahmaputra. Tall and sturdy teak trees in the large and open yard of the darga cast an air of tranquility over the shrine. Behind the shrine was the modest home of the *khuddām*—the caretaker of the holy tomb. Many Hindu and Muslim devotees who regularly visited the shrine were personally known to the khuddām.

Opposite the Panch Pīrer Darga, on the bank of the great river, were two recreational parks, one for men and the other for women. However, male and female family members accompanying women and children could enter both parks.

Beyond the iron railings of the parks was the fast-flowing Brahmaputra. The vast span of the river mirrored the blue of the sky. In fair weather, the silhouette of the mountain kingdom of Bhutan appeared on the skyline beyond the river. During the monsoon rains, the river swelled up to its brink and rushed in a tumultuous tantrum. My hometown then resembled an island in an ocean. It was a breathtaking experience to watch the Brahmaputra in its frenzied deluge.

During winter, the water level of the Brahmaputra receded, and the bank-to-bank span of the river became shorter. A long and deep flight of cement stairs running from the roadside down to the river would appear right by the legendary footprint of Netai Dhopanir Ghat.

In my childhood, an irresistible proclivity brought me to the ghat on idle afternoons when no one was there to interrupt in my fanciful moments. The swooshing sound of flowing waters enthralled me. A faraway, gentle breeze, the sibilant breath of the Brahmaputra, rustled the leaves of tall trees on the bank. The ambience was perfect for reverie. I would slip into my dreamland.

One afternoon at Netai Dhopanir Ghat, I found a bearded old man, wearing a pair of blue pants and a knitted pullover, sitting on one of the lower steps of the stairway. The presence of the stranger disrupted my solitude. I resolved to ignore him. But time after time, my eyes inadvertently fell on him. He greeted me with a smile and winked his invitation to join him.

I never knew what charm he cast on me; I stepped down like a mesmerized being to where he was sitting. He asked me to sit down and introduced himself as Abdul Sattar. Despite the great difference in our ages, we became friends because of our common interest in the river. Over the course of many successive meetings on the riverbank, I came to know the thoughts and feelings of the lonesome man. I would never have known many things had I not met Abdul Sattar. I called him Sattar Miyan.

Sattar Miyan was born into a handloom weaver's family in Jangipur, on the bank of the Bhagirathi River in the Murshidabad district of northwest Bengal. From his childhood, he enjoyed swimming and boating on the river. As he grew up, his parents moved to Mymensingh in East Bengal. While in Mymensingh, Sattar Miyan became interested in large rivers like the Meghna and the Brahmaputra, known as the Yamuna in Mymensingh. Sattar Miyan already knew many Baul songs and other Bengali folk songs while he was in Jangipur. Then he learned Bhatiali songs from the East Bengal boatmen.

After briefly attending a madrassa in Mymensingh, Sattar Miyan took a job in a jute trading company at the river port of Narayangang, near Dhaka. He loaded bales of jute into barges and steamboats. In the process, Sattar Miyan came to know many steamboat workers, including steamboat crewman Abdul Khalek. Khalek helped him get a job as an apprentice crewman in the English-owned River Steam Navigation Company, generally known as the RSN Company. Sattar Miyan spent his entire career as a *khalasi*, or crewman, on the RSN Company's steamboats. He navigated on steamboats plying the watercourses of eastern and northeastern India.

After retirement from service, he felt nostalgic and came back to his birthplace, Jangipur. But he was utterly disappointed to find that his home village was no longer the same village he had known in his childhood. Everything was so different; everything was changed. Sattar Miyan could not recognize his birthplace.

The palms that had produced luscious juice that made jaggery were no more. The *doel* and *koel* songbirds were gone. The fabulous tamarind trees and the dainty pomegranate plants too were no more. Tile-roofed mud houses had been replaced with tin-roofed cottages; metal roads had been substituted for pastoral paths. The *haat*, a weekly bazaar that had been the traditional rendezvous of neighboring villagers and the meeting-point to exchange mutual happiness and sorrows, was held no more in Jangipur. The rattling of handlooms on which village weavers wove the famous Murshidabadi saris was heard no more. Nobody knew how and where the weavers had gone.

Brokenhearted, Sattar Miyan could not find any of his childhood friends to tell him about the many changes. Some had migrated to other places; others had left this world forever. Shops and stalls, eateries and inns lined the new and busy road, turning Jangipur into a highway halt and a trucker's joint.

In his disappointment, Sattar Miyan decided to quit Jangipur in search of a peaceful place to spend the rest of his life. Mymensingh and Narayangang were too crowded and too expensive. He liked my picturesque hometown on the bank of the Brahmaputra, the river he had come to know so well during his career on the steamboats. So he moved to my hometown and decided to spend the rest of his life there.

He said he found peace whenever he came to the riverside. He was a pensive old man who gave the best part of his life to the RSN Company. He had his own convictions and a strong sense of likes and dislikes. I loved to listen to him as we sat on the bank of the Brahmaputra. I loved the reflective and confident manner in which he told me about his life and his thoughts. He sang to me in his natural country style. I discovered in him a sincere and unpretentious man. His affinity with the river was absolute.

Steamboats from the company Sattar Miyan had worked for cruised up and down the stream of the Brahmaputra. These smartly built steamboats had exotic Indian names boldly inscribed on their chimneys; some had white bands around the circumference of their flues. These boats were large and strong enough to navigate in the turbulent Brahmaputra, often with two flatboats loaded with cargo tugged along the sides. Sattar Miyan knew most of these steamboats and many of the *sarengs*, or boatswains, by their names.

Most members of the crews of the steamer company boats were Muslims from East Bengal. English companies operating steamboats in India preferred Muslims for their unfailing loyalty and familiarity with East Indian rivers. Many came from the boatmen and fishermen communities. Although Sattar Miyan was born to a weaver's family in northwestern Bengal, his religious and elementary general education had been in Mymensingh in East Bengal, where he spent his adolescence and youth. Thus for all practical purposes, Sattar Miyan too was an East Bengal Muslim and a boatman.

Sattar Miyan once called the Brahmaputra "Wild Yak Bull." I thought that he was comparing the turbulent nature of the Brahmaputra with the wild yaks of Tibet. He later elucidated his reference. He said, "Once we went upstream to Sadiya. We were on a navigability survey, an adventurous cruise upland against the force of the waters. It was not only difficult but dangerous. We had to find the furthest point of navigability on the Brahmaputra. The more we cruised upstream, the more we found silt-filled areas. We had to be particularly cautious to find a navigable course and not hit upon a submerged rock.

"On that particular trip, a young sahib was the captain of the boat and old Suleman Ali was the sareng. The young sahib called the river Wild Yak Bull, probably because of the river's tempestuous nature and its origin in the Tibetan region of the Himalayas. The young sahib was very angry at the wildness of the river. He expressed his anger by shooting deer and waterfowl that came within range on the banks.

"With our small lifeboats, most of the time it was very difficult, sometimes impossible, to pick out game from the thicket of weeds and shrubs on the jungly riverbanks. *Insha'Allah*—God willing—in spite of all the hazards of the rough cruise, we collected enough game birds and deer through the skill of the young sahib. We enjoyed cooking and eating waterfowls and venison. For the young sahib, we specially cooked spice-free dishes because he could not take our type of hot and spicy food."

Sattar Miyan went on to say that the young sahib asserted that, had the Brahmaputra been a river in his country, people would never have allowed it to behave so wildly. They would not have granted so much liberty to the river to inundate such vast areas of land every year, to change its course so frequently, and to impede navigability with sand and silt unpredictably transferred and deposited from one end to another. He chuckled. "The young sahib was our boss, a white man. Besides, he never ill-treated us because we were natives. So we quietly listened to whatever he said."

Then, in a sardonic tone, Sattar Miyan added, "Sahib did not know that human beings can never control rivers. White men are fortunate that Allah did not create rivers like the Brahmaputra in their country to rush through such intricate courses from the Himalayan heights, traversing ravines and forests and carrying so much rainwater and silt."

I didn't like to interrupt him with my textbook knowledge of the many turbulent rivers that flow in countries beyond India. Neither had I any particular interest in the young sahib, his opinions, and his activities. I was only interested in the stories of Sattar Miyan. Perhaps my presence provided a good opportunity for the lonely man to vocalize his thoughts and memories to a receptive listener.

His long association with some of the major Indian rivers had convinced him that rivers are animate entities. He thought that rivers behaved according to their natural instincts and that their movements were regulated by an ultimate power. He regretted that the white men and most of his own countrymen did not know this obvious truth. He believed that the Brahmaputra yearned to join his mate, the river Meghna in East Bengal, to flow together and then drain out all earthly exuberance and despair into the Bay of Bengal. That, he believed, was the underlying truth that prompted the rivers to merge with the ocean, the eternal waters.

He said, "East Bengal boatmen understand the rivers and articulate their feelings in their songs. The young sahib did not realize that Indian rivers never accepted the steamboats as they accepted indigenous country boats. How could one tame a river? Rivers are expressions of nature. Human beings can temporarily destroy some natural phenomena but can never tame nature, because nature is controlled by the Almighty."

After a whole lifetime of cruising the great rivers of India, Sattar Miyan pronounced his profound comprehension. Fixing his eyes on the waters of the Brahmaputra, Sattar Miyan sang for his own delight an East Bengal folk song. The imagery of the unknown songwriter was that the enigmatic river mirrored the form of the formless and the sense of the essence—the supreme substance.

Sometimes, addressing the Guru, or God, he would sing a song that contended that when in a whole lifetime the songwriter couldn't fathom the river's mind, how he could he fathom the immense grace of the Guru? So he vowed to live in the river and die in the river, swinging and floating all the while until the Guru rescued him and took him home. Traditionally, these songs were sung by the Bauls, fakirs, and boatmen, engrossed in their own cognition of love, life, nature, and the ultimate reality. It never mattered whether they were born as Hindu or Muslim, Vaishnava or Sakta, Shia or Sunni. They expressed similar feelings in their spontaneously composed songs.

The Bauls are traditional wanderers, dedicated to singing and dancing. Their compositions are full of pastoral imagery and spiritual metaphors, which they passionately intonate in rich folk forms. Bauls are beyond the bounds of any conventional religion. They are only devoted to the Baul perception of human life and the ultimate reality.

Bauls have come to be known as a sect. Many Bauls are artists and philosophers in their own right, acclaimed and appreciated by the rural folk as well as the sophisticated. Some of the outstanding Baul songs are compositions of Fakir Shah or Lalon Fakir Shah, who lived and sang his songs in nineteenth-century Bengal. Baul themes and forms appear in many of the songs of the mystic poet Rabindranath Tagore.

Sattar Miyan also sang Bhatiali songs. These compositions were also replete with mystic imagery and sung by professional boatmen who live normal domestic lives. In a few Bhatiali songs, the romantic aspects of human love, happiness, and sorrow often attain aesthetic and even spiritual heights. Many of these compositions are classic in nature and highly popular as a distinctive tradition of folk songs of Bengal. These songs epitomize the instinctive genius of bucolic boatmen expressing the fleeting nature of human life. I recall Sattar Miyan singing, in the typical high-pitched Bhatiali tone, a song in which the songwriter says that had he known before, he would have never boarded the scuttled boat, symbolizing the transient nature of human life.

These compositions also signified the river as the river of life. To the all-powerful moon, the helmsmen appealed for protection and success in their sailing expeditions. Although temporal love was the most familiar theme of these songs, the lyrics often related to mythology, particularly the Viraha-Bhakti aspect as applied to temporal life.

This was where Bhatiali and Baul songs differed in content. Baul songs were essentially devotional, even though they spoke of the worldly aspects of life. Baul songs invariably invoked highly philosophical thoughts. Bhatiali songs related to mundane aspects of life, especially love and the pangs of separation, though they occasionally spiritualized human love. Musically, the two forms had different styles, but both were rendered in identifiably folk patterns.

Sattar Miyan told me, "Rivers come streaming down the hills and flow from higher to lower levels of land, traversing the country before merging with the ocean. It is the wide outlet to the ocean that welcomes the rivers to merge with the ocean. The moon causes the ebb and tide of the rivers. When the river is in *joar*, high tide, it surges and becomes restive. It is like the restless exuberance of youth, when ambition and desire overwhelms. People want to have everything and forever.

"During the *bhata*, the ebbing tide, the river is calm and relaxed. It is like the poise of realization that life is only a fleeting phenomenon and desire is mere illusion. Men cannot have everything they crave, and at last they realize the truth of life. Bhatiali songs portray that realization. They accept human destiny as the absolute truth of life. Along with the ebbing tide of the river, Bhatiali songs flow calm and relaxed, reconciled to fate like a boat sailing down the ebbing stream. All smiles and tears, all loss and gain, all hope and despair flow down the Bhatiali songs, wide and doleful. It is like the waters rushing from the mountainous height of illusion to the level of reality—the ocean."

He said that the Baul, on the other hand, would sing his metaphoric compositions that picked up the ordinary aspects of rural life and lifted them to the numinous height of transcendental realization. The Baul liked to carry on with the affairs of everyday life, while at the same time maintaining detachment from the illusory lures of life.

Sattar Miyan often sang a composition in which the songwriter said that the entire universe was a great void. How could one think of making a house in the pervasive emptiness? I did not know if Sattar Miyan too was a Baul. I only knew that he had unfailing faith in the Almighty, whom he named variously in his songs as Allah, Guru, Gosaīn, and Saīn.

One day, I asked Sattar Miyan about Panch Pīrer Darga. I wanted to know who the pīrs were, resting in the tombs. Sattar Miyan replied, "The pīrs and fakirs are holy men; they possess the supernatural power that passes to them from the Prophet himself."

I told him that I had seen the fakirs who visited our home on Saturdays. Each held in his hands a twisted cane studded with colorful beads and a tin can fixed to its handle, together with a *shanī*, an icon of Saturn carved in a small sheet of tin. They chanted lines from the "Shanīr Paņchali"—Bengali folk verses about the legends of the Shanī, sung to exorcise evil for the welfare of the household. Whenever a fakir came to our home, my mother or Grandma dropped a few coins into his tin can. He would then bless everyone and leave for the next house in the neighborhood.

Sattar Miyan chuckled and said, "Well, the so-called fakirs who visit domestic houses are mere vagrants. Genuine fakirs do not beg from door to door; they are holy men."

After a pause, he said, "It is difficult to explain to you all about each of these categories of holy men. They are mystic saints. They perform miracles. They can cure the incurable and enhance the well-being of those who attend their resorts and listen to their talks with devotion."

Sattar Miyan smiled and explained further, "Those who attend the holy men with absolute faith and devotion, listen to their divine discourses, and seek their blessings will get all their material and spiritual desires fulfilled. Even after the holy men die, those who come to their shrines and pray with devotion get their problems solved and wishes fulfilled. That is why they are called *zinda pīrs*—ever-alive saints. Their holy spirits remain alive even after their bodies are placed into graves. Their bodies pass away, but their holy spirits don't. So their tombs are holy shrines."

"How do their spirits remain alive when they go to their graves?" I asked.

"Their existence is spiritual. Many righteous people have seen rays of divine light over the tombs of these holy men. Many have seen miracles. I told you they are mysterious. Ordinary people cannot realize the greatness of the saints. Although we are unaware of their powers, many such holy men always live in this world. A devout person may invoke the holy spirit of any one of them, whether living or resting in the grave. Righteous people get blessings to fulfill their material and spiritual needs."

Sattar Miyan left an unforgettable mark in my mind.

6

One afternoon, Grandma was sitting all alone in her bedroom, looking at her old photo album. As I came in, she closed the album and put it back into a drawer in her timeworn cabinet. For some reason, she was in a great mood that afternoon. Her happy mood encouraged me to ask her to tell me a story.

She replied with an indulgent smile, "Am I a story wizard to instantly produce stories on demand?"

I begged her in my usual manner. "Grandma, you've never told me anything about yourself. Today, please tell me your own story. What did you do when you were going to school like Anita and me? Tell me about your pals and playmates—I mean, all about you only."

"I am your grandma; isn't that a great story?" She chuckled.

"I know, but please tell me what happened when you were not a grandma," I urged.

"I was wedded to your grandpa when I was a student in the primary school in my home village. That is my story."

Her face changed. I looked at her in surprise. After a silent while, she smiled, and I collected enough courage to press her for more details. "Tell me about your wedding with Grandpa, please, Grandma."

For a while, Grandma was sunk in her thoughts. I eagerly waited for her to begin. Slowly, her face assumed an aura I had never before seen. She smiled quietly without a word as I looked at her with expectation.

Then she began, "You know, your grandpa is a very learned man. He spent most of his student life away from home, living in college and university hostels. When he was studying law, his father, your great-grandfather, visited our home and discussed the marriage of his son with my father. Together they decided that I should be wedded to your grandpa. I didn't meet your grandpa before my wedding to him; I didn't know him."

She took a pause and then said, "After their decision, one day your great-grandfather, together with some others, came to our home to see me ceremonially, as was the custom. Then the *ashīrvad*, the betrothal ceremony, was held at our home. Your great-grandpa blessed me with a pair of oversized *kangkan*, traditional gold bangles, and I was engaged to your grandpa without knowing him. How do you like that?" she asked me with grin.

To be doubly sure, I asked her if she had seen Grandpa before the betrothal ceremony.

"No, I never saw him at any time before I was wedded to him. Your great-grandpa came to perform the ashīrvad ceremony, not with your grandpa, but with some other elderly men. I was terribly scared. I cried. I never wanted to get married. I wanted to be with my mother, my brothers, and my playmates. I wanted to continue with my studies in school. I didn't want to leave my home. But in those days, girls like me had no choice. We had to wed our grooms whether they were old or young, ugly or handsome, and they were chosen by our fathers or elder brothers, whoever was a girl's guardian."

This seemed incredible to me, so I asked her again, "Your wedding with Grandpa was fixed even before you saw him?"

She smiled with a glow of contentment and affirmed it. "Absolutely, and I have no regrets. I had a happy life with your grandpa in the many phases of our conjugal life, sometimes good, sometimes not too good."

An expression of tranquility was on her face. She plunged back into her thoughts. After a while, I reminded her that she was supposed to tell me about the ashīrvad ceremony. Grandma came back, perhaps with tons of memories overwhelming her. She resumed her story.

"Oh, yes. After the ashīrvad ceremony, my wedding date was fixed on an auspicious day and at an auspicious time determined by the priests and pundits, who knew the auspicious dates and times."

She suddenly became quiet again, too soon for me, because I eagerly wanted to hear more. After a while, she narrated how she had to go through many traditional rituals, such as the turmeric bath and other prewedding ceremonies, with women and girls singing as they brought pitchers of water from the nearby river. She said that all those rituals were great fun.

I listened attentively as she drew from the deep well of her memories.

"As the wedding date drew near, the atmosphere of our home changed. Relations from other villages and towns poured into our home. There were a lot of new faces and lots of children. Ornaments, saris, and many more things were brought from Dhaka as wedding gifts for me, for the bridegroom, and for other members of his family. My parents, uncles, aunts, elder brothers, and cousins all got busy arranging various aspects of the wedding ceremony. Preparations for the reception of the all-important groom and his party and the customary feasts for the invited guests were going on in full swing. A big canopy was put above the courtyard. *Purahits*, or priests, pundits, jewelers, cooks, and sweets makers all came. And a *nahabatkhāna* too was erected."

"What is a nahabatkhāna, Grandma?" I wondered.

"Well, a nahabatkhāna is something like a makeshift loft set up on the top of the reception gate, on which the musicians sat and played. In those days, there were no readily available bands of musicians for hire. It was a luxury to have a nahabatkhāna made for a wedding. An *ostad*, a maestro, came from Dhaka with his disciples to accompany him in playing *shehnai* music. They were great musicians who took high fees. They were traditional gurus with many disciples. They played only classical raga music. It was my father's desire that there be shehnai music played by a well-known ostad's ensemble during my wedding. I was the only daughter of my parents."

"Oh, that's great, Grandma! I didn't know that! I love to listen to shehnai music. I've heard Ostad Bismilla Khan's shehnai recitals on gramophone records. Did Bismilla Khan come to your wedding?"

"I only remember that a nahabatkhāna was made and shehni music was played. I never knew who the ostad was who led the music party," replied Grandma.

She smiled when she looked into my astounded eyes. She said, "I never felt that it was *my* wedding for which all these arrangements were made and for which so many people came to our home. I and my friends were enjoying watching all the hectic activity in the house. I was playing around, having fun with the goings-on and the festivities. After all, I was just a child.

"My cousin Bibhabati was already married. She came from a nearby village to attend my wedding. One evening she took me to a corner and told me that I must not run about like other children. She said I must behave like a bride or else people would say that I was an immodest girl, a tomboy.

"Her advice fell on my ears like molten lead. I cried out in anger and fear. Until that moment, I had not taken the wedding as a serious matter. Although my mother and others soothed me with their loving words, from that moment I realized that my upcoming marriage was not only a serious matter but also a vital turn in my life. I had to keep myself aloof from others and within the confines of the house. I had to surrender helplessly to my fate. It was a strange feeling . . . it is very hard to explain. I felt as if I was not wanted in my own home anymore. It seemed as though I was being gifted out to some strangers. It's a terrible feeling . . . you can't understand."

Grandma appeared lost in her faraway thoughts. I felt sad and sorry for her. Both of us kept quiet, holding each other's hands. I didn't know what to say.

On her own, Grandma came back and then resumed her narration with a smile. "And then, on the wedding day, the groom's party arrived. They were given an uproarious reception. There were many paraffin lamps flooding the entire area with bright light, and all the festivities were accompanied by the joyful sounds of shehnai music and conch-shell blowing.

"I did not go out, and I did not see the reception. I could only feel the hilarity and the hubbub outside my lonely room. I had been told to fast the whole day, and I had not eaten anything since morning. I quietly stayed inside the room like an inanimate object.

"From time to time, girls and women from the neighborhood came to see me as though I were an exhibit. They babbled; they teased me; they cut jokes and laughed. But nothing really interested me.

"They were dressed in their best saris and had put on all the ornaments they had. They wrapped me in a gold-embroidered sari and put a lot of gold jewelry all over my body. I felt fettered in gold and messy in the heavy sari. They made up my face with powder and things. They lined my eyes with *kajal*, a homemade eyeliner to brighten my eyes. Finally, they decorated my face with the typical designs of *alaka-tilaka* made with sandalwood paste.

"I was crying in hunger. My tears washed away all the sandalwood dots on my face. At last my mother, ignoring convention, somehow brought me a glass of hot milk and a few pieces of sweets. I gobbled all the sweets she brought and quaffed the glass of hot milk."

Grandma could hardly suppress the explosion of her feelings as she recounted the situation with mixed emotions. In her efforts to control her imminent outburst, she stopped for a while and then exclaimed, "Can you imagine the scene?"

I tried seriously to visualize all that she had described, but I was having difficulty doing so. It seemed hard to believe that she, the bride, had been made to suffer hunger and wait alone.

Grandma seemed to enjoy recounting the memory overall, but at one point she abruptly wound up her narration. She only said, "Anyhow, the wedding was over as if in a spell of stupor. I really do not remember much of it. Perhaps most of the time, I was in a state of slumber, doing whatever I was asked to do. I was led to do things that are required in performing the wedding rites."

Grandma again became lost in thought. I coaxed her to tell me what happened after the wedding rites. She related how emotional and nervous she felt while leaving her parents, her brothers, her cousins, and her playmates after the wedding was over.

"The very thought that I would be leaving my mother and other loved ones at home and that I would be going away with the groom, a stranger, was a devastating feeling. I was scared. I was all in sobs, as was my mother, who never wanted to send me away. I was her only daughter and still just a child! But it was inevitable; it was the custom, an inviolable social rule that daughters must be wedded young and sent out from their family homes to live with their grooms forever. Marriage was a matter of destiny for young girls, not a matter of choice."

Grandma said that soon after her wedding and the emotional parting with her family, she sailed with her husband to her new home, where she was destined to spend the rest of her life. She did not know how to behave as a wife and daughter-in-law, especially with unknown people in an unfamiliar setting. She said she felt extremely scared.

She recalled how, clad in a gold-threaded Banaras-silk sari and bedecked in heavy gold jewelry, she sat on a bed in an exclusive cabin in the *bajra*—a privately owned, luxury country boat with cabins, used for sailing by river from one village to another.

The only other familiar person in the cabin was her attending maid, an elderly woman who had worked in her parental home for many years. The maid was a kind woman. She had looked after the children and done household chores in the family home. She was sent along with Grandma to escort her, guide her, and look after her as Grandma went to her in-laws' house. It was a customary practice among landholders to send a housemaid with a just-wedded daughter. Old and experienced maids functioned as the bride's caretaker.

Grandma described the interior of the cabin she and her maid shared during the cruise. She said that the flower garlands she had exchanged with her groom during the wedding ceremony now lay wilted before her on a small table fixed to the cabin floor. Also on the table was the *mukut*, the bridal tiara she had worn, and the *topor*, the conical cap of the groom, both made of white Indian sponge wood.

A portmanteau placed on the floor contained her new saris and the add-ons, silken and woolen wrappers, and many other necessities and luxuries. Her many items of gold jewelry were packed in a red velvet casket, along with a few silver coins in a pouch and other valuable items presented by her parents, brothers, cousins, and wedding guests. A leather attaché case placed over the portmanteau contained her toiletries and cosmetics. A brand-new leather suitcase and an umbrella packed in its original paper wrapping were also near the portmanteau. The umbrella and the contents of the leather suitcase were customary gifts offered to the groom during the wedding celebration.

She said that more than anything else, she constantly felt conscious of the vermilion dabbed on the furrow of the parting of her hair and of the vermilion dot on her forehead, essential signs of a married Hindu woman. The other symbol of a wedded Bengali Hindu woman was the conch-shell bangle she wore on her wrists. This bangle was conspicuous among many gold bangles of various designs. Every time she moved her hand, the bangles on her wrist tinkled, giving her a strange sense of awareness that she was now a married woman. All these and the marital rites performed before *Agni,* the god of fire, as the witness to the union, cast on her a strange spell of responsibility that she didn't know how to bear. She was confused and very scared.

The boat was sailing on the Padma, the river that features prominently in Bengali literature and many pastoral songs of East Bengal. Other than Grandma and her old maid, the rest of the people in the boat were men. The youngest among them was her groom's only brother, Yadav. Her groom was with his cousins and friends, who accompanied him as *bar-yatri,* somewhat like the groomsmen in a Western wedding. They were on the rooftop. Seniors and elders relaxed in the only other cabin in the boat. Others were on the front deck, playing cards or chess or engaged in chats. Thus, the men instinctively divided in groups according to their ages and conventional etiquette.

From time to time, an attendant would hold out before the seniors' platters full of *paan*, or betel-leaf. Neatly folded, paan leaves were filled with thinly cut pieces of betel nut and seasoned with dashes of edible lime, catechu paste, cardamom, cinnamon, and other aromatic fillings. The leaves were pinned with a clove at the center. Paan was an essential element of Indian culture. Offering paan for chewing was a common custom both at home and on ceremonial occasions. Sometimes, offering paan was part of the formal process of initiating important proposals. Other times, offering paan was a gesture of respect. Paan was invariably offered during the worship of goddesses. For many men and women, chewing paan was an addiction, with or without the mild narcotic preparations of tobacco. A paan-chewing housewife was a symbol of prosperity, like *Lakshmi,* the goddess of prosperity. Grandma, however, was not used to chewing paan.

Smoking an aromatic native tobacco mix in a *gargara,* now commonly known as hubble-bubble, was an aristocratic addiction, especially among seniors and middle-aged men. There were various grades of native tobacco in terms of flavor, strength, and price. Most boatmen, peasants, and ordinary folk smoked the common man's handheld *hookah*, a coconut-shell water pipe. Important men smoked gargara through long, flexible rubber tubes fixed to a water-filled metal container. This container was fitted with a vertical wooden tube with a detachable earthen bud on the top, which contained tobacco sprinkled on burning charcoal cakes. This ingenious smoking device probably originated in Persia and was introduced in India during Mughal rule.

Smoking tobacco in any form in the presence of one's elders and superiors was considered a gross discourtesy. Fashionable young men smoked cigarettes, one of the first things the British introduced in Bengal. Never in his life, however, did Grandpa take paan or tobacco in any form; nor did he ever drink alcohol.

I asked Grandma, "Wasn't Grandpa with you in the cabin?"

Now back to her normal mood, she replied, "He was sailing in the same boat, of course, but not in the cabin I was in. In those days, it was considered highly immodest for young husbands and wives to hang around one another, especially when others were in sight. We had just been married, and there were many elders and others in the boat."

The corners of her lips curled upward in amusement, and she gleefully said, "Your grandpa's younger brother, Yadav, came to me from time to time to inquire how I was doing and to ask me if he could bring me things I needed. Many times, he offered to bring me food and drink. Later, I came to know that your grandpa was sending Yadav. I did not feel like taking anything. I only felt awkward and worried."

I had never before found Grandma in such an engagingly reflective mood. She was recollecting the precious moments of her early years and perhaps the most memorable time of her young life. She recounted that while sitting inside the cabin, she could feel the rolling waves of the Padma rocking and swinging the large boat. She said that she had no mind to listen to the incessant babbling of her attendant maid. The rhythmic sound of the rowers' oars and the splashing of water created a soporific ambience.

Lost in her thoughts, she felt nostalgic, recounting the emotional parting from her parents and others at her parental home from which she had been sent away forever. She did not know what awaited her in the unknown environment of the family home of her husband and her in-laws. She hardly knew her husband, whom she had thus far only been with on their nuptial night. On that night, he had appeared decent and polite. But that was when she was in her parental home. Now she would be in an unknown atmosphere. If she was mistreated, no one would come to her rescue. She had been solemnly consecrated to her groom for life by the sacred mantras of the wedding rite. She must bear whatever she might encounter.

Again, she thought that she was now the duly married wife of a respectable young man. She had to feel confident in her role as an equally respectable wife and the eldest daughter-in-law of a traditional family of high heritage. After her marriage was settled, her friends and her mother had told her that she was very lucky to be the bride of such an eligible groom from such a well-known family. She knew that her mother would never have told her that unless her mother knew it for sure. She tried to think that she must be proud because she had such a highly educated and decent husband.

Her mental state was as wavering as the waves of the Padma. She was too exhausted to think. She felt tired due to the long spell of stress she had just endured. When she couldn't think anymore, she sank into slumber.

She didn't know how long she slept. She could only recall that the maid shook her to wake her up. When she opened her eyes, the maid whispered to her, "We are nearing the bank. Soon the women of your father-in-law's place will come to receive you. Please wake up and wash your face. I have to get you dressed. I have to get your hair done, too. Your hair is a mess. Look!" The maid held out a small looking glass.

I could visualize how, with slumber still lingering in her eyes, the child-bride must have felt perplexed. Grandma said that she gave herself up to the maid's ministrations. The maid washed her face and wiped it with a towel. With meticulous care, she dressed her step by step and from top to toe, changing her clothing to a gorgeous new sari, combing and braiding her hair, then arranging it into a traditional coiffure fastened with a tassel and fixed with a jeweled hairpin. She made up the bride's face with cosmetic cream and powder and highlighted her eyes with lines of kajal. Next, she painted her feet with *alta,* a liquid lacquer, and put ornaments on her arms, neck, ears, wrists, feet, fingers, and head. The maid also put a fresh vermilion dot on her forehead and sprayed perfume on her from a jasmine bottle.

After completing details of the intricate process, the maid looked at the beautiful child-bride from different angles. Finally, she lifted the young bride's face by the chin, smiled, and with a deep sense of satisfaction, said, "Now my child looks like the image of the goddess Durga; nobody would be able to deny that."

Grandma looked bashful as she recounted the maid's comment. Clay modelers of Bengal have perfected the image of the goddess Durga as the paragon of feminine beauty. Decorated women were typically compared with the goddess by way of complimenting them.

"You're indeed pretty, Grandma," I told her.

Old Grandma blushed at my comment, took me in a hug, and pressed her wrinkly cheek against mine. Moments later, she continued, "The boat berthed on the river bank. As soon as the boatmen laid the landing planks, a host of women making *uludhvani*, a customary auspicious sound made by twirling the tongue, poured into the cabin. I was led slowly off the boat, walking side by side with your grandpa. He was dressed in the finest available dhoti, a Garad-silk kurta overlaid with a lush wrapper, silk socks, and shining leather shoes."

Grandma told me that her nervousness was intensified by the loud shehnai music, the uludhvani sound made by the womenfolk, and the general mood of hilarity that prevailed. She was sweating and her legs were trembling. The couple was put into a palanquin. As the bearers lifted the flower-bedecked palanquin to their shoulders, the rhythmic spacing of their steps and the repetitious whirring sound put her in a stupor.

She said she could only recall that at the decorated gate of her father-in-law's house, which was lit by gaslight, some ladies helped her alight from the palanquin amid a jubilant crowd of mostly women and children. Her groom came to stand by her side. The newlyweds were ceremonially received amid the bewildering din. There was a strange ambience of dissonance rather than celebration.

An elderly woman slowly wiggled around Grandma's face the *baran dala*—a woven, round, flat tray with a burning earthen oil lamp and other propitious items. After the ceremonial welcome was over, someone whispered in her ear that she must bow down and touch the feet of her mother-in-law and the other elderly women to show respect to them. She did not know who was who, and so she bowed and touched the feet of every woman standing nearby. They blessed her and put more and more vermilion on the parting of her hair. They also put on her head grains of paddy rice and tender shoots of auspicious *durba* grass, smeared with sandalwood paste and other aromatics. These grains and shoots were symbols of prosperity in agrarian Bengal. Grandma recounted that as she continued to bow down, she fainted.

When she came to senses, she found herself on the lap of an old woman in a crowded room. The old woman was sitting on a white sheet spread over a thick area rug on the floor. There were bolsters to lean against. Another woman was fanning her with a handheld palm-leaf fan. Grandma tried to sit up on her own. The elderly woman, however, held her on her lap.

A woman from somewhere in the crowd made a shrill comment. "Oh my, *didi* (elder sister), after such a great search you have brought into your home a sick daughter-in-law for such a gem of a son? This is exactly what is called buying glass-bits for gold!"

Several female voices jeered, giggling and enjoying the prickly comment.

Another woman said, "Looks like a case of epilepsy; hold an old shoe before her nose."

The motherly woman on whose lap Grandma was sitting ignored the sarcastic comments and the giggling of the womenfolk. She softly asked her, "Are you okay? Are you feeling better?" Then she kissed her head and said, "Never mind. I know you are exhausted."

A young woman brought a glass of fresh coconut milk and held it to Grandma's lips. "Please drink. It will do you good," said the motherly woman.

As she described these events, Grandma seemed amused. "And you know, I drank the full glass of coconut milk like a child in her mother's lap. After the drink, I felt much better. I remember that it tasted so good that I drank all of it from the tumbler held to my lips."

Grandma seemed to be struggling to hold in her emotions as she recounted these painful memories. I felt annoyed at the womenfolk who had ridiculed her. After a pause, she said that the motherly woman then gathered Grandma's fingers and slid onto her wrist an iron bangle anodized with gold. It was customary for Bengali mothers-in-law to offer an iron bangle as their first gifts to their daughters-in-law. The traditional amulet was supposed to ward off evil and bring good fortune to the family, especially to the son who had brought the bride home.

Some critics of this custom, however, said that the iron bangle was a symbol of the shackles of slavery, signifying that daughters-in-law were treated as slaves by their mothers-in-law.

Whatever the bangles might signify, I gathered from my grandma that after her mother-in-law put the ceremonial iron bangle on her wrist, a young woman held out a gold necklace. Her mother-in-law put the heavy gold necklace around Grandma's neck. Next, she put into Grandma's hand a jewel box and said, "You may use these ornaments whenever you like."

At this point, another woman's voice said, "We haven't seen what is inside the box. Why not show us?"

The young woman, first cousin of the groom, picked up the old family jewelry box, traditionally handed down to the wife of the eldest son. She unlocked it, and one by one, she held out before the thronging womenfolk a collection of heavy and old-fashioned gold jewelry.

After showing the jewelry, Grandpa's cousin put the pieces back into the box, secured it by a lock, and then put its key on Grandma's palm. Grandma's maid took the key for safekeeping.

Another woman sitting close by audibly whispered to Grandma, "She is your new mother," meaning that the woman who held her on her lap was her mother-in-law. "You must touch her feet," the woman added.

Bewildered at this suggestion, Grandma attempted to get up to touch her mother-in-law's feet, but her mother-in-law held her on her lap and said, "It's all right. You have already done it."

It was difficult for me to envisage the situation narrated by Grandma. I felt for her as the young girl she was at the time in such a grown-up situation.

She said that soon thereafter she was led to another room, where she was asked to sit side by side with her groom. Before them was a large copper plate on which were arranged auspicious and ceremonial items, such as grains of paddy rice, shoots of grass, and sandalwood paste.

The reception ceremony resumed. Her father-in-law and other senior relations, both men and women, ritually blessed the newlyweds, each of them presenting the bride with ornaments, *mohurs* (gold coins), saris, and other articles of value, depending on the nearness of their relationship and individual ability.

Grandma finished by saying neatly, "And that is the story of my wedding. How do you like it?"

"It was wonderful, Grandma, but you didn't tell me anything about what Grandpa did!"

"You must ask your grandpa to tell you all that he did," replied Grandma. "Remember, we were kept apart from one another most of the time."

I realized that Grandma felt exhausted after narrating so many details for such a long while, and now there were many emotions surging within her, stirred from her memories. I gave her a loving hug and a kiss and left her to rest.

* * *

One day I collected the mail from the family mailbox. I gave a letter to Grandpa, addressed to him in an envelope with a Pakistani postal stamp. Instantly Grandpa opened the letter and attentively read the contents, handwritten in Bengali script. He looked sad and worried after reading the letter.

"Anything wrong, Grandpa?" I asked him.

He attempted a smile and said, "No. It's a letter from my brother, Yadav."

Later that afternoon, when I entered Grandma's room, I found Grandpa sitting on the old couch there. I would have gone out, but Grandma showed me her bed and asked me to sit down. The envelope I had given to Grandpa earlier that day was on the bed beside Grandma. Although I felt somewhat awkward to be in the midst of their conversation, I had to sit down. I heard Grandpa speaking aloud his thoughts to Grandma.

"So many times I have told him to come with me, but he never cared to listen. He stuck to his obstinate vow to live and breathe his last on the ancestral land. Now he seems to be in real trouble. The *rayats*, the tenants, refuse to pay their share of the crops or anything whatsoever. They say that the land belongs to them and they have no obligation to pay anything to anyone. They claim ownership rights over the lands they plow."

Grandma listened quietly without any comment. Grandpa continued, "I knew that such a situation would arise; he won't be able to live there in peace. But he is such an adamant fellow! He still insists on living on that worn-out and collapsing property, surrounded by hostile people. I don't know what to do with him. He will make me go mad."

Grandma suggested, "Do you think I should write to him?"

"You might," replied Grandpa. "But I don't think he will change his mind. I wrote no less than a dozen letters to him, but he went on harping on the same point. Now he is under threat, especially due to political developments. What can he do? How can he cope? He is all alone . . ."

Disturbed and preoccupied with his adamant brother's plight, Grandpa restlessly exited from Grandma's room. It was obvious from their conversation that Grandpa's only brother was in a very difficult situation in the East Bengal ancestral home.

Later, Grandma told me the sequence of events that had taken place in the course of only a few years after her wedding. "Your grandpa had many dreams. He thought he would practice law in Dhaka and make his residence on the bank of the Buriganga stream of the Dhaleswari River. He also made plans for developing the ancestral property into a profit-yielding farm in the Manikganj subdivision of the Dhaka district. He thought of finding a pretty girl from a high family for Yadav to marry, and then in the course of time, he would put his brother in full charge of the estate. He dreamed that he would establish himself and then ask his father to retire, so that we two could take care of the old couple."

Grandma described historical developments after the Indian mutiny of 1857–58. That was the rebellion of the joint forces of Hindus and Muslims of India against British colonial rule. It shook the very foundation of British rule in India. The rebels enthroned the last Mughal emperor of India, Bahadur Shah Jafar, and he virtually ruled India for nearly a year.

The British realized that the joint forces were capable of overthrowing colonial rule. The Royal British Army raised in India was replenished with large contingents of white men from Britain. They quelled the rebellion by ruthless repression. Bahadur Shah's sons, nephew, and grandson were slain by a British captain named Hudson. Their severed heads were presented to Bahadur Shah.

Shah was imprisoned, tried for treason, and banished to Burma as a prisoner, where he breathed his last. Rani Lakshmi Bai of Jhansi gave her life fighting the British, along with thousands of others. The East India Company was dissolved on charges of lenience to the Indians, and Indian administration was taken over by Queen Victoria as the empress of India.

The queen made many promises to the loyal Indian princes and the people. The British government in India, however, did not implement most of her promises. Instead, they diplomatically implemented a policy of divide and rule by creating a wide rift between Hindus and Muslims. The policy was also to frustrate the growing popularity of the Indian nationalist movement.

Bengal was divided in 1905. The Muslim League was formed in Dhaka in East Bengal in 1906. East Bengal was already overpopulated with poverty-stricken Muslim peasants, who represented the overwhelming majority in most districts in the eastern part of the province. Proprietors and landowners, however, were mostly Hindus. The British strategy worked very well. Muslim tenant farmers, called *rayats*, demonstrated their defiance of Hindu landlords, challenging their hereditary rights as proprietors. Communal disharmony became an everyday affair in East Bengal, with sporadic eruptions of Hindu-Muslim riots.

Grandpa's father could not bear the situation. Suddenly, a cerebral stroke took him away from this world. Grandpa's dreams turned into a nightmare. As a wise man, he had to take the hard decision to abandon his ancestral home in the strife-torn land. He decided to migrate to a peaceful place with his wife and mother. It was very painful to leave behind the traditional home that bore countless memories of many generations. However, it was a timely decision to relocate and start a new life.

His loving younger brother, Yadav, despite Grandpa's and his mother's ardent requests, decided to stay on in the crumbling feudal structure, hoping against hope that things would change some day. Yadav wept like a child when Grandpa decided to leave, said Grandma, lamenting that her affectionate and only brother-in-law, in spite of everything, stood firm in his decision to remain in his ancestral home.

7

Navigable by country boats, a breakaway stream of the Brahmaputra flowed gently past a new sector of our town. The area was known as *Baluchar*, a name meaning "sandbank." It grew up due to the accretion of alluvial deposits carried by the mighty river. Baluchar was on the outskirts of the town. It developed erratically with the building of warehouses by merchants dealing in jute and rice. There were wooden piers on the riverbank for boats carrying these goods. Overloaded bullock carts and overused trucks strenuously clambered up the gradient to join the gravel road. Except for the piers and the connecting road, Baluchar was comprised of pure green pasture used for cattle grazing.

Soon after the winter months, the riverbank at Baluchar came alive with freshly grown vegetation of various shapes and forms. An endless array of wild shrubbery thickened into woods. The entire panorama, dotted with wildflowers and wild berries, turned into a stunning vista of untainted nature. Streaming waters mirrored the images of the trees.

Because there were no hills in the landscape and no rocks embedded in the stream to obstruct the flow, the watercourse meandered through many miles of vegetation and villages, and then rejoined the main stream of the Brahmaputra, called the Yamuna in East Bengal. Long-winged, fork-tailed kites, red-crested kingfishers, and many other birds flew above the stream; chirping little birds flocked in the woods.

Boats, large and small, floated by, some with sails inflated by wind, others rowed by boatmen. There was always a flotilla of fishing boats. Fishermen threw their nets and then slowly drew them back with fresh catches. Rafts of bamboo floated along, bound for faraway paper mills. Soft timbers were sent to the matchbox factory on the fringe of our town. On each raft was a solitary rafter, who had a small shed of bamboo and thatch raised on the raft where he could cook his rice and rest for a while. The stream thus was a boon from the Brahmaputra, or the son of Brahma, to earthly beings to meet their worldly needs.

On some tranquil afternoons, a cowherd boy would tend a herd of cattle or sit under the shade of a tree. He invariably held a stick of bamboo in his hand or was heard playing on a bamboo flute.

The natural setting of Baluchar reminded me of "Vrindavana," the legendary scene of the dalliance of Krishna. It evoked the imagery of the pasture of *Vrindabana*, where the cowherd Krishna played his bamboo flute under the *kadamba* tree.

Krishna as an incarnation of Vishnu, the Supreme Being, first featured as Bashudeva-Krishna in the Chandogya Upanishad, dating to the period from circa 900 to 700 BC. Krishna prominently features in the Mahabharata, the Bhagavad Gita, Harivamsa Purana, Vishnu Purana, and Bhagavata Purana. The imagery and iconography of the tenth-century Bhagavata Purana, however, is the most exclusive and idealistic in its narration of the legends of Sri Krishna and Sri Radhika. The legends emphasize *bhakti*, the cult of devotion. In fact, the text combines Vedic nondualism and Vaishnava devotionalism. The tenth canto of the text describes the life of Krishna.

Vishnu, in his Gopala Krishna imagery, is a delightfully naughty child, a mysterious prankster in the cowherd land of *Braj-bhoomi*. He steals butter from the butter churn of his foster mother Yashada, annoying her and yet charming her at the same time. Mother Yashada's love for the child Gopala Krishna intensified into an ecstatic feeling of devotion, leading to the realization of the ultimate reality. Maternal love was exalted to the transcendental height of devotion, leading to deliverance.

Murali-Monohar, or the flute-playing cowherd Krishna, on the other, lured the *gopinies*, cowherd wives of Vrindavana, with the charm of his flute. Elated by their love for Krishna, they danced on the bank of the Yamuna. Krishna dilly-dallied with them but remained elusive and mysterious. Immersed in her love for Krishna, the cowherd wife Radha, or Sri Radhika, became one with Krishna. This approach to deliverance through the experience of apparently romantic love elevated the worldly experience of love to an aesthetic height of realization of the absolute. Here, love is devotion, a *pantha*, or a means to attain union with the ultimate reality, as variously elaborated in Vaishnava literature and in the "Bhakti Yoga" of the Bhagavad Gita.

The notion is similar to the Upanishadic concept of *ananda*, out of which flows all cosmic phenomena, some perceptible and some imperceptible, dissolving back into eternity and orchestrated to the dynamics of *stristi*, *sthiti*, and *loy*—creation, sustenance, and dissolution. The imagery of Krishna as the pastoral cowherd playing on his bamboo flute and enchanting the wives of Vrindavana is purely metaphorical. The image of the Supreme Being as a boy in a pasture on the bank of the Yamuna illustrates the idea that the Supreme Being could be as simple and ordinary as that.

In fact, the pasture on the bank of the Yamuna represents the eternal and boundless pasture of time and space. The familiar bamboo flute is the cosmic flute. Its tune represents the awareness that apparently trifling and insignificant things are also within the dynamics of the *leela*—the all-pervading scheme of the eternal dynamics. Thus, the imagery of an ordinary cowherd playing a bamboo flute in the pasture of Vrindavana could invoke the feeling of compelling love, leading to absolute devotion to the personal godhead of the devotee as an incarnation of the Supreme Being. It could be elusive and mysterious like the dalliance of Krishna with the cowherd wives. But the inner theme sublimates the imagery in to *bhakti* or absolute love leading to liberation.

The gopinies symbolize the souls of ordinary human beings. Enthralled by the overwhelming spell of Krishna's cosmic flute, they leave behind all the bondage of *samsara,* or worldly affairs, and dance in rapturous joy whenever they perceive the call of the cosmic flute. Every human soul is enchanted for a moment by the Supreme Being in some form or the other. The compelling call is so captivating that one forgets everything else and runs to join it in the ecstasy of ananda, or bliss. But the moment the call is no longer perceptible, the elusive spell of *maya* again entices human beings into the fetters of the *samsara.* The gopinies go home and forget Krishna.

Radha, on the other hand, symbolizes the soul of the awakened one, absorbed and exalted to the absolute extent in loving the ultimate soul. Therefore, she can ignore her husband and overlook every other mundane and social constraint to join Krishna—not only when the call of his flute is audible; not only when Krishna, in person, is present and discernible; but all the while and forever. This aspect of love is known as *viraha-bhakti*, which denotes the overwhelming pangs of separation for the lover, who can never forget the all-consuming aspect of love.

The *Leela-Kunja*, or pastoral bower of Vrindavana, signifies the notion that a devotee does not need a temple to worship his or her personal god, who exists everywhere and in all situations and environments. The urge of love as the awakening of devotion needs no specific precondition of time, space, or causality. Similarly, realization of love as absolute devotion is free from all restraints of financial status, social class, caste, and color.

Vaishnavism is the philosophy of universal love. A Vaishnava does not need a Brahmin to guide him or her through a ritualized process to seek his or her Bhagavan, or godhead. The duality of the lovers as Radha and Krishna represents *bhakta* (devotee) and *Bhagavan* (the Supreme Being).

A popular analogy here is that of the flame of a burning lamp and its shadow. When the lamp burns, there is both light and shadow. When the lamp doesn't burn, there is no light and no shadow. The lamp thus produces the duality of light and shadow, but the lamp remains as one entity. When the bliss of fulfillment in the absolute sense is attained, the devotee and the divine are one and inseparable. It is maya, or the apparition, that creates the illusion of duality represented by Radha-Krishna in the leela, or involvement with the phenomenon of the cosmic dynamics.

The *viraha-bhakti,* or pangs of separation, have been the greatest inspiration of all forms of Indian art and culture. The charm of the Radha-Krishna legend inspired many illustrious devotees, songwriters, composers of Indian classical music, dancers, and painters.

The *alvar* saint-poets of Tamil country popularized the aesthetic aspect of the bhakti cult. The Tamil word *alvar* has been translated as "immersed in the realization of the godhead." There were twelve alvar saint-poets, including one woman. They came from all walks of life and from all strata of society. They did not discriminate between castes. They sang their songs in praise of the Supreme Being visualized sometimes as Vishnu, sometimes as Shiva, as they traveled from place to place, temple to temple, between the fifth and the ninth centuries. They composed some four thousand Tamil verses during the ninth and tenth centuries.

The poet Jayadeva, in a collection of only twenty-four songs that comprise his immortal work *Gitagovinda* (Songs of Krishna), circa1200 AD, eternalized the perception of the viraha-bhakti theme. He composed his immortal verses while in the Jagannath temple of Puri in Orissa. Legend has it that the temple dancer Padmavati was his inspiration. *Gitagovinda* had a spellbinding impact on generations of devotees and connoisseurs of ecstatic love songs and dance forms all over the world. Translations of *Gitagovinda* are available in many Western languages, including English.

Vidyapati and Candidasa of Bengal strung their verses into the colorful garland of *Vaisnava-Padavali,* extolled and popularized, particularly in the fifteenth century and before the advent of Sri Caitanya of Bengal.

Vaishnava spiritual perceptions diversified into many strains and schools. Vaishnava imagery inspired the seventeenth- and eighteenth-century Rajasthani and Pahadi paintings. Kavir, Tulsidas, and Mirabai are some of the immortal songwriters of *bhajans*—devotional songs of the bhakti cult. From the Bhagavata Purana to *Gitagovinda* and the lyrics and songs of Sri Caitanya, Vidyapati, and Candidasa, all exalt the eternal glory of absolute love that transcends worldly bondage to merge the devotee into Krishna.

Vaishnava philosophers hold that there can be no greater force to realize human awareness of Brahman, the Vedic-Upanishadic Supreme Being, than through the power of love. In their search to find the ideal way to escape from the cycle of rebirth, they visualize the path of absolute devotion to Vishnu or Krishna as *Īśvara*, the Supreme Being, personalized as *Bhagavan.* Devotees worship him through the medium of absolute love. The concept is to realize the essence of the

Vedic-Upanishadic perception through the simple approach of love, an exalting perception via the rapturous imagery of various art forms. The concept of viraha-bhakti or the yearning for absolute love in its final state is beyond all the boundaries, limitations, barriers, and restraints of traditional society. It is absolute and unconditional.

This is also the point from which the concept of the relationship between the personal god and the devotee originated, described and popularized in different schools and cults of Vaisnavism. The philosophy of *Visistadvaita* is the essence of the concept of qualified nondualism. In the state of realization, the devotee sees himself as all beings and sees all beings as the Supreme Being.

Ramanuja's commentary on the Vedānta-sūtra explains this concept. Ramanujacharya, or Ramanuja, was a theologian and philosopher in the years from 1117 to 1137 BC. Sankara Bhagavatpadachrya, or Adi Sankaracarya, or simply Sankara, of the ninth century AD, further elucidated the concept with slight variations. The Upanishads and the Vedānta-sūtra explicate the Hindu philosophy of nondualism (Hindu monism). This is comparable to the Vaishnava philosophy minus the centuries of irrelevant outgrowth, as in all Hindu cults. There is no doubt that such outgrowths overshadow all Hindu philosophies, constantly proliferating deities to overcrowd the Hindu pantheon.

8

While shattering Europe and bringing many great nations to their knees, World War II extended to Asia. Japanese armed forces occupied the Indian Ocean islands in the Bay of Bengal and Burma (Myanmar). A volatile political situation developed in India. Muhammad Ali Jinnah, in the 1940 Lahore session of the Muslim League, submitted his Pakistan Resolution. The resolution had significant political impact in India and Britain. Lord Linlithgow, the British viceroy in India, declared that India was at war with Nazi Germany and the Axis powers.

Radical leader Subhas Chandra Bose escaped from house arrest and managed to reach Germany. From there, he was transferred to the Japanese navy via German submarine. In a radio broadcast from somewhere in Asia, he announced the establishment of *Arzi Hukumat-e-Azad Hind*—the national government of free India—and the formation of the *Azad Hind Fauz*—the Indian National Army (INA). He declared war against British rule in India and announced that the INA, in collaboration with Japanese forces, was advancing toward the northeastern mainland of India. He claimed that the INA had already set up posts in Kohima in Naga Hills and Imphal in Manipur state.

I was then in school, too young to understand the implications of war and politics. One morning in our school assembly, teachers and students gathered before classes began. The headmaster, in a short speech, said that the Allied nations, including India, were at war with Nazi Germany and the Axis powers. He said that there might be air raids and bombing by the enemy.

river became totally out of bounds for us. Rows of army vehicles replaced the floral landscape of the park. The caterpillar treads of tanks abraded the surface of the tarmac road. Telephone lines and power cables were strung all over the area. The park was fenced with canvas sheets fortified by barbed wire. A dynamo constantly droned within the encampment. The marble statue of Queen Victoria holding a scepter in her hand was no longer visible from the road. The district authorities requisitioned all schools and other public places for use as army camps. Allied personnel were everywhere in our district and elsewhere in the country.

The sky-blue uniformed air-raid precaution (ARP) was a locally raised squad. They included schoolteachers, college students, and young men and women of the town. Trained ARP personnel educated and assisted the civilian population in taking precautions against possible air raids and bombing attacks. They hired day laborers to dig trenches everywhere—on roadsides, front yards, and backyards of government offices, courthouses, and other public buildings—completely defacing the beautiful town. The ARP helped householders to get private trenches dug at their own cost. We had two trenches dug in our courtyard. Squad personnel instructed us to prepare emergency kits consisting of a battery-operated flashlight, a kerosene lantern with a half-blackened chimney, matchboxes, a first-aid kit, some dry food, cans of cookies, and bottles of drinking water, all put into handy bags.

They also taught us how to clench wooden pencils or rubber erasers between our teeth to protect them from breaking and to put cotton wool in our ears to protect our eardrums from cracking at the bangs and blasts of bombardment. All glass panes of doors, windows, and skylights were painted black to conceal light that could be visible from outside. We stuck paper tape on the glass panes to prevent splinters of glass from exploding out during a bombardment. Black paint covered the upper half of the headlights of all motor vehicles. Concealed streetlights hardly gave much light. Army checkpoints were set up to prevent entry of spies and enemy agents into our town. Antiaircraft guns installed at strategic points completed the preparation to combat the enemy.

Throughout the day and night, aircraft filled the sky. Carrier airplanes took off from a hurriedly constructed aerodrome within a forested area a few miles outside of the town. These airplanes carried supplies to the war fronts close to India's northeastern frontier.

Air-raid signals wailed sporadically, traumatizing the entire population. On some days, the scream of the siren drove terror-stricken men, women, and children to cram themselves into the Z-shaped trenches. After a breathless lull, the all-clear signal would be blown and the huddled masses of humanity crawled out from the raw, muggy holes. Those who had private trenches went into them immediately upon hearing the air-raid signal, which often sounded on curfew-crippled, blackout-blinded nights. Those who had no trenches near them had to resign themselves to their fate.

The town came under full control of the army somewhat like a besieged territory. In the terror-stricken atmosphere, the normal activities of everyday life came to a standstill. Civil administration, including the police department, had to work under instructions from the army. Military personnel frequented everywhere, some on patrol and transportation duty, some just moving around the town. Gum-chewing, off-duty Allied army soldiers strolled about the streets, frolicking and joking with the bewildered natives, interacting through gestures and other body language.

While the soldiers were interested in enjoying their free time, the unprivileged locals were interested in whatever little they could earn in such a hard time. To the common men in India, American GIs were powerful strangers with pockets full of dollar bills. They offered candies, chewing gum, and cigarettes to anyone they liked. Gestures and body language were more effective ways of communicating than spoken words.

Traditional modesty and fear stymied middle-class women and girls from venturing out into the open. The poor and the illiterate had no alternative other than to toil for survival. Most householders in the town kept their doors and windows tightly closed. Sometimes, on a bleak evening, a stray, drunken GI would swear and thump on the bolted door of a residential house. Those who had telephones in their houses rang up the army command. Soon after the phone call, motorcycle-riding officers of the military police would appear on the scene and take away the delinquent GI to the makeshift barracks.

It was a common sight to find special trains and convoys of motor vehicles carrying Allied army personnel from one place to another. Some were from the Republic of China. They wore sandal-boots woven with braided ropes. Goods trains carried army supplies, including mules and ponies for use on the sub-Himalayan mountain trails to fight the Japanese army.

That was how things turned out in and around my hometown. Thus, in a way, India was involved in the war, as Viceroy Linlithgow declared.

On some nights, there was a total blackout all over the town. Passing flashes of motor vehicle headlights and the whizzing of army vehicles intensified the uncanny stillness of the night. The sudden howling of the cacophonous air-raid signal in the middle of the night shattered the eerie silence. My mother would nervously stand, clasping all her children like a mother hen tending her chicks to protect them from imminent danger. Father would lead us to hurriedly pick up the emergency kits and rush into the trench. If the siren sounded during the day when Father was at work in the courthouse, I would take his role, soothing my mother and sisters and taking them to the trench.

There were days and nights when we would go into the trench after the air-raid signal sounded and wait for a long while with no all-clear signal. We would cluster together inside the dark hole like a family of rodents. After a long wait, the all-clear signal would sound, and we would presume that the droning sound we heard was of Allied air force fighters searching for the airborne enemy. We would come out, wash ourselves, and change our soiled clothes.

Vexed and upset, Mother would desperately question, "Why must there be war at all? Why should human beings destroy their creations and their kin? Isn't war the absolute antithesis of civilization? I really don't understand! I hate war. I feel like coming out with open protest against war."

We quietly nodded, most sincerely appreciating her feeling. Under the prevailing circumstances, Father could neither condemn the war nor support it. In his own loving way, he emotionally soothed Mother.

Prices of all commodities shot up. Food and other essential items of daily need came under rationing, giving rise to much malpractice.

Many essential items were not available at all. The Allied army depended on civilian contractors and suppliers for basic logistics and the supply of provisions. Construction of roads, bridges, aerodromes, aircraft hangers, cantonment sheds, and other such construction were taken up at breakneck pace as war efforts. Contractors worked around the clock under the supervision of garrison engineers and army commanders. Contractors and suppliers took full advantage of the situation. They received payments at exorbitantly high rates based on the US dollar. Spiraling inflation caused total imbalance in the traditional agrarian economy. Civilian contractors emerged as a neo-rich class with plenty of liquid cash in hand, causing further imbalance in the economy.

The war came to an abrupt end when atomic bombs were dropped on the Japanese cities of Hiroshima and Nagasaki. The war left behind far-reaching sociopolitical effects in India. For the great multitude of the poor, what mattered most was survival. Historically, India had a hierarchical society comprised of landowners, peasants, and artisans. In the course of time, with the rising population and scarcity of cultivable land, society swerved to generate semiagricultural labor and an educated middle class. Out of the traditional aristocracy emerged a few England-educated political leaders of the time. Many self-made, educated members of the middle class also took over popular political leadership roles. The war-bred neo-rich walked the corridors of power. Economic malpractice, including hoarding, profiteering, and black-marketeering, pervaded the country as the inevitable concomitants of a postwar state.

The most shocking instance of manipulation and malpractice was the great famine of Bengal during 1943. Due to hoarding by unscrupulous speculators, the price of rice in Bengal rose to an unprecedented level, causing a devastating famine. This man-made tragedy took a toll of one and a half million lives. Many political analysts, both within and beyond India, believed that the ruling politicians of the Muslim League in Bengal were involved in the manipulations that created the famine. Nobody, however, was accused of being responsible, and nobody was punished for committing such a horrendous crime against humanity.

* * *

World War II had the most significant effect on India's political scenario. The war definitely turned the nation's struggle for independence into divisive politics. Indian nationalism was born out of the Hindu Reform Movement in the early nineteenth century, initiated by Rammohan Ray, founder of the Brahmo Samaj or the Society of God. Rammohan, besides discarding many atrocious practices of Hindu society with the help of India-loving Englishmen, initiated the process of liberating Hindu women.

A galaxy of distinguished people in all fields of life and culture adorned the period of Indian history known as the Bengal Renaissance. It is an oft-quoted comment that the renaissance in Bengal began with Rammohan Ray (1775–1833) and ended with Rabindranath Tagore (1861–1942).

After the Battle of Plassy in 1757, the British East India Company set up their first post in Bengal. Gradually, English education and Western liberalism brought in waves of changes in Bengal. A cluster of renowned personalities, such as Isvar Chandra Vidyasagar, Sri Aurobindo, and their contemporaries, devoted themselves to reforming Hindu society and restoring dignity of life for all human beings.

Next in succession was the great reformer, Swami Dayananda Sarasvati (1824–1883). The swami introduced the Arya Samaj movement, a widely accepted reform in Hinduism that discarded idolatry and the Hindu caste system, besides many more reforms. Revolutionary leader Lala Lajpat Rai (1865–1928) joined the Arya Samaj movement together with other social leaders. The spirit of reforming Hindu society kindled the spirit of Indian nationalism, thus leading to organized efforts to liberate the country from the bondage of British colonial rule.

Historically, the Indian struggle for independence had its origins during the time of World War I (1914–1918). Underground revolutionary parties made organized efforts to terrorize and compel the British to quit India. Well-known revolutionary philosopher Sri Aurobindo (Arabinda Ghosh) was one of the pioneer leaders of the underground radical movement.

With a view to stop the spread of the movement, the British gagged the vernacular press and vernacular literature and sought to replace them with English. They founded the Hindu College in Calcutta in 1817 and renamed the institution the Presidency College in 1855. Calcutta University was founded in 1857.

The British government in London, however, did not appreciate the India-loving attitude of the British East India Company. They held the company responsible for laxity in administration that had made the 1857 rebellion possible by the Hindu and Muslim masses. The British crown dissolved the British East India Company in 1874, and the British *raj* took over the administration of India. The British administration imported large contingents of British forces instead of relying on India-raised forces.

A retired officer of the Indian Civil Service, Allen Octavian Hume, who had seen the nature and extent of the 1857 mutiny, addressed a letter to the graduates of Calcutta University. In his letter, he conveyed the message that education played a key role in avoiding revolts like the one in 1857. Some historians regard Hume as the father of the Indian National Congress Party. In 1883, Hume's advice led some seventy-odd England-educated barristers and social elite to form the party.

The organization submitted petitions to the British government, seeking representation in the viceroy's legislative council, a greater share in the Indian Civil Service, protection of Indian industries, and reduction of unproductive public expenditure. Unlike the revolutionaries, the Indian National Congress Party initially did not have a manifesto to overthrow British rule in India or to wage a struggle for independence. The elite organization only asked for certain privileges. Hume's letter thus succeeded in raising a parallel, peaceful movement against the radical leaders of the struggle for independence, named by the British as anarchism.

After the dissolution of the East India Company, British policy in India shifted to "divide and rule" by creating a wide rift between the Hindus and Muslims. They partitioned Bengal in 1905 and made a new province by amalgamating Muslim-majority East Bengal and Assam. Almost simultaneously, in 1906, the All India Muslim League, as the institution was then known, came into being in Dacca (Dhaka).

A popular movement against the partition of Bengal, known as the *Swadeshi* movement, spontaneously generated under the leadership of national leaders.

In 1907, Congress split into two distinct groups known as the moderates and the extremists. The moderates believed in English institutions and lucid presentation of demands to the British authorities. Surendranath Banerjee, Dadabhai Naoroji, and Badruddin Tyabji led the group.

Muhammad Ali Jinnah, who joined this group in 1906, later became dubious about the policies of Congress. He, however, retained membership in Congress while joining the Muslim League. Later, as the president of the Muslim League in 1916, he attempted a compromise between the two political parties. He was the architect of the Lucknow pact between Congress and the League. But the pact did not yield any feasible result.

Jinnah formally quit Congress in 1920 when M. K. Gandhi took over leadership. He resigned because he could not endorse Gandhiji's favorite song, "*Ramdhun,*" and his manifesto of establishing *Ramrajya* after the model of the Ramayana. He considered all these directly opposed to the Congress manifesto of secularism.

In context, it is relevant to mention that the poet-philosopher Sir Allama Muhammad Iqbal (1877–1938) first introduced the two-nation theory in 1931. Muslim modernist and reformer Sir Syed Ahmad Khan joined him. Their contention was that Islam is not merely a religion but a way of life. Indian Muslims, irrespective of their ethnicity, language, and culture, constituted a nationality other than the Hindu nationality. The contention was that the two nationalities could not coexist peacefully within India. They advocated for total transfer of the Hindus and Muslims in a partition of India.

Muhammad Ali Jinnah, who initially was a secular person and was not really interested in politics, later took over the leadership of the Muslim League and led the effort to make Pakistan a reality. But creation of the Islamic Republic of Pakistan could not fulfill Iqbal's dream of a total transfer of population. After the partition, secular India continued as the home of both communities. A substantial number of

Indian Muslims refused to leave their homes, thereby proving that the two-nation theory was a myth.

* * *

The extremist group in Congress demanded *Swaraj*—self-rule. Revolutionary nationalists Bipin Chandra Pal, Arabinda Ghosh (Sri Aurabindo), and Baal Gangadhar Tilak led this group. The movement spread all over India. Many illustrious figures, including the poet Rabindranath Tagore, joined the agitation.

The movement began with boycotts of British and foreign goods and the burning of those goods in bonfires. Both the Bengali and the English press in India supported the movement, and both Hindus and Muslims joined it. In street processions, people sang *"Bande Mataram"*—"Hail to Thee, O Motherland," and chanted the slogan *"Allah-ho-Akbar."* The British administration let loose ruthless repression. They prosecuted Arabinda Ghosh and Bipin Chandra Paul and banned "Bande Mataram."

Underground revolutionary activities intensified, particularly in Bengal and Punjab. The so-called Morly-Minto Reforms of 1909 created separate electoral districts for Muslims, and Muslims only could vote for the Muslim candidates.

Nonetheless, the Swadeshi movement compelled the British government to reunite Bengal in 1911. With a view to avoid the nerve center of the struggle for freedom, the British shifted the capital of India from Calcutta to Delhi in 1912. The Montagu-Chelmsford Report of 1918 recommended reserved seats for the Muslims as the next attempt to isolate the Hindus and Muslims of India. The Government of India Act of 1919 legalized the Montagu-Chelmsford report.

In 1920, M. K. Gandhi took over the leadership of Congress and patched up the rift between the moderates and the extremists. A new division surfaced between the groups known as the leftists and the rightists. Pandit Jawaharlal Nehru and Subhas Chandra Bose were the most prominent leaders of the leftist group. Gandhi, with his obvious penchant for the rightists, continued to be the overall leader of Congress, now a well-organized political party.

Subhas Chandra Bose joined the Indian Civil Service in 1920, and while he was a probationer in England, resigned. Soon thereafter, he joined the Bengal Provincial Congress Party under the leadership of Chittaranjan Das as the president. Bengal Congress was the *de facto* legislative wing of the Indian National Congress Party. Bose became the youth educator and commandant of the Bengal Congress Volunteer Corps. Bose had to face imprisonment in 1921 on charges of antigovernment activities. After his release in 1924, Bose, then a journalist, became the chief executive officer of Calcutta under Chittaranjan Das as the mayor. The British imprisoned him once again and deported him to Burma. They released him in 1927. He came back to India when Chittaranjan Das was no more in this world. He started rearranging Bengal Congress. The British arrested him again in 1930. Calcutta citizens elected Bose as the mayor of Calcutta while he was in British prison.

The hanging of the revolutionary freedom fighter Sardar Bhagat Singh in 1931 on charges of antigovernment activities is believed to have been the cause of disagreement between Gandhiji and Subhas Bose. In an article in the *Young India*, Gandhi paid tribute to the patriotism of the young martyr Bhagat Singh, but he disagreed with his revolutionary method.

The British administration proclaimed the so-called Communal Award in 1932 that assigned specified numbers of seats to various Indian communities. Provisions for similar reservations existed in the Government of India Act of 1935.

From 1932 to 1936, Bose campaigned for India's independence in his travels throughout Italy, Germany, and France. He met Mussolini, Felder, D. Valera, and Roman Rolland. While in Europe, he published his book, *The Indian Struggle, 1920–1934*. The British government in India banned Bose's reentry. He defied the ban and entered India in 1936. Immediately upon entering India, he was imprisoned.

Meanwhile, the Government of India Act of 1935 conceded provincial autonomy. Elections to provincial legislative assemblies took place in 1937. Congress won the majority in seven out of eleven provinces of British India. Upon his release from British prison, Congress members unanimously elected Bose as the president of Congress in the Haripura session in 1938. In his presidential speech, Bose emphasized the revolutionary potential of the party that had formed ministries in seven out of eleven provinces.

On the eve of the World War II, Bose was reelected Congress president in the Tripuri session of 1939. Once again he announced his revolutionary manifesto of struggle against British imperialism. In his presidential address, he proposed that the British government be served with a six-month ultimatum asking them to either grant complete independence to India or face massive demonstrations and acts of civil disobedience by the people.

Party veterans such as Sardar Vallabhbhai Patel, Babu Rajendra Prasad, Jivatram Kripalani, and four other members submitted a countermanifesto seeking Indian independence through peaceful means and in a phased program, beginning with dominion status. Gandhi supported this group, and Pattabhi Sitaramayya was set up as the group's candidate to contest the leadership with Subhas Chandra Bose. In the election, Bose again won the presidency of Congress by a majority.

The majority group, known as the leftist group, supported Bose's proposal of massive civil disobedience against British rule. Earlier, the rightist group supported the Gandhian resolution that Congress would support the British war effort if the British committed to grant India self-government after the war ended. The rightist group now asserted that they would not be able to work with Bose as the president of the party. Twelve working committee members submitted their resignations in protest against Bose's reelection as president.

Pandit Jawaharlal Nehru, who was a proclaimed leftist, neither supported Bose nor resigned from the party. While Nehru believed in peaceful means, Bose was a radical leftist. Nehru's socialism was best reflected in his post-independence policy of nationalization of basic and key industries and in five-year plans for development. Bose, on the other hand, had a drastic approach. He believed in total revolution.

On April 29, 1939, Gandhiji wrote a letter to Bose from Rajkot, contending that since there were fundamental differences between Bose and the rightist group, Bose might choose his own working committee.

Bose resigned from the presidency of Congress and formed a new block within the party called the Forward Block.

On July 9 of the same year, he gave a call to protest against the All India Congress Committee's resolution to support the British war effort.

By way of retort, the All India Congress Committee resolved to remove Bose as president of the Bengal Provincial Congress Party and barred him from holding any office in Congress for the next three years. Congress thus ousted Bose from the party. He made the Forward Block a separate party, hoping to rally the radical elements in Congress. The British government took advantage of the situation and promptly arrested Bose in July 1940.

Bose went on a hunger strike. After eleven days of fasting, his health deteriorated alarmingly. For fear of a countrywide revolt that might get out of hand, the British released him from prison and kept him under house arrest. On January 7, 1941, Bose escaped from house arrest and went to Germany, trekking the difficult route through Afghanistan and Russia.

On April 9, 1941, he submitted a memorandum to the German government outlining his plan of cooperation between the Axis powers and the freedom fighters of India. Hitler concentrated his focus on Europe and was not interested in involving Germany with the Indian struggle for independence.

In November 1941, Bose established the Free India Center and Free India Radio in Germany. In 1942, he formed the first Indian legion, also in Germany, consisting of forty-five thousand volunteers to fight the imperial British. From Germany, he went to Japan, and from there he formed Azad Hind Fauz and established free India's government while in exile.

In India, the British administration welcomed the Congress resolution supporting the British war effort. Viceroy Lord Linlithgow proclaimed in a memorandum that India would be granted dominion status after the war ended. The British prime minister, Winston Churchill, and the native princes of India opposed Linlithgow's memorandum. Congress ministries in the provinces resigned in protest against the British prime minister's opposition to viceroy's announcement. A political stalemate ensued.

Gandhiji, who had supported the British during the Boer Wars and the First World War, now felt that the Second World War was an unparalleled catastrophe, similar to the great war of *Kurukshetra* in the Mahabharata. Gandhi was no longer prepared to offer anything more than moral support to the British war effort. He asked his compatriots to face the advancing Japanese forces in a nonviolent manner. Pandit Jawaharlal Nehru, on the other hand, thought it proper to cooperate with the Allied forces.

The people of India were exasperated with the ever-increasing scarcity of food and other essential commodities, spiraling price rises, and rampant corruption in the government-administered supply and distribution system. Furthermore, the existence of Allied army personnel deep inside towns and villages caused the populace to reach a state of desperation.

The news that Subhas Chandra Bose was advancing toward India with the Indian National Army sparked a strong sense of national pride among many Indians. Patriotic speeches delivered by Bose and similar other broadcasts through secret radio stations roused popular support in favor of Bose and his Azad Hind Fauz. People in India acknowledged Bose as *netaji*—a respected leader.

With the unfolding of these events, Gandhiji changed his mind and personally drafted a long and drastic resolution, contending that since the British had not come to the negotiation table, they must quit India immediately. The Congress working committee and most other Congress leaders, including Pandit Nehru, could not approve the resolution at that time. After a great deal of debate and discussion, Gandhiji agreed to change his resolution from a mass *satyagraha* to an individual *satyagraha*, which in fact had no political impact.

In 1942, Singapore, Rangoon, and the Andaman Islands fell to Japan in quick succession; the constant onslaught of propaganda and radio broadcasts overwhelmed the people of India. The influence of Netaji and his charisma was felt everywhere in India.

In a call for mass noncooperation, Gandhiji asked the people of India to "do or die." On July 14, 1942, the Congress working committee passed the historic Quit India resolution. A statement instantly issued by the committee declared that if the British did not quit India immediately, Congress would launch a massive nonviolent struggle on the widest possible scale. Nonetheless, some members of Congress were skeptical about the nonviolent aspect of the proposed struggle, especially in view of the developing situation with the Japanese forces advancing toward the Indian mainland and the rising charisma of Bose.

On August 8, 1942, the British governor general in Delhi declared that Congress as a political party was not the mouthpiece of the people of India. Yet in the interest of securing their own dominance and in pursuit of their totalitarian aims, the leaders of Congress constantly impeded British efforts to bring India to full nationhood after the war ended. Gandhi and all other leaders of Congress were arrested.

On July 4, 1943, with the help of the Japanese government, Bose established free India's national government in Singapore, called the *Arzi Hukumat-e-Azad Hind*, and he took over as the supreme commander of the Azad Hind Fauz, or INA. He declared war against British rule in India. He also founded the first women's regiment of the INA, named after the princess of Jhansi, Rani Lakshmibai, who gave her life fighting the British in the Indian Rebellion of 1857.

On July 6, 1944, Subhas Chandra Bose, in a broadcast on the Azad Hind Radio addressed to Gandhiji, proclaimed that India's last war of independence had begun. In this holy war, he sought the blessings and good wishes of Gandhiji as the father of the nation. Bose named one of the INA regiments Gandhi Regiment.

Bose had no military training. He rose to the stature of charismatic leader on his own merit, organizational ability, leadership, and personal sacrifice at a time when the people of India desperately needed someone to lead them out of the mess of a situation that had affected their lives for far too long.

Bose believed neither in the Gandhian philosophy of nonviolence nor in parliamentary democracy. He believed the Indian National Congress Party was suffering from lack of unity and weak leadership. He believed in revolution. He believed that out of the revolt stirred by the left wing, a full-fledged new party would emerge with a clear ideology, program, and plan of action.

Bose had declared his policy of a synthesis between socialism and fascism as far back as 1930, in his inaugural speech as the mayor of Calcutta. He was convinced that such a synthesis would foster justice, equality, and love when applied with efficiency and discipline.

Fourteen years later, in a speech in 1944 to the students of Tokyo University, he asserted that India must have a political system characterized by authoritarianism—a synthesis between socialism and communism. In his book *The Indian Struggle, 1920–1942*, Bose wrote that he believed that India needed a new form of government, one of total equality, in which every citizen would be treated equally in terms of politics and economics. Ultimately, he wanted to unite India into a federation with a strong center that would function with military discipline.

After the Quit India resolution, Congress passed another resolution on August 8, 1942, at the Gowalia Tank rally in Bombay, resolving that if the Congress leadership was removed by arrest, every Indian who desired freedom and strived for it must be his own guide. It motivated an upsurge of anti-British activism. The British authorities reported to London that the outburst was a deliberate fifth-columnist conspiracy intended to strengthen the Axis powers.

The British, beset by the Japanese in skirmishes along the Indo-Burma border, arrested Gandhi and put him in Aga Khan Palace in Pune. All other members of the Congress working committee, including Pandit Nehru, were held in the high-security Ahmednagar Fort. The next day, on August 9, 1942, the young activist Aruna Asaf Ali presided over a Congress session and hoisted the flag. The British administration in India banned the Indian National Congress Party.

The British actions roused strong patriotic passion among the masses of India. Despite their lack of organized leadership, large-scale protest demonstrations were held all over the country. Workers went on strike. Bombs exploded in a few places, and transportation came to a standstill. Power and communication lines were snapped.

The struggle no longer remained nonviolent or in Gandhiji's control. The extensive nature of the Quit India struggle is evident from a letter seized by the British authorities. Congress Socialist leader Jayaprakash Narayan wrote from Deoli jail urging that Congress Socialists should enter into alliance with the underground revolutionaries. He asked for coordination with illegal organizations to do illegal acts.

The British viceroy wrote that the Quit India movement was the most serious physical challenge to British rule since the Great Rebellion of 1857. The British administration came out with ruthless repression. Some one hundred thousand people were arrested, collective fines were levied on townspeople and villagers, demonstrators were publicly flogged, and innocent people were killed in police and army actions. The Royal Air Force dropped bombs and used machine guns to fire at civilians from fighter airplanes.

The revolutionaries and Congress volunteers together plunged into the struggle. Educated students and illiterate peasants resorted to terrorist activities, sabotage, and guerrilla warfare. Parallel national governments were set up at Tamluk in Midnapore in Bengal, Satara in Maharashtra, and Talcher in Orissa. Many national leaders went underground and broadcast messages to the masses from secret radio stations. Activists of parallel underground governments encouraged the struggle to liberate India and distributed pamphlets.

The entire body of Congress leadership, already in prisons, were cut off from the rest of the world for the next three years.

Prof. Judith M. Brown, in her work on the Quit India movement, observed that Gandhi's call definitely resulted in a tumultuous, countrywide struggle, both nonviolent and violent. In terms of gain and loss in attaining independence from Britain, the Quit India movement led Congress into the political wilderness.

The British government had assured Indian leaders since 1940 that an undivided India would be granted independence at the end of the war. On March 30, 1942, the British government issued a white paper contending that the British government would concede Indian independence with a certain conditions, including the formation of a constituent assembly to draft the future constitution of independent India with sufficient safeguards for minority communities. The white paper also put forward the policy that any state not interested in joining independent India would not be forced to do so. Such a state would be allowed to maintain its own entity and administration.

With the above declaration, Sir Stafford Cripps came to India and submitted a plan of granting independence to undivided India by transfer of power, but keeping more or less the same administrative structure as set forth in the 1935 Government of India Act. At that time, neither Mr. Jinnah nor the Muslim League had any plan of dividing the country into India and Pakistan.

Theoretically, Cripps's plan could have created an undivided, independent Indian dominion, with options for states that would like to have a different constitution. The expression *state* in the white paper must be construed as referring to the princely states, because the other units of British administration in India were known as provinces. The princely states were not within British India, and so the British government did not like to take any decision about their futures without their consent. The white paper only kept the option open for the princely states to participate in the constitution-making process, which in reality had to be a constituent assembly of popular representation. It was also provided in the white paper that if a particular province desired to have a separate constitution, that would be considered by the constitution-making body.

Sir Stafford Cripps came to India to negotiate with the Indian political leaders for the propositions contained in the white paper. In this context, it is pertinent to recall that in 1939, Subhas Chandra Bose, as president of Congress, gave a call for the all-out noncooperation movement to compel the British to quit India. Party veterans like Sardar Ballababhi Patel, Babu Rajendra Prasad, Jivatram Kripalni, and four other working committee members did not accept the proposal. They desired dominion status through peaceful means. But when the same proposal of dominion status was mooted by Sir Stafford Cripps, Gandhi, Jawaharlal Nehru and others in Congress rejected the proposal.

They did not accept the plan and refused to negotiate further on the grounds that the plan kept the native states (princely states) beyond the scope of the plan for Indian independence. The native states were out of British India, and Britain had no authority to force them to come under the plan. The white paper, however, provided for the native states to send their representatives to the constituent assembly if they so chose. In the event, when India was partitioned and Pakistan came into existence, more than five hundred native states were independent and remained out of India and Pakistan. Subsequently, most acceded to either India or Pakistan. Of the two large native states, Jammu and Kashmir acceded to India with certain preconditions, and Hyderabad had to be acquired by force.

Cripps returned to London after being rejected by the Indian leaders. In a statement in the *Times*, Cripps stated, among other points, that Gandhi asked the British government to walk out of India and leave the Indian people to settle their differences among themselves, even if it meant chaos and confusion. Cripps hypothesized what this chaos and confusion would actually mean. All government institutions based on the existing constitution would immediately cease to exist. There would be no viceroy, no executive council, no legislative assembly, and no civil service with any legal authority. He broadcast a similar statement through the Columbia Broadcasting System on July 26, 1942.

Sri Aurabindo, from his ashram in Pondicherry, wrote to Sir Stafford Cripps on June 15, 1945, that he had heard Cripps's broadcast. He wrote that as one who had been a nationalist leader and worker for India's independence, though his activities were no longer in the political but in the spiritual field, he wished to express his appreciation of all that Cripps had done to bring about the offer of independence of India. He welcomed the offer as an opportunity for India to determine for herself and organize in all liberty of choice her freedom and unity, taking an effective place among the world's free nations. Sri Aurabindo, by a telegram also dated June 15, 1945, urged Dr. Syed Mahmood, a member of the Congress working committee, to urge upon Gandhi and other leaders of Congress the acceptance of Cripps's proposal.

After the Quit India movement, Jinnah and the Muslim League had a clear field, not only to build up local strength, but to build a national presence unchallenged by any counterclaim by Congress or other Muslim leaders of India. The Muslim League was thus given a full and unobstructed opportunity to put their politicians into the formal institutions of political consultation and control by forming governments in Bengal, Assam, and Sindh.

Feeling emboldened, Jinnah's Muslim League demanded Pakistan. The timing of this demand was critical, as it came amid the restless commotion stirred up by the Quit India movement. After widespread bloodshed and destruction due to the movement and British repression, Jinnah's call for Pakistan caused frequent Hindu-Muslim riots, which served to divert attention from the national struggle for independence to many localized communal struggles.

After the war ended abruptly and Japan surrendered, Bose was mysteriously lost. The INA battalions, mostly comprised of the Japanese prisoners of war and officers and men of the Royal Indian Army, were brought to India as prisoners to be tried for treason. A powerful movement sprang into action spontaneously all over India in defense of the INA prisoners. The Indian press denounced the government plan to inflict harsh punishments on the INA detainees. All political parties, including the Muslim League, the Sikh League, and the Hindu Mahasabha, joined the protest and demanded clemency.

In February 1946, the united forces of the Royal Indian Navy staged a strike in Bombay in protest against the INA trial. The struggle spread to barracks in Thane and Delhi and to ships anchored in the ports of Karachi, Calcutta, and Vishakhapatnam. Two hundred thousand factory workers in Bombay put down their tools and ceased work in a demonstration of solidarity with the striking forces of the navy.

The British government took to mass arrests. The death toll due to police actions alone reached seventeen hundred. Thus, the navy strike not only upheld the cause against the INA trials, but also emboldened the Indian masses to rise against the British.

The British realized that they could no longer rule India. They turned their attention to the *modus vivendi* of granting independence to India. The fight for the independence of India, already plagued by communal politics and the struggle for power, resulted in a situation of total confusion.

In July 1945, the Labour Party came to power in England with Clement Attlee as the prime minister. The situation in India became overwhelming due to a conglomeration of factors that gave the idea of independence an undeniable momentum: the trauma of the great famine of Bengal, the charisma of Netaji and the Azad Hind Fauz, the Quit India struggle, the INA trials, and the rebellion of the Royal Indian Navy.

Reminiscent of the Indian Mutiny of 1857–58, the events of 1945–46 proved once again that the people of India, regardless of their diverse faiths and castes, could unite for a national cause as Indians. Political leaders, however popular they might appear to be, could not bring about such unity. The British government decided to grant independence to India with sufficient safeguards for Muslims.

A British cabinet mission consisting of Sir Stafford Cripps, Baron Frederick Pethick-Lawrence, and A. V. Alexander came to India on March 24, 1946, to negotiate with the political leaders and the viceroy for a consensus regarding the independence of India. The mission, after a great deal of deliberation, submitted its proposal on May 16, 1946. It proposed an interim arrangement for a united, independent India in the form of a loose federation. The mission proposed three groups: the Muslim-majority provinces of Baluchistan, Sindh, Punjab, and the northwestern frontier provinces; Assam and Bengal; and the Hindu-majority provinces in central and southern India.

The mission proposed a central government that would administer foreign affairs, communication, and defense, while all other powers would remain with the provinces, coordinated by the groups. The mission also proposed setting up a constituent assembly with representatives from all sections of the people of India. The assembly would draft the constitution and define the powers and functions of the federal and state governments, consistent with the communal groupings that the mission had delineated.

This plan would have necessitated the sharing of power by the leaders of two rival political parties, namely the Indian National Congress Party and the Muslim League, then respectively led by Pandit Jawaharlal Nehru and Muhammad Ali Jinnah. Such sharing of power was inevitable, at least until the elections were held, the people chose the leader of the federal government, and the constituent assembly drafted the constitution.

On June 16, 1946, the mission submitted an alternative plan suggesting that India could be divided into Hindu-majority India and

Muslim-majority Pakistan. The princely states of India, nevertheless, remained independent and could accede to either of the two nation-states.

Initially, members of the Congress working committee and Mr. Jinnah and the Muslim League accepted the first plan of May 16 to create a federation of undivided India. Gandhi, Pandit Nehru, and some other Congress leaders objected to the communal groupings. But they did not raise the question of the independent princely states that were outside British India. They believed that neither of the plans was conducive to India's integrity, nor would either plan foster peace between the two religious communities. The second proposal would create two nation-states out of India, which in all probability would be at odds with each other. Between the two proposals, therefore, the first proposal of an undivided federation with a constituent assembly was preferred by both Congress and the Muslim League.

Suddenly, on July 10, 1946, Pandit Jawaharlal Nehru, as the president of Congress, declared in a press conference in Bombay that Congress had agreed only to participate in the constituent assembly, and regarded itself free to change or modify the cabinet mission plan at will and as needed.

Immediately upon learning of Pandit Nehru's statement, Jinnah withdrew his support of the plan on the grounds that the proposed constituent assembly would obviously have a Hindu majority, since Congress was a Hindu-majority party. Congress would dominate the constituent assembly and frame a constitution that would substantially alter the cabinet mission plan. He contended that such a situation would be opposed to Muslim interests. He demanded the creation of Pakistan.

At that time, the Muslim League ruled Bengal. On August 16, 1946, Jinnah gave his call for observing a direct-action day. That day and the next four days witnessed unprecedented communal riots in Calcutta, known in history as the *Calcutta Killing*. This was followed by a series of communal riots in East Bengal. Gandhiji went on a fast and held prayer meetings in Calcutta.

On February 19, 1946, British prime minister Clement Attlee declared the British government's decision to grant independence to India. On March 24, Lord Mountbatten took over as the last British viceroy of India with a brief to partition India by slicing out parts of Punjab and Bengal to form Pakistan, winding up His Majesty's government in India by June 30, 1948. British Field Marshal Sir Auchinleck satirically suggested that if Pakistan became a reality, it would need a British garrison to defend it against Afghan and maybe Russian encroachment.

At midnight on August 15, 1947, the nation was partitioned between India and Pakistan, and the two parts of India became independent nation-states. The border of the truncated nation was drenched in a horrendous bloodbath. Some twelve and a half million people were uprooted from their homes as refugees.

In October 1947, Pakistan attacked India; on January 30, 1948, Gandhi was assassinated. On his deathbed on September 11, 1948, Jinnah expressed his regret to his personal physician, Colonel Illahi Baksh, and his sister Fatima that the creation of Pakistan was the greatest blunder of his life.

9

In our family, there was no tradition of music. My mother, however, encouraged me and my two sisters to sing *Rabindra Sangeet*—the songs of the poet Rabindranath Tagore. Once, my sister Anita and I sang *Rabindra Sangeet* to our father. He immensely appreciated us. A couple of days later, he appointed a music teacher for us.

Our music teacher, Adhir Ray, did his postgraduate studies in Hindustani classical vocal music at the well-known Bhatkhande Music Institute in Lucknow. Thus we had a music guru. We called him Master Mashai, meaning respected teacher. My two sisters and I started learning Hindustani classical music step by step and systematically. Master Mashai believed in the conservative tradition of north Indian classical music that had no *bandish* (composition) in *thumri*—a melodious, semiclassical form of music. He taught us dhrupad, khayal, and bhajans, but no thumri. I, however, liked thumri because of its melodious rendering and the romantic nature of its compositions.

Raja Vairab Narayan was the last surviving heir of a native estate in the district. He lived in a mansion in my hometown with the members of his large family. Only his wife had already passed away. He was not only a light-skinned, hefty old man, but also a social and political heavyweight. Nonetheless, he had a rustic air of vanity about him that made him look more like a village headman.

During the winter mornings, he would often be seen sitting bare bodied in his front yard, enjoying the warmth of sunlight. His trusted servant Tepu would be seen giving him an oil massage. Vairab Narayan smoked country tobacco in a hookah. Tepu fixed the earthen *chillum* with tobacco mix called *tamak*, which was placed upon smoldering charcoal cakes at the top of the hollow pipe of the smoking device. In sharp contrast to his master's burly look, Tepu looked like a lanky totem pole with protruding teeth. Because of his teeth, people always thought he was smiling. If anyone asked him how old he was, he replied that when his master took to smoking hookah, he (Tepu) could punt a boat.

Vairab Narayan's granddaughter, Veena, was my sister Anita's classmate in the local girls' high school. Veena too learned classical vocal music, but from a different guru. Her guru, Ostad Pannalal, dressed in skin-tight *churidar* pajamas and knee-length kurta. He also sported a Gandhi cap and a Jawahar coat. When he walked on the road, unmindfully humming some musical tune, people who did not know him gave him a salute, thinking that he was a political leader. He knew excellent thumri. He, however, did not have a deep voice like my guru.

Every evening, his only disciple Veena audibly learned thumri as he accompanied her on the tabla. The learning sessions used to be in the rearmost room of the mansion, behind a heavily curtained door and windows that were always closed. The particular room faced a narrow lane. There was a low wooden gate and a flight of three cement steps leading to that room. Veena had a sweet voice, and she sang thumri very well. But Vairab Narayan never allowed his granddaughter to sing at any public function, probably as a matter of orthodox princely custom.

Pedaling my bike slowly on the lane around Vairab Narayan's house, I carefully listened to Veena's recitals. In fact, I became a secret admirer of her thumri renderings. She generally ended her learning sessions with a composition in Maithili relating to the Radha-Krishna legend. The refrain of the song was "*Sakhiri, kawn galee gayo Shayam*"—"Oh, my friend, [tell me] which way Shayam has gone?"

I had never met her personally, although I saw her going to school carrying a bagful of books. Somehow, I liked to think that she knew that I biked around Vairab Narayan's house to listen to her thumri recital. I used to think that she knew that I especially liked the particular song she sang every evening as the last number of her learning session. I even fancied that she sang that song only for me.

Vipul Choudhury was the chairman of the town's municipal board. His wife, Monorama Choudhury, an imposing woman, was popularly known as Minu Di. She was the principal of the local girls' high school. The couple was childless. People believed that they were from some princely family of the local Rajbangsi tribe. Both of them had been educated in Calcutta. They spoke Bengali and were accustomed to Bengali language and culture.

Vivacious Minu Di was very fond of *Rabindra Sangeet*. She would call me to her place whenever she found me biking on the road near her house. She would ask me to taste a slice of cake she'd baked or a samosa she'd freshly fried, and then would ask me to sing some *Rabindra Sangeet* to her. Minu Di and I thus had a very cordial relationship.

By the time I was in the tenth standard, the last and final class before the matriculation (school graduation) exam, I had learned quite a bit of classical music from my guru. On a Saturday morning, Minu Di invited my parents, my sister Anita, and me to a musical soiree and dinner at her place.

Father was away from the town. Mother didn't like to go without him and, in a phone call, politely regretted her inability to accept the invitation. Minu Di then asked her to let Anita and me join the function. My mother did not like to let Anita go, as such functions normally ended late at night. She said that she had no objection, however, if I would like to go.

She handed the telephone receiver over to me. Minu Di heartily extended the invitation to me to attend the party. I accepted. Although I was busy preparing for the exam, I thought that it might be a good change for me to relax for a while with music.

That evening, as I stepped into her residence, I found a lot of musicians and artists, including Veena's guru Ostad Pannalal, the violinist Nirmal, and the renowned tabla player Ostad Ram Lagan Pande, were already present. Only my guru was not there. He normally avoided such private soirees. I exchanged greetings with everyone present. The artists were already making the atmosphere musical as they tuned and stroked their instruments.

Suddenly, Veena emerged from inside the house. Her presence gave me a spark of thrill—an inexplicable feeling of delight. I had never before been in such close proximity with her. She looked stunningly beautiful.

I greeted her and she reciprocated my greeting. For a moment a strange sense of edginess overwhelmed me. I couldn't look at her directly.

Everyone was sitting on a carpet covered with a white sheet of linen on the living room floor. Minu Di introduced all her guests and artists, especially mentioning Veena and me.

Ostad Pannalal was plucking the strings of a fine-tuned *tambura*. Other stringed instruments set to the same scale reverberated. Instinctively Veena and I stole glances at each other. Every time our eyes met, I felt a sense of thrill.

Slowly, Ostad Pannalal hummed the notes of an evening *raga*. Other musicians followed him with strokes of their instruments. That evening Ostad Pannalal was interpreting the raga, not in his usual thumri style but in the style of *khayal*—a heavier style of classical music. He was doing well except for his not-too-good voice. The violinist Nirmal charmed everyone with a few rapturous strokes of his violin and then winked at me to join, his chin on the chinrest of the violin.

Music always had a compelling effect on me. I was already tempted to join. When I got the hint from Nirmal, I picked up the cue and started slowly humming *vistar*—the prelude in the raga initiated by Ostad Pannalal. Throwing my voice as finely as I could—slowly, note by note and stroke by stroke—I tried to develop the structural pattern of that particular raga.

Ostad Pannalal now concentrated on plucking the strings of the tambura he held. Nirmal accompanied me on the violin. Someone stroked the strings of a *saramandal*, a type of Indian harp.

Suddenly, I was elated to find Veena joining us. She drew the harmonium toward her and started following me. As the resonance of the music permeated the atmosphere, creating an absorbing mood, she also joined me vocally. Music did its magic. All of us were engrossed in the melody of the raga. I felt as if we'd been making music together for our whole lives. I was now in full control of the modal vibes of the raga pervading the atmosphere of the connoisseur-packed room, with Veena accompanying me.

With a couple of expert strokes by way of fine-tuning the tabla, Ostad Ram Lagan Pande joined us. I intently interpreted the refrain of a khayal to join the ostad in the complicated timings of "Vilamvit Ektaal," a typical succession of slow rhythms. The ostad's swinging beats inspired me. Nonetheless, I became very careful lest I miss any beat of the sophisticated *theka*, or meter, played by him. At the same time, I felt a sense of triumph at being accompanied by Veena, my dream girl, and an expert tabla player, Ostad Ram Lagan.

We were repeatedly complimented by the connoisseurs of classical music. Following the convention of Hindustani classical music, I completed the recital by rendering a khayal in *madhaya laya*, or medium timing, and concluded my performance in *drut* or fast rhythm. Appreciative listeners fervently applauded me.

After a short pause over cups of hot tea, hands changed as Ostad Pannalal gave another tuned tambura to Veena and he took the harmonium. Nirmal added his nimble strokes of fillers. Veena sang a khayal and then my favorite thumri, "*Sakhiri, kawn galee gayo Shayam.*" Nirmal and Ostad Ram Lagan accompanied her. The session ended with Nirmal playing a few solo numbers on the violin with Ostad Ram Lagan accompanying.

As the session of music ended, most of the guests slowly moved toward the makeshift bar in the corridor connected to the living room. Veena and Minu Di went inside the house and Nirmal went out to smoke a cigarette. I felt left out and awkward.

I went to the quiet veranda at the rear of the house. I stood on the shadowy side of the deck beyond the dimly lit area of reflected light. After a while, I sensed the rustling of silk and fragrance of feminine perfume. As I looked back, I found Veena standing next to me. Her unexpected presence near me in the secluded back veranda astounded me. I forgot to greet her; she too didn't say anything. We stood side by side, holding the wooden railing. A strange feeling of delight mixed with nervousness overwhelmed me. I didn't know how to welcome her or what to say in a situation like that.

Before I could think of anything, Veena whispered in a soft and husky tone, "You sing so well. I simply love your voice and your style. I've heard you singing *Rabindra Sangeet* at public functions. I told Anita that you sing so well. Today, I came to know how well you do in raga music too. It's wonderful meeting you; I'm so happy. I wish I could learn from you. Would you teach me *Rabindra Sangeet*?"

I was sweating, despite the cool breeze blowing. I managed to reply, "I'll be only too happy if I can help you in any way. You too sing so well, so sweetly. I want to learn thumri from you. Would you teach me?"

"As though," she whispered bashfully. Then she seemed to change her mind about what she was going to say. "You know, I always feel your presence whenever you're outside on your bike. I feel a sort of happiness about singing. I don't know how to tell you. I feel as if I am singing to you only. But I cannot ask you to come in. My ostad is always near me whenever I practice singing. Besides, my grandpa too is generally about the place. I feel so bad because I cannot call you inside." She lowered her face.

"I too like to meet you, listen to you, and sing with you. This evening I felt very happy to sing with you," I replied.

Standing close to her on the open veranda, I felt a strange surge of emotion. I didn't know how to act in such a situation, being so near to the most desired one. In the solitude, when she virtually tendered her feelings to me, I didn't know how to respond or what to tell her. The encounter, as it were, was a challenge to my manhood and also to my sense of modesty. I was struggling within, not knowing how to court my dream girl.

Suddenly, someone turned the light on, astounding us. Instantly we looked back to find Minu Di. She exclaimed in her usual manner, "Oh, you are here? I was searching everywhere for both of you." Then with a smile, she politely said, "Please come in. Dinner has been spread."

After dinner, I bade good night to all, and I came back home still floating in the stream of delight. I didn't know if that was the first feeling of love. For the rest of the night, I thought of her.

Next morning as I woke up, I resolved that I must control my emotions in view of the imminent practice exam I had to take before the matriculation exam. Nonetheless, recollections of the musical soiree and the moments with Veena on Minu Di's rear veranda often diverted my concentration from my studies.

I resolved that I must prove that I was worthy of the indulgence my father had given me by offering the opportunity to learn music. I recounted his words: "Music will only add luster to your life." I was determined not to let music distract me from the mainstream of student life. I didn't go biking around Raja Vairab Narayan's house anymore. I wrote the practice exam, which was spread over days.

On the morning after the exam ended, I lingered on my bed lazily. I didn't want to think about exams anymore. Neither did I feel any urge to go out biking. I felt a strange state of void: a state of mind in which nothing works, not even one's dearest thoughts.

Anita had gone to her school and Father to the court. Mother was somewhere in the house, maybe in the kitchen or in her bedroom. I had just come out to the hallway when suddenly the telephone rang. I lifted the receiver. From the other end whispered a familiar voice. "Hi. Is there anyone else near you?" It was Veena.

"No," I replied.

"How was the exam?" she asked.

"Not too bad, I think," I answered.

"Could you come to the park on the riverside?"

"Now?" I asked with surprise in my voice.

"Please, if you can," she whispered.

"Okay," I replied instinctively.

"I will be there within an hour. Would you please wait for me?" she asked.

"Sure," I whispered. My lethargy vanished in a moment.

It was electrifying to think that I would be with Veena secretly in the serenity of midday in the riverside park. My heartbeat quickened. Hurriedly, I shaved and put on aftershave. Then I felt my cheeks to make sure I had shaved properly. I changed into the best clothes I could, combed my hair, and looked at myself in the mirror from different angles to make sure that I looked my best. Stealthily, I took out my bike and set out for the tryst, my first-ever secret meeting with a girl.

The autumnal sky was clear blue. Noontime sun flooded the town. I pedaled my bike to reach the park as fast as I could. I wondered why she had called me so suddenly to meet her. Perhaps she was missing me because I didn't go biking around her place for so many evenings after my last meeting with her. I didn't hear her singing "*Sakhiri, kawn galee gayo Shayam.*"

I pedaled harder on the tarmac road that ran parallel to the Brahmaputra. I reached the riverside and entered the park. I left my bicycle slanted against a tree. It was shady and cool inside the park with a riverine breeze blowing. She had not yet come. I looked at my wristwatch. I had made it in less than twenty minutes. She had said she would be there within an hour. I had arrived sufficiently ahead of time, I thought.

But how would she come? It was impossible to walk all alone from her place to the park. She would have to take a rickshaw. An old man rickshaw puller was already there, leaning on his rickshaw under the shade of a tree on the other side of the road, near the shrine of the five pīrs. It flashed in my mind: could she have already come in that rickshaw? No. She had asked me to come to the park. So she must have intended to come to the park and not go to the shrine of the the pīrs.

Nonetheless, I came out to the road and went near the sleeping rickshaw puller. With his body on the footrest, his head on the seat, and his feet on the ground, the old man was fast asleep. I hesitated to disturb him. Let him sleep, I thought. If she had come by that rickshaw, the rickshaw-puller wouldn't already have been in such a fast sleep.

I went back to the park. She must be on her way, I thought. I had to wait for her. Who knew—she might have been delayed; she might not have found a chance to escape from Vairab Narayan's vigilant eyes. I was worried about how would she get to the park secretly and all alone in broad daylight.

Suddenly, it occurred to me that the park was a public place. If we were found together, it would be an awful scandal. I searched for a suitable point at the riverside-end of the park where we could hide ourselves. It had to be a safe place, a foolproof place, where no one would be able to find us.

The park was fenced by a wire net on the riverside. There was no hiding place within that boundary. I thought that we might go down the eroded end of the park to the river's edge. There was an opening in the wire-net fencing.

I stepped down, using the exposed roots of a huge tree as footholds, and found a place below the park at the water's edge. The point was not visible from the road nor from the park, which were at a much higher level. I felt sure that nobody would come up to the eroding edge of the park for fear of falling into the river along with chunks of loose earth.

I planned how we could safely go down, carefully stepping on and holding the exposed roots, avoiding the loose earth. The tree had deep roots that must have spread over a wide stretch of soil underneath the park. I made sure by pushing the tree with all my strength and found that it was firmly rooted to the ground. It would never fall down.

I sought out the thickest part of the exposed root at the river's edge. I scraped the root with twigs and removed the layers of dirt sticking to it. I dusted it clean with my handkerchief. Now I felt sure that it would not soil Veena's sari or whatever she might be wearing. We could sit on that particular root and nobody would be able to find us.

I imagined how she would alight from the rickshaw and run toward me. She would feel shy and lower her eyes. I felt sure that she would give me a beaming grin. She would be blushing, radiating her glow all over her face. Before I could greet her, she would put her finger on her lips, signaling me not to speak.

Then she would throw her arms around my neck, putting her cheek against mine. I would hold her close and plant kisses on her soft, plummy lips. Her entire body would be throbbing like a warm dove, caught in my hands. I remembered the fragrance of the perfume she used on the evening we met in Minu Di's place.

But would she be able to get down, stepping over and holding the exposed tree roots? She would be scared, I knew. I would help her to slowly and carefully climb down the tree roots; I would hold her tightly so that she would not be scared. Then, sitting together on the tree root by the rushing stream, we would be lost in ecstasy. I would smell the enchanting scent of her hair. I would hold her hand and listen to all she'd tell me.

A large bird flopped on the top of the tree, breaking my reverie. I looked at my wristwatch. It was already an hour since I had come to the park. She must have come and, not finding me, left the park. I shouldn't have gone down to the river's edge. I repented of my stupidity. It was too frustrating to think that she had come and gone.

I looked around outside the park. No one was anywhere within or outside the park. Even the sleeping rickshaw puller was no more. I pedaled my bike as fast as I could from end to end of the riverside road. There was no rickshaw in view. I felt sure that she had come and gone without finding me. I felt miserable thinking that she would believe I never came; she would think that I didn't care enough to honor her request.

There was no way to contact her. I didn't know how I could convince her that I came to the park, selected the safest place to sit, and waited for her for more than an hour. Again I thought, how would she get a rickshaw to come at that hour of the day? She might have been caught by Vairab Narayan, the rustic old man. And then she couldn't come.

I waited until three o'clock. She did not come. Disappointed, I slowly pedaled my bike toward home.

After going a little distance, I turned and came back to the park again. She might have been delayed; she might not have been able to get a rickshaw in time. I thought I must wait for a little while longer. I waited outside the park's gate so that I wouldn't miss her. I stood, leaning against my bike, on the paved sidewalk by the road. Both sides of the road were visible.

Another rickshaw puller appeared, pedaling his tricycle-rickshaw with no one on it. He stopped near me. He gave me a sealed envelope with no name or address written on it. He stood waiting, as if he wanted something back. Anxiously, I opened the envelope, expecting that it would contain a message from Veena. Yes, it did. Inside it was a slip of paper containing a few words hurriedly scribbled in a feminine hand.

"Sorry, couldn't come to meet you. Hope you understand and excuse me. See you some other time. Good luck with your exam result."

The message was neither addressed to anyone nor signed by the sender. I knew it was from her. I realized there must have been some genuine difficulty that prevented her from coming. I had no chance to know why she wanted to meet me, and I had no chance to know why she couldn't come.

I went biking around Vairab Narayan's place. I did not hear her singing thumri, nor did I see her anywhere outside the house. Not only was my first assignation in vain, but I saw and heard no sign of her anywhere for a long time afterward.

I wrote the answer scripts for the matriculation exam for ten days. After the results came out, I would have no more school. It saddened me to think that I wouldn't meet or hear Veena; I wouldn't meet my classmates and friends anymore. On the other hand, the idea that I would be going to a university excited me. If I went away to Calcutta for higher studies, however, I wouldn't be able to meet Veena. Yet I would come home on vacations. I could meet Veena then. Flickers of thoughts crisscrossed my mind.

Then one morning, the beating of *dhaks*, a traditional large barrel drum, reverberated, reminding me that it was time for the Durga Puja, the greatest annual festival in Bengal and eastern India. The Durga Puja mood began with the first beat of the dhak on Mahalaya, the new-moon day preceding the festival. Mahalaya is the day of invoking the goddess Durga. In all the households in town, Puja shopping, the meeting of friends and relations, and the making of sweets and eats bring irresistible hilarity.

Traditionally the Puja season was the time of homecoming, of giving and taking of love, affection, and gifts. My mother, together with my sisters Anita and Sunita and housemaid Saudamini, all dressed in new clothes, went to the Hari Sabha temple to offer welcome to the goddess, a ceremonial invocation. Anita asked me if I would like to come with them. I told her that I would go later. I just avoided them.

Durga Puja was celebrated in the Hari Sabha and in many other *barowari* or community pavilions and private houses in the town. Drumbeats were heard from near and distant places. Durga Puja was also celebrated in the houses of traditional aristocrats as a status symbol. Raja Vairab Narayan celebrated Durga Puja in his house with great éclat.

Puja pavilions were particularly crowded during the *arati*—the evening session of offering salutations to the goddess. Priests would first offer the ritual arati to the goddess with rhythmic waving of smoke-giving incense pots, fire pots, and butter lamps, together with the chanting of mantras and beating of dhaks. After the rite was over, it would be open to young boys and men and to everyone else to offer arati to the goddess. Those offering arati would dance, displaying their best sense of rhythm and creativity, holding earthen incense pots in hands to adore the goddess with incense smoke.

On the evening of Navami Puja, the last evening of Durga Puja, I moved around the town and met many of my classmates in various Puja pavilions. In spite of their company, crowds of Puja revelers, and much hilarity, light, and sound all around, I felt a sense of loneliness. I only wanted to find Veena. Her mysterious silence after the message she sent through the rickshaw puller roused my anxiety and the urge to meet her. I wanted to know for sure what had gone wrong. Why was she so silent? I also wondered why she was not singing thumri anymore. But I couldn't find her anywhere.

I sneaked apart from others and entered Raja Vairab Narayan's Puja pavilion. The entire area was brightly lit and thronged by visitors. A crowd of people was watching arati. I managed to get a place to stand right in front of the enclosed area for the drummers, just below the dais. The *dhakis* were dancing to the beat of their drums. In front of the glittering image of the goddess on the dais, two young men were offering arati.

Suddenly, a spark of thrill stirred me as my eyes met Veena's. She was standing near the wing on one side of the dais, from time to time throwing incense dust into the fire pots held by the pair of young men swinging to the rhythm of the drumbeats and offering arati. She looked like another goddess.

In the next moment, I felt a strange fit of indignation. I felt betrayed, humiliated, insulted. But there was hardly anything that I could do. I quit the place with a sense of disgust.

I avoided the glow of light and the stream of people on the main road facing Vairab Narayan's Puja pavilion. Instead, I took the obscure lane running by the rear of the house. I hated myself for wasting so many evenings biking on the lane to listen to Veena's thumri recital. I felt convinced that she was not a truthful girl.

As I was walking by the lane precipitously, a silhouetted human figure obstructed my passage. I was startled at the touch of a human body. In the opacity of the lane, I could barely make out that it was

Veena standing before me, blocking my passage. As I stopped, she spread her hands around my neck. Before I could speak, she pleadingly whispered, "I know you're angry with me. Believe me, I just couldn't help it. I don't know how to tell you. I'm really sorry, very sorry. Please don't misunderstand me, please . . ."

For a moment we stood quietly, hugging each other. I felt her firm and soft body against my chest; her warm breaths fell on my neck. Her emotion-filled whisper and the touch of her tear-soaked cheeks instantly broke all my barriers of anger and ego. An intense feeling of love urged me to soothe her. My body and soul desired her all over again. It was a strange sense of ecstasy that made me forget everything else.

Clasped together, we went through the rear gate of Vairab Narayan's house and slumped on a step in front of the room in which she practiced singing thumri. After a few moments, a sudden snapping sound of an unlocking door latch alerted us. Veena tore herself away from me with a push to release herself from our entwined position. She hurried inside, shutting the door she had opened to come out to me.

I strode at a quick pace and reached the road at the other end of the lane. I managed to mingle in the crowd of people, carefully observing to make sure that no one was following me. Impulsively, I stopped a cycle-rickshaw and got onto its seat. Unable to decide where to go, I asked the rickshaw-wallah to just move out of the crowd. As the rickshaw came up to the crossroads, I told him to turn left and again turn right, not knowing where to go.

The rickshaw entered the bazaar road. I remembered a Bengali sweetshop-cum-restaurant on that road. I knew its owner, a friendly man. On that evening, everyone was out to revel on the last evening of the Puja, and there was no customer in the shop. I got down, paid the rickshaw-wallah, and walked into the shop as nonchalantly as I could.

The shop owner greeted me. I reciprocated. He asked me how I enjoyed the last evening of the Puja. He said, "You look tired. Did you do some arati?"

I had no alternative other than to affirm his guess by a nod.

The shopkeeper chuckled. "I know it's very tiring; let me give you some hot tea. Would you like something to eat? I have some freshly made *lalmohans*." He pointed to a large bowl filled with sugar syrup and deep-fried red balls of *chana*—curd cheese, floating.

"These lalmohans were just brought to the shop; they are still hot," he added. He didn't wait for my reply and put two lalmohans on a plate. He placed the plate on a table and started making tea for me.

I was familiar with the setting of the shop. I walked to the washbasin and a small mirror fixed to the wall. I turned on the light, washed my hands, face, and neck, and wiped up with the common, not-too-clean hand towel hanging from a hook. It smelled of stale sweat. I managed to wipe off the lipstick marks from my face. But there were at least two marks on my shirt. I soaked my handkerchief in water, rubbed it against the piece of soap, and slowly wiped at the stains. Nonetheless, faint traces remained.

The shopkeeper called to me, "Your tea is already cold. What are you doing?"

I combed my hair to make myself as presentable as I could and then came back to the table. I turned on the ceiling fan at full speed. The shopkeeper looked at me in surprise. I told him, "My shirt is wet. Let it dry under the fan."

The shopkeeper smiled and said, "Don't take that tea; it's cold. I'll get you a fresh cup."

I was feeling better in a safe place. The shopkeeper came with another cup of tea, placed it before me, and sat down in the chair across from me at the small table.

"Is this the first time you did arati? Where did you do it? I presume you did it in the Hari Sabha, where your grandpa used to go every day. That is the best place; that's everybody's place. Everyone goes to the Hari Sabha during the Durga Puja," said the shopkeeper.

I nodded.

He continued, "Let me tell you that the best thing to do after offering arati is to take a shower. Then you feel fresh and relaxed." After a pause, he continued his soliloquy. "Tomorrow is Vijaya Dasami. I have so many orders for sweets that I don't know if I will be able to keep all my commitments. My *karigars*, sweet-makers, will work throughout the night. I promised to give them wages at double the rate."

Unmindful, I listened to his prattle. After he stopped, I said, "Thank you very much. Let me go now; my shirt has dried."

"Where are you going? Are you going to watch *Jatra Gan*—folk opera?"

"No. I'm going home," I replied.

"Then why bother? After performing arati, everyone feels like that."

I couldn't tell him that I was offering arati to the goddess of love. I paid him with thanks and walked toward home. Quietly I entered my bedroom, unnoticed by anyone. I felt triumphant winning Veena's love. Every moment I thought of her, I desired to be with her again and again and tell her how enormously I loved her.

But what had been that snapping sound, I wondered. Why was Veena so scared, running inside the house as if for fear of her life? The thought haunted me. I never wanted her to be in trouble.

* * *

The next morning and day after day I went biking around Vairab Narayan's house, hoping to meet her. But I neither saw nor heard Veena. My eagerness turned into anxiety. Was she all right? Was she out of the town? I thought I must find out. I biked aimlessly, not knowing where to go, what to do, or how to find Veena.

One day I saw Minu Di standing on her balcony. Spontaneously, I gave her a smile. She acknowledged it with a smile. I thought that since she was the principal of Veena's school, she might know about Veena. I got down from my bike and walked to her house. We exchanged greetings and I followed her to her living room. We sat down facing each other in her living room. I noticed that on that day, Minu Di was unusually lukewarm in receiving me. What has happened to Minu Di, I wondered. She was never so impassive. I asked her, "How are you, Minu Di?"

"Not too bad; how are you?" she asked me in reply.

"Are you all right, Minu Di?" I asked her again.

"Oh yes, I'm fine, How are you?" There was a touch of slight in her tone. I was surprised. Before I could say anything, she said, "How about a cup of tea?"

Without waiting for my reply, she stood up and went farther into the house.

I sat quietly, wondering what might be the reason for her to be unusually laconic on that day. After a while, she came back with two cups of tea and a plate of crackers on a tray. She offered a cup to me and put the other cup on the small table by her side. She settled down and then nonchalantly observed, "So, the ordeal is over at last—I mean, the exam. How did it go? You must have done very well. The paper on math was rather stiff, wasn't it? But you're a good student; you must have done well. Some girls found it hard to answer, particularly the intricate and rather lengthy equation."

"I really don't know, Minu Di, how good or how bad my answers were. I answered all the questions, including the equation," I replied normally.

After a few moments of calmness, Minu Di broke the silence again. "Wintry weather is setting in. Do you take a morning walk? If you come very early in the morning, you can see dewdrops on the grass. Fragrant *sephali* (jasmine flowers) are profusely blooming in my backyard. At night we feel the sweet fragrance, and in the morning the ground under the tree is covered with the flowers shed. Every morning girls flock around the tree to collect flowers to knit garlands."

I felt sure that Minu Di was fishing for something to speak about. She didn't speak about music; she didn't ask me to sing *Rabindra Sangeet*.

After some more hesitation, she blurted out, "I want to tell you something, if you don't mind and don't take it too seriously."

"Sure, please tell me. I won't mind," I replied.

"Actually, it's a bit serious, but I must tell you because you should know."

I felt concerned at her tone. Could it be something about Veena, something about our meeting on the evening of the Navami Puja?

Seemingly, she guessed my feeling. She said, "Don't worry. I am only telling you as a matter of my duty. Nobody knows anything in the matter, not even your parents. Did you meet Veena on the evening of the Navami Puja?"

"Yes, I did," I affirmed.

"Where?" was the next question.

"We met at Raja Vairab Narayan's place."

Minu Di recomposed herself and then in the same low tone said, "I don't know how it reached him, but someone told my uncle about you and Veena. Perhaps they also mentioned your secret meeting on the evening of the Navami Puja."

"Your uncle?" I uttered in surprise.

"Yes. Veena's grandpa, Raja Vairab Narayan, is my uncle. As you know, he is an old-timer. He was very angry and wanted to tell your father. With a great deal of persuasion, I appeased him. I convinced him that I know for sure that you two only appreciate each other as artists. It's nothing unusual and nothing to be taken so seriously. Artistes do admire one another. People always have the tendency to exaggerate things. I assured him that I would personally ask you, and I was sure you would tell me the truth. I am glad that you told me the truth."

She chuckled and then continued, "I won't ask you to tell me any more details of your meeting. Veena also admitted that she met you. Both of you are of an age when interest in the opposite sex naturally develops. In your case, it must be your common interest in music that aroused mutual admiration and the urge to meet. This is exactly what is called infatuation."

I lowered my face and looked at the floral rug under my feet, wondering what her next accusation would be. I tried to think why she used the expression *infatuation*. What had Veena told her?

"You know, as principal of a girls' high school, I know the psychology of girls. I know how young girls fall in love with young and attractive boys and consequently get victimized. All adolescent love affairs end up in the same way. Boys fly away like birds in the bush, and girls suffer mutely as victims."

I felt insulted at her generalization that directly hurt my ego. I was not a bird in the bush; I genuinely loved Veena. Just because Minu Di was principal of the girls' high school, she had no right to scorn me and ridicule my love for Veena.

But before I could protest, Minu Di said, "I don't mean to offend your feelings, but this is how scandals spread. Someone gave my uncle, maybe, a twisted and exaggerated report about your affair with Veena and your meeting on the Navami Puja evening. He got infuriated. Nobody wants a scandal to spread involving their dear and near ones. There is no dearth of gossipmongers in the town. They can easily wreck the life and future of an innocent girl.

"Please don't misunderstand me. I don't mean that you have done any wrong, but when, in the course of time, such infatuations wither, the boys escape and the girls bear the brunt. Their lives are ruined. You could take offence at what I am telling you. But I am telling the inevitable consequences of all such love affairs. I am telling you from my experience of dealing with schoolgirls for so many years."

She didn't give me a chance to say anything but continued, "We don't live in a permissive society like in the Western countries. We do not recognize any intimate relationship between a boy and a girl as friendship. In our society, love is recognized only after a boy and a girl are united by marriage."

I kept quiet, restraining my urge to counter her points.

Minu Di took a sip of tea and then resumed. "Marriage in our society is a social institution, a permanent alliance between two families rather than mere union of a man and a woman. It's a traditional institution that holds and perpetuates the ethos and culture from generation to generation."

I was just about to speak when Minu Di raised her hand to stop me from interrupting her. She continued, "When Uncle came to know, he said something to Veena, and she reacted rather stubbornly. As a grandfather, Uncle didn't expect such behavior from his loving granddaughter. He called me on the phone, and immediately I went to his place. I somehow managed to pacify him and checked him from taking up the matter with your father. I took the responsibility to speak to you. I assured him that you're a reasonable boy and that if I spoke to you, you would care for my words. Today when I saw you, I thought, 'Let me call him and tell him about the matter.' It was good that you came in of your own; I didn't have to call you.

"When I went to my uncle's place, I found Veena all in sobs, hysterically babbling the words every girl in similar circumstances babbles. I felt so sorry for the poor thing. She was ever so jolly, so innocent, and as you know, she is very talented. Her mother was my cousin. She died a premature death. Her father married again. My uncle brought her to his place and looked after her as his beloved granddaughter. He never refused anything to her. Veena too loved Uncle very much. I don't yet know what my uncle told her that could bring about such convulsions in her. I also don't know what exactly she told my uncle that enraged him so much."

I looked to her anxiously and asked, "What did she tell you; what did she do?"

"She told me that she loves you. I told her that she should understand that you are only a student now. You have a long way to go in higher education, and by the time you're on your own, she will be rather too old to be married. You know, girls grow up faster than boys. And who knows whether you will still be interested in her like you are today? Besides, there are many other social barriers."

I was fuming in anger. But I didn't know what to tell her. Perhaps she understood how her words humiliated me, how her conclusions hurt my ego. Lest I express my feelings, she again raised her hand with an insipid smile, gesturing at me to keep quiet. She continued now in a more complaisant but palliative tone, "I know you're a good boy, a good student with every promise of a bright future. You also come from a good family. But I had to tell her, as woman-to-woman advice, that boys of your age are like clay on a potter's wheel, yet to take shape. If one tries to take the pot in hand before it is done and dry, it will only fall apart. But she wouldn't listen to the honest advice that I gave her in her own interest."

With a great deal of effort, I controlled my reactions as Minu Di went on surmising. Nonetheless, I couldn't help telling her, "I'm sorry to say it, Minu Di, but aren't you generalizing about the entire class of young men, proclaiming them unreliable, birds in the bush, clay on the potter's wheel, and so on? Aren't you judging our relationship and our feelings for each other without really knowing anything about it, without hearing us? You never thought that she and I too could have something to say? Everyone might not be a bird in the bush."

Minu Di now laughed and exclaimed, "Well, this is the common dialogue delivered by all heroes of such affairs, whether in real life or in the movies. Please don't forget that I'm the principal of a girls' school. I have seen oceans of tears shed by unfortunate girls. Veena could only add to their numbers."

Minu Di's caustic tone hit me very hard. A feeling of resentment pervaded me. I never expected such abrasive comments, such a harsh stance from Minu Di. Her words broke my patience. Nevertheless, I controlled my feelings and asked her, "What did Veena say?"

"What could she say? She is too simple a girl to realize the hard realities of life."

"How is that? You told her so many things. You gave her so much advice, and she just listened to you and said nothing? You would agree, Minu Di, that it sounds very unusual," I retorted.

Minu Di was surely angry but maintained her calm. Slowly she uttered, "I know you're an intelligent boy, and that makes it all the more difficult."

A few moments of silence ticked by as my blood flew faster in my arteries. Both of us became conscious that our conversation was overshooting the parameters of etiquette. Minu Di resumed with the words, "Besides, nobody knows what the reaction of your parents would be if they knew. You know my husband and I have a very good relationship with your parents. I prevented my uncle from speaking to your father both in the interest of maintaining the same good relationship and to protect you from getting into any unpleasant situation. But if you too become unreasonable and adamant, it will only complicate things rather than solving the problem. There is no point arguing. I hope you understand?"

Minu Di could not have admonished me more severely. Her words sounded like a threat. Conscious of the developing dialogue, I kept quiet.

Minu Di took another sip of tea from her cup. Then, referring to our social relationship, she said, "Besides, there cannot be any matrimonial alliance between us. As you know, we belong to two different communities. To be very frank about it, we belong to the royal family of the former Kamata kingdom. Kamata kings ruled southern Assam from the thirteenth century. You come from a family of immigrants from Bengal. There's no doubt that we have many common things in our cultures, and both families generally follow the prevailing standard of education and culture. Nevertheless, we have two different ethnic and social identities. So the best course is to nip the affair when it is in the budding stage, before it blooms into a poison flower. You know what I mean?"

She quaffed the rest of the caffeinated concoction from her cup that went cold as her statement heated up, flaming the fire of resentment in me.

"Nice to know, Minu Di, that you have royal ancestry. But I'm afraid it would be going beyond our education and culture if we identified people in terms of their ancestry and community. Indeed my grandfather emigrated from Bengal when this district was a part of northern Bengal. My father and all his siblings were born here after the area was incorporated with Assam, probably as far back as 1874. Every educated person of our district, including you, has been educated at Calcutta or Dhaka Universities of Bengal. And every educated person has been imbued with the same language and culture they learned in the course of their higher education in Calcutta. Going back to Kamatapur would be going back to the Middle Ages instead of looking to the common and progressive culture you and we profess. I hope you agree with me?"

Minu Di stood up from her seat and uttered in a satirical tone, "Your outlook is indeed very broad. I wish everybody could think in the same way. Unfortunately, they don't, and that is the reality. I can only wish you the best of luck."

Minu Di unceremoniously left the living room. Disgusted, I exited from her place like a mute, wounded animal.

After my encounter with Minu Di, I had no opportunity to meet Veena or hear from her. From Anita, I learned that Veena's music coach, Ostad Pannalal, was no longer teaching her. Anita also told me that she learned in her school that Veena had gone to live in Raja Vairab Narayan's original home somewhere around the neighboring Cooch Behar-Gauripur area. I had no opportunity to know anything more about her until the time I left for Calcutta for higher education.

Sometime later, I encountered Veena by chance when I came home from Calcutta on a vacation. Presumably, Veena came to our place to meet her ex-classmate Anita. She greeted me just like any other friend of my sister would have acknowledged me. I noticed that she had put on some weight and had a vermilion mark on the parting of her hair. Before I could get over my vague, intuitive grasp of the situation, she hurried to leave with the plea that her rickshaw was waiting outside. I never met her again.

The questions of castes, subcastes, and the difference between various communities of Hindus in India still persists, despite the tremendous progress achieved by the nation in many other socioeconomic spheres. Veena, however, represents the social situation of a time decades ago.

10

I called Nirmal Bhattacharya "Nirmal Da" because he was older than I. He was a handsome young man, a fairly good student, and a keen violinist. Nirmal was the eldest son of a well-known practicing physician in our district. Nirmal was an extremely moody person. Sometimes he would do anything for someone he liked, and sometimes he wouldn't do a thing for someone else he didn't like.

Nirmal's father, being the eldest of his brothers, was the head of the joint family. Nirmal had an exclusive room in the large ancestral house, with a door facing the road. Dolly, a neighborhood girl, was his childhood playmate. As they grew up, they maintained the same friendly relationship. Whenever Nirmal picked up a new tune or a new composition, he played it to Dolly in his exclusive room.

Those days, the free mixing of adolescent boys and girls was not acceptable to Bengali middle-class society, especially in small towns like ours. Nonetheless, nobody spoke against their relationship because everybody needed Nirmal's father's help as the best physician of the town. So Dolly continued to visit Nirmal to listen to his violin recitals.

Nirmal's physician father was totally preoccupied with his professional engagements. He hardly had any time to bother about who visited his son. Nirmal's loving mother was too simple to suspect any unwanted relationship between her darling son and his childhood playmate, even though Dolly was growing up into a beautiful damsel. She addressed Nirmal's mother as *mashima*, aunt, a customary address by young people to motherly neighborhood women. The old woman was fond of Dolly, especially because of her winning nature and acquiescent disposition. Dolly often visited her neighborhood aunt on her way home from her school, particularly when Nirmal was at home. Nirmal's mother did not speculate on Dolly's keenness in listening to Nirmal's violin recitals in his room. She only felt proud of her son whenever someone admired his talents.

Dolly too was the eldest child of her parents. She was dearly loved by them. She was a good student and one of the most popular girls in the school. Her father, a rich jute merchant, was also busy with his trade, while her mother looked after the household and her four children. She was proud of her daughter, who scored high marks in school exams. Dolly's mother likewise never worried about who Dolly was mixing with.

Nirmal was a through introvert. He preferred to remain at home playing on his violin rather than mixing with his classmates and friends. In fact, he would allow into his room only a chosen few, those who were genuinely interested in music. Rarely, he would be seen outside the house, biking, with a bunch of old gramophone records in a canvas bag dangling from the top tube of his bike. These old gramophone records contained treasured renderings of instrumental and vocal recitals of Hindustani classical music by the well-known maestros of the previous generation. He had standing permission from the last legatee of a local native estate to borrow as many gramophone records as he liked from his ancestral manor in our town. Nirmal thus learned quite a bit of Hindustani classical music and played the pieces in his own way on his violin.

I can hardly recall how and when I became close to him. Perhaps our common passion to learn music instinctively brought us close to one another. In fact, aside from Dolly, I was the only person who had open access to Nirmal's music-filled room. In the process, I too became acquainted with the original styles of rendering the ragas and raginis as the basic musical patters of Hindustani classical music.

After Nirmal matriculated from school, his parents desired that he should go to Calcutta for higher education and become a qualified medical doctor to succeed his father. Accordingly, Nirmal prepared to proceed to Calcutta. Before leaving for the railway station, he clumsily took leave from Dolly. Both of them were in their salad days. Dolly wiped her tears and managed to whisper good luck to Nirmal. Nirmal felt a strange sensation of emotion he had never known before. He only pressed Dolly's hand with a feeling glance. Perhaps for the first time, they realized how deeply they were enamored of one another.

In Calcutta, Nirmal studied science, including biology and chemistry, in a residential missionary college. The Irish pastor of the college chapel was a violinist. He picked up Nirmal because of his musical talents. The pastor taught Nirmal how to play violin in Western style. Nirmal took it up with fervor and learned to read music from Western staff notations.

As a token of his appreciation of Nirmal's quick progress in learning music, the priest presented him with an Italian violin. Nirmal could now play some Indian and some Western music, bowing and fingering his violin in Western style. He became a real violinist.

He came home on vacations. With strokes of his violin, he charmed the music lovers and his many fans, particularly of the opposite sex. He became the most sought-after person, not only in our town, but much beyond it. He was frequently invited by music lovers to play violin at public events and in private soirees.

Nevertheless, he couldn't think of anyone else in place of his childhood playmate and admirer, Dolly. As before, he played exclusively to Dolly in his room whenever he came home on vacations. He played for her many new pieces of music on his Italian instrument. Dolly, now a student of the local college, continued to visit Nirmal whenever he came home on vacation.

After completing intermediate science, as his course was called, Nirmal joined the Calcutta Medical College. He continued to come home on long vacations. Dolly, as usual, visited him and listened to his violin recitals in his room. Although their mutual admiration had spontaneously developed into love, it remained unrevealed all the same. Perhaps for them it was too delicate and too dear a feeling to bring it down to the mundane level.

Even so, Dolly's classmates and friends started gossiping about their relationship. Their gossip reached Dolly's mother and, necessarily, her father. They not only became suspicious but were alarmed that the gossip among the girls might break out into a real scandal, ruining their daughter's future. Besides, Nirmal and Dolly belonged to distinctly different castes and classes in traditional society. While Nirmal came from a pedigreed Brahmin family, Dolly belonged to a Vaishya family. Their relationship, therefore, could not end in a family alliance.

Slowly, it came about that whenever Dolly came to her neighborhood aunt's place, her little brother Chintu appeared as the emissary of his mother, carrying the message that their mother had asked Dolly to come home at once. Humiliated and embarrassed, Dolly had to abruptly leave Nirmal's company and go home.

On certain occasions, disgusted Dolly flouted her mother's command under the indulgent umbrella of Nirmal's mother. Consequently, the matter took a serious turn. Dolly's parents not only prohibited her from visiting Nirmal and his mother, but also threatened that they would withdraw her from the college and get her married off to someone from a faraway place. Dolly quietly tolerated everything because she never liked to upset Nirmal and distract him from his studies and his dedication in playing violin.

Chintu knew the exact times of Dolly's going to college and coming back home. With a view to avoiding Chintu, Dolly started skipping classes and secretly visiting Nirmal. Nirmal's mother and Nirmal had no idea about what was going on between Dolly and her mother. Nirmal eagerly waited for Dolly's visits so he could play new tunes for her.

Suddenly and for some days, Dolly didn't visit Nirmal. Nirmal was worried about her. He could neither go to Dolly's place to inquire about her, nor concentrate on his violin. For the first time, he realized the social taboo that an unrelated young man and young woman were prohibited from visiting each other. He desperately tried to contact her over the phone. Every time he dialed Dolly's home telephone number, someone else lifted the receiver, only to say that she was not available. Probably no one in the house told Dolly that Nirmal rang up to talk to her.

Just about the time when Dolly stopped visiting Nirmal, his loving mother suddenly developed acute colic pain. His physician father and all other medics available in the town, including the civil surgeon, couldn't diagnose the cause. She was rushed to Calcutta for specialized attention and treatment.

In a Calcutta hospital, after various investigations, specialists and surgeons decided to operate on her. Alas, she expired on the operating table. For Nirmal it was the most shocking disaster.

Her body was brought to the town for the last rites. I recollect how Nirmal and his two younger siblings grieved inconsolably over the lifeless body of their mother. My parents and many other friends and family relations visited the place to pay their last homage to the departed soul and to offer condolences to the bereaved family. It didn't miss my notice that Dolly was conspicuously absent from the scene.

I kept in touch with Nirmal throughout the period of his sudden bereavement. A few days after demise of Nirmal's mother, I came to Nirmal's place to look him up. The door of his room was ajar. I pushed the door and was about to step into the room. I dithered at the scenario inside the room.

Nirmal, with two weeks' growth of beard on his cheeks, was spacing out on the floor of his room. Dolly, in a disheveled state, was sitting on a wooden chair, burying her face between her arms obliquely placed on the desk in front of the chair. As she raised her head at the sound of my steps, I noticed that her eyes were swollen and her face drenched with tears.

I was perplexed and didn't like to disturb them in such a situation. Before anyone could utter a word, I came out. I got on my bike and pedaled off.

But I could not be at peace. I was dying to know what had happened to upset Nirmal and Dolly so much. The next day I again went to Nirmal's place. This time I knocked at the door. In a grave tone, Nirmal asked me to come in. As I entered the room, I found a melancholy Nirmal sitting on a chair. He gestured to the other chair for me to sit. I drew the chair near him and asked him as warmly as I could, "How are you doing, Nirmal Da?"

In a gloomy tone he replied, "Okay."

I felt hesitant to broach the topic that was bothering me. A tight silence prevailed for a few seconds. In my effort to start a conversation,

I asked about the arrangements for the impending *sraddha*—the Hindu obsequies ceremony, performed for the peace of the departed soul. Nirmal didn't reply to my question. He looked depressed.

Wondering over unknown anxieties, I didn't know what to say or how to break the stillness. After a while, I ventured to apologize to him for my unannounced entry into his room on the day before.

Suddenly animated, Nirmal fumed, "Can you believe that they"—obviously meaning Dolly's parents—"are forcing Dolly to wed someone she doesn't even know?"

"How come, all of a sudden?" I anxiously asked.

"I don't know. Her parents have fixed up her marriage without her consent. You saw her yesterday; she really doesn't know what to do. She won't even be able to sit her exam. I feel like knocking down such people who torture their daughters just because they are born as girls." Nirmal was really angry.

I was shocked to hear the news. I didn't know what to say. Nirmal stood up, paced a few steps within the room in his impatient excitement, and then sat down on the chair. I too felt a raging anger against Dolly's parents.

I didn't know what to say; I didn't know what to do. Although Nirmal never told me in so many words, I knew for sure that they were deeply in love with one another. I don't remember how long I was musing over the matter.

Nirmal asked me, "What do you think we should do?"

I asked a counter question. "Have they fixed the date for the wedding?"

"Oh yes, they have fixed the date. It is the same auspicious day on which my mother's sraddha ceremony would be held. Can you imagine?"

"Brutish!" I sputtered.

After some thinking I suggested, "Could Dolly go away someplace to escape the wedding, at least till the sraddha ceremony is over and you are able to join her?"

"I already discussed that with her, but she could not think of any safe place where she could go. Besides, if she runs away, her father would surely inform the police. The cops would find her and bring her back. If I joined her, I would be arrested and charged for kidnapping or abducting a girl, you know what I mean?"

Nirmal continued, "I discussed the situation with Uncle Vimal. [Vimal was a young cousin of Nirmal's father, friendly with Nirmal.] He consulted his lawyer friends. They advised that any such move would result in a court case, which in all probability would end in favor of Dolly's father. Uncle Vimal also asked them if Dolly could take any legal action against her father."

"What did they say?" I eagerly asked.

"They said that it would be very doubtful, if not impossible, to convince a judge to take legal action against her father, especially when Dolly is already above sixteen and has crossed the legal age of minority for the purpose of marriage. There cannot be any action on the ground of marrying a girl before she reaches the age of consent. And again, if Dolly files a complaint that she is above eighteen and she doesn't consent to the wedding, her father would surely place her horoscope before the court to prove that she is below that age. Horoscopes can be easily manufactured with the help of the so-called pundits. The irony is that courts always accept horoscopes as good proof of age. So either way the law would go against her. As you know, educational institutions do not mention the age of a girl in their examination results and certificate."

"Do you know what Dolly's real age is?" I asked.

"I never asked her. She's now a college student; she must be about eighteen or nineteen. But you never know. She could be much less than that, according to her horoscope," scoffed Nirmal.

I did not see Dolly anywhere. I was regularly in touch with Nirmal during that time. I felt extremely sorry for Nirmal and Dolly. We didn't know what to do in a situation like that. From my own sources, I gathered that Dolly was not attending college anymore.

After a few days, I found a printed invitation letter issued by Dolly's father, inviting my father to attend his daughter's wedding and the feast, together with his family and his friends. The groom's name was mentioned in the letter. The letter lay on my father's office table. I went running to Nirmal to tell him that I knew the name of Dolly's groom from the invitation letter distributed by Dolly's father.

But my enthusiasm died down at once when Nirmal, in a flat tone, said, "I already know his name, and also his father's name and his address. But what do I do with all that when I haven't seen Dolly? I don't know what she is doing. I don't know if she has changed her mind."

"She's not attending her college. Could it be that she has been confined at home by her parents? Nobody seems to have seen her." I tried to soothe Nirmal.

"Aren't we living in the same town? She could have sent me a note or a message through someone. She could have telephoned me, dropped a line by post. She did nothing. Who knows? She might have consented to the wedding."

I kept quiet.

A few days passed. There was no news and no event concerning Dolly. Then the momentous day arrived. The quivering tunes of the *shenai* resonated in the air, proclaiming the ceremonial commencement of Dolly's wedding. I witnessed shaven-headed Nirmal and his younger brother Bimal chanting mantras led by a priest, offering oblations in the sraddha ceremony of their departed mother. Nirmal's only sister, seated nearby, was quietly shedding tears. I felt the pinch of defeat for my inability to help Nirmal.

The next morning when I came to see Nirmal, I was told that he had left for Gaya early in the morning, carrying the ashes of his departed mother to consecrate to the holy Falgu River, convergence of two hill streams called Niranjan and Mohana in Gaya in the Bihar state of India. Legend has it that Lord Rama consecrated his father King Dasaratha's ashes into Falgu River. Falgu thus is considered by the Hindus as the most holy river for consecrating the ashes of the departed souls.

I was surprised and also felt hurt because Nirmal had never told me he would be going to Gaya. Perhaps it was a last-minute decision, I thought. Perhaps he wanted to get away from the town before Dolly and her husband were given a ceremonial send-off in a pompous procession. I was told he had left by car early in the morning to catch the express train from the nearby railway junction.

Thus the episode of the love affair, like innumerable such affairs, ended on a tragic note. Like most such lovers, Nirmal was expected to rejoin his college and come home on vacations. But for a long time Nirmal was neither seen nor heard from. When I asked his brother whether Nirmal had gone back to Calcutta, he replied that he didn't know. He could not even tell me where Nirmal was or when he would come home.

Life in our town went on as usual. Sometimes, when I heard music or I hummed a tune I had picked up from Nirmal, I missed him. Nobody knew his whereabouts. Or perhaps someone knew but didn't like to disclose the information.

Nearly two years later, one evening I saw a dim light in Nirmal's room. I tiptoed up to the door, unsure if Nirmal or someone else was in the room. The door was slightly ajar. I whispered, "Nirmal Da?" hoping that he might have come back.

"Come on in," uttered a familiar voice that was doubtlessly Nirmal's.

I entered the room and exclaimed with open arms, "Welcome home, Nirmal Da! Have you come home on vacation? How was your exam? How is everything?" I asked him all my questions in my natural exuberance.

Nirmal didn't stand up from the chair where he was sitting. He didn't respond. He only showed me a stool to sit down. He didn't reply to my greetings and my ardent questions.

Neither of us spoke for a while. I felt embarrassed, also uncomfortable. At last Nirmal said in a plain, emotionless tone, "How are you?"

Surprised at his indifferent attitude, I looked at him intently. Nirmal was holding a glass of drink in his hand. A bottle of whiskey was under the table on which he rested an elbow. He looked different.

"Care to try some whiskey?" he asked me.

I waved my hand, gesturing that I wouldn't like to drink. Before I could ask him anything more, Nirmal said, "I don't know how, but I had a premonition that you would come. Did you know I joined the violin maestro Pandit Bhajanlal Vandetkar as his student? From him I learned some ragas and styles, including his masterpiece, "Rag Jog."

He took out his violin from its case, adjusted the fine tuner screws at the tailpiece, and started playing on it. He was playing "Rag Jog" exactly as I had heard the famous maestro playing it in a radio broadcast. Within moments Nirmal was absorbed in music. Nirmal with his violin was the same person, now definitely more perfect.

Suddenly, he stopped and put the violin carefully in its box. He didn't utter a word. He poured some more whiskey into his glass. I guessed that he was unable to set his mind to anything. He gulped the whiskey. Perhaps he badly needed someone to share his thoughts, someone he could confide in.

After a few moments of silence, he opened up and told me details of what had happened during his absence from the town. After consecrating his mother's ashes to the Ganges in Gaya, he went to nearby Banaras just because he didn't feel like returning home.

Banaras was the home of Indian classical music. In fact, there was a tradition of Indian classical music known as the Banaras *gharana*—the style of the traditional maestros of Banaras. Gharanas, or styles, were somewhat like the ancient Indian *gurukul*, or institutions centering on the tradition of a guru's style of interpreting Hindustani raga music.

Native princes and rich merchants traditionally patronized the professional songstresses and danseuses of Banaras in nightly entertainment houses. A few professionals from these entertainment houses also became famous and are remembered for their exquisite styles of interpreting dance and music. Nirmal was already acquainted with the recitals of some of the historic musicians of the Banaras schools from the gramophone records he had played.

While in Banaras, he accidentally came across a connoisseur of Indian classical music. Nirmal's violin recital impressed the stranger. He took Nirmal to a professional *nautch ghar*, or entertainment house, where nightly recitals of classical music and dance were regularly presented to patrons.

The handsome young man with a fine hand on the violin was welcomed by the madame of the nautch ghar. Nirmal visited the place again on the following evenings and joined other musicians accompanying the dancing girls.

Nirmal badly needed a change. The musical environment of the house fascinated him. He also wanted to learn the *bandish*, musical style of Banaras, directly from the musicians of Banaras. He was amazed at the stunning, durbar-style decor of the nautch ghar, the masterly musicians accompanying the celebrated chanteuse interpreting raga music, the youthful danseuses performing the dances, the seductive maidens coltishly serving wine to guests from Mogul-style ewers.

He joined the professional musicians as an amateur violinist. He looked upon a particular *sarenghi* player as his guru. Drinking alcohol was a common custom in the house. Drinks, snacks, and chewing paan were served for free during the nightly sessions. Patrons appreciated the dancers and singers by throwing bundles of hard cash. In no time, Nirmal became a popular player in the nautch ghar.

He forgot that he had to attend the medical college in Calcutta; he forgot his home and everything else. Nirmal was lost in the milieu of music in the entertainment house.

The madame of the house, a shrewd professional, found out that Nirmal was not an affluent young man. Professionally, she was interested in entertaining men who could give away handsome amounts of cash. Nevertheless, initially she didn't object to his coming and participating in the music. She treated him like one of her musical hands.

As time passed, the madame's vigilant senses didn't miss the fact that the youngest and prettiest dancer of her house had definitely developed a weakness for the handsome and talented stranger. The madame came out in her true colors. Not only did she insult Nirmal in filthy words, but she asked her gatemen to throw him out of the house. Others laughed and enjoyed his humiliation as he was treated like a losing fighter driven out of an ancient amphitheater. Nirmal learned the harshest lesson of his life.

Mortified and exasperated, he took the first available train to Calcutta. He couldn't forget the humiliation and the insult meted out to him by the madame of the entertainment house. He could only think of music and the insults. He firmly resolved that he must earn enough money to be able to throw it in the face of the Banaras madame.

He realized that wealth ruled the prosaic reality behind the divine facade of music. He had no other capital, he thought, other than the four strings and the bow of his violin. He held his violin to his heart and promised himself that he would devote heart and soul to gain mastery over the violin, to earn money like famous violinist Pandit Bhajanlal Vandetkar.

It did not occur to his mind that he was in Calcutta to complete his course at the medical college and become a qualified medic.

He resolved to professionalize his talent and immediately earn money on his own. The violin maestro Pandit Vandetkar lived in Calcutta but enchanted his fans everywhere within and beyond the country. It was not difficult to find an opportunity to personally meet the violin maestro. The busy and professional ostad agreed to admit Nirmal as his disciple, but only on payment of his high fees.

Nirmal had no money. An agent of a large pharmaceutical firm knew Nirmal as son of a popular practicing physician in his hometown in Assam. The firm was searching for a suitable person who could augment their business in North Bengal and Assam as a sales representative. Nirmal had all the qualities. He was a handsome young man, son of a well-known physician. Above all, he had the special quality of charming people with his violin recitals. The company offered to finance Nirmal for six months to learn violin from Ostad Vandetkar if Nirmal would sign a contract to serve the company, initially for a period of five years.

Nirmal didn't hesitate. He signed the covenant. In his urge to become a famous violinist and to earn enough money to throw in the face of the nautch ghar madame, he overlooked the fact that he had signed an indenture of bondage to the pharmaceutical company.

By the time the news leaked out and reached Nirmal's father, six months' time was almost over. The company asked Nirmal to take up his job as per the terms of the covenant. Nirmal now realized that, in an unguarded moment, he had fallen into the company's trap. They had literally bought him for a song. Now, he had to give up all hopes of earning enough money with his violin. His music lessons remained incomplete.

Suddenly, Uncle Vimal appeared on the scene as the emissary of Nirmal's father. He tried his best through his lawyers to revoke the contract signed by Nirmal. Uncle Vimal's lawyers argued before the arbitrator that the company had fraudulently obtained the signature of an emotionally overwhelmed young man. The company, on the other hand, had a stronger case with documented evidence. After a great deal of arguments and counterarguments, a compromise was struck, under terms of which the company agreed to make Nirmal's headquarters at his hometown in Assam.

Those were the circumstances under which I found Nirmal back in his lonely room, drinking whiskey. Perhaps he was repentant for his mistake.

A few days later, his father rented out to the company Nirmal's room in the house, just because he didn't like his son to live outside the house. The pharmaceutical firm, at their cost, remodeled the room, virtually converting it into a miniature suite. It now became an independent unit consisting of an office-cum-living room with a small storage space for samples of the company's products, and a bedroom. Freshly painted, carpeted, and furnished with all new furniture, curtains, and effects, the room now became the office of the company's sales representative.

Nirmal's father still hoped that good sense would prevail with his son. He believed Nirmal would soon be tired of a profession of constant travel, resign from the job, and resume his studies. In fact, his father was prepared to pay any amount of compensation to the company if his son changed his mind and quit the company.

Nirmal now became the roving sales representative of the pharmaceutical firm. He continued to live in his room while working for the company. However, he could hardly stay in his new suite for more than a couple of days in a month. He had to frequently go out on tour to promote sales within the territorial limits allotted to him by the company.

He used to go out from his home office dressed like an executive to travel from place to place, carrying a bagful of drug samples and advertisement literature. However, he never forgot to take his violin—his inspiration and symbol of his distinction. The company provided him with a station wagon and driver-cum-assistant. I hardly ever found him in the town playing violin.

* * *

Years passed, and meanwhile I matriculated from my school and went to Calcutta for higher education. Once during a vacation, I came home. After the initial excitement of meeting my parents and my sisters and my brother, I dusted off my old bicycle, took it to the nearby bike shop, got the tires inflated and the wheel hubs oiled, and set out around the familiar town. I thought of looking up Nirmal if he was home.

As I knocked, a beaming Nirmal opened the door and welcomed me. I found him a completely changed man, not the moody and pensive Nirmal I knew. He had gained weight. His flourishing midline was discernible. His neatly shaven cheeks were glowing with content. His mature face was accentuated with a pair of lenses fixed to a dark brown frame. We hugged each other most cordially as Nirmal showed me in.

"Hi. What a surprise! How are you doing? When did you come? Have you come on a vacation? Welcome home." He asked the same questions in the same manner I had asked him when he came back after years of self-imposed exile.

I replied, "I am doing fine. I have come on vacation and thought to look you up if by chance you were at home. How nice to see you. Hope everything is fine with you."

"Oh yes, we're fine. I too am very happy to see you. Please take your seat."

I was surprised to find his company-made suite completely changed. The parlor-cum-office had now been converted into a small living room, separated from the bedroom by a removable Kashmiri partition. A new sofa set, complete with a centerpiece and side tables, was placed over a Mirzapuri area rug. Fancy lamps, a low bookshelf with a few famous titles, a miniature bronze of the Nataraja on its top, and a Kangra Valley painting on the wall embellished the setup. I carefully observed the new setting and appreciated the tastefully made arrangement. There was a touch of trendy style everywhere. The businesslike look of Nirmal's former company-made suite had been replaced with homely elegance.

"Wonderful, Nirmal Da. I see a lot of changes in you and also in your suite! It's so nice to see everything so different, so tip-top. You seem to be perfectly settled," I observed.

"You're most welcome," replied Nirmal, bypassing the implication of my comment. Visibly excited, he peeped beyond the partition, calling someone in a low voice, "Hello, where are you?"

His manner and the words he used were typical of the customary way in which a husband called a wife in our kind of traditional homes. Although outmoded, the old-time practice was somehow still considered modest and mannerly, especially for the newlyweds of traditional families. I felt sure that Nirmal was calling his wife. But who she could be?

Nirmal turned his face, and as I looked at him, he blushed and then blurted out with a grin, "You know, I got married. Everyone insisted that I must get married. I never took the idea seriously. My father is now getting old. When he desired to have a daughter-in-law in the house, I couldn't disregard his wishes. You know what I mean."

"You have done the right thing, Nirmal Da. I am very happy to see you settled. I can see that you're happy; you're now at home in the true sense of the expression."

Nirmal's newlywed wife bashfully entered the room through the partition door. She was in a fine handloom sari, symbolically covering only the bun of her hair at the back of her head with the carelessly thrown *anchal*, or upper end of the sari. She wore a thin vermilion line in the parting of her hair and a tiny dot on her forehead. Dazzling gold bangles on her wrist tinkled as she drew the veil a little more. I stood up and greeted her with a *namaskar.* She returned the greeting in the same manner. Nirmal asked her to sit down as he closed the door behind her. She sat down and we followed suit.

Nirmal introduced me, "Mala, this is my friend I mentioned to you so many times." He added, "You need not put on the veil before him. He is just like my younger brother. He is now studying in a Calcutta college. He has come home on vacation."

I felicitously said, "It's a great pleasure meeting you. May I call you Mala Baudi?"

"By all means; may I call you *dada* instead of *thakurpo*?" she asked me in turn, with a modest smile. "I think thakurpo—husband's younger brother—is too old-fashioned. What do you think?" She didn't wait for my reply and said, "I have heard about you so much from your dada that I feel as though I already know you personally."

I immediately understood that she was a modern and intelligent woman. She also looked urbane and educated.

"Rightfully and surely you may if you like. I, for myself, would be too happy if instead suffixing dada, you call me just by my first name."

"Oh, wonderful. That would be really great. Why don't we both call each other by our first names?"

"Excellent idea; thank you, Mala," I replied.

Nirmal said, "That would be fine. There's no formality between us. We are not yet so old as to go back a century in etiquette. Isn't that right?"

All of us joined in laughter. After a while Nirmal told me, "You appreciated the new setup in the room. I had no contribution in it. This is all her creation. She handpicked everything. You may tell her how you like the setting in the room."

Before I said anything, Mala demurred, "I don't think there is anything so special here. This is just a little room to sit down when we have some exclusive guests like you. Your dada always has a tendency to overstate things about me. I hardly know anything of decor and style."

"You have very good taste, indeed; the setup is so elegant," I observed.

A happy Nirmal, by way of further introduction of his wife, said, "Mala and her parents hail from Bardhaman. They are now settled in Calcutta. Mala graduated from Calcutta University. She sings *Rabindra Sangeet* very well."

"As though," she said in a typical manner.

We had tea together. I casually asked Nirmal, "How come you never informed me about your marriage? You didn't ask me to join you in the groom's party; you seem to have totally forgotten me. I would have been the first person to accompany you."

"I knew that you would reasonably accuse me because I didn't invite you to my wedding. But, believe me, I couldn't help it," replied Nirmal. "You have to pardon me. I went to your father to ask him your Calcutta address. He said that you were extremely busy preparing for your exam. He added that any interruption at that time would cause serious dislocation to your studies because you would surely like to attend the wedding. He courteously said that, while he appreciated my genuine friendship with you, he would consider it a great favor if I didn't send you any invitation to my wedding.

"I couldn't disregard him, as you know. And he added that after the examination, you would have your vacation. You were likely to come home, and then you would surely visit me to meet my wife. After he said so, especially when he put his words in such a polite manner, I had to give him my assurance that I won't let you know. When I assured him, he smiled and said that he knew that I was a good boy," explained Nirmal.

I asked Nirmal if he was still with the company. He replied, "Yes, but I have shifted my office to a rented house. I have to be there every day from morning till evening. Only on Saturdays and Sundays do I find some time to rest. And again on those days we have to meet people socially. Sometimes we have to go out to visit relations and friends; people invite us to dinner."

From the rest of the conversation, I gathered that Nirmal had been promoted to area sales supervisor of the company. He now had more desk work than touring.

I congratulated him on his promotion.

11

My classmate Sunil Sen Gupta was a brilliant student and a plain-speaking fellow, but sometimes he could be arrogant. Both of us went to Calcutta for further studies. I was studying economics in one college and Sunil was studying commerce in another college.

At one point, he underwent surgery at Carmichael Medical College Hospital in Calcutta. I visited him every evening while he was recuperating in the hospital. After his recovery, Sunil returned to his hostel. Meanwhile, the annual exam approached, and both of us got busy preparing for it. We could not see each other as often as we had before the exam. After the exam was over, I went to his hostel to find out how he had done.

I did not find him. On asking other boys in his hostel, I came to know the incredible news that Sunil had not taken the exam and that he was no longer a resident in the hostel. He had been expelled from the college and the hostel because he had not paid his fees. No one, however, could tell me where he had gone.

To me, it appeared absurd that of all students, Sunil could be expelled simply for not paying his bills. Surely the college could have worked out a payment arrangement for him, especially because he was such an exemplary student.

I left his hostel with a deep sense of sorrow that slowly turned into anger against Sunil. I felt offended because he had never told me anything about the problem. If he had done so, I would've tried to help him. But he never told me anything. He never asked me for help or advice, even though he knew that I was very much in the city. But there was hardly anything that I could do when Sunil was not there to tell me what had really happened. It was impossible to search him out in the vast city of Calcutta.

After my first reaction subsided, I felt worried about him. I wrote a letter to his home address, but there was no reply. I wrote to my sister, and she replied that she had no idea about Sunil's whereabouts. I had no other alternative than to reconcile to the situation.

My childhood friend Sunil thus vanished without a clue. He was the only child of a widower father, a bank manager in my hometown, who loved him dearly.

Years later, I stumbled upon Sunil in the hub of Guwahati city in Assam. Sunil looked lean, and he seemed somewhat high strung, wearing a jazzy Hawaiian shirt. Impulsively, we hugged each other. Sunil smelled of alcohol. It was just about eleven o'clock in the morning. Almost incessantly, I asked him all the questions that had accumulated in my mind since he had vanished so suddenly from college.

Sunil appeared indifferent and unresponsive. He coolly avoided all my questions and said, "Come, let's have some tea. We're meeting after a long time."

I agreed because I didn't want to leave his company with my question unanswered. He led me to the nearby cooperative canteen of the local post and telegraph employees union. We sat together at a small table in the far corner of the hall. I expected that he would open up over tea, but Sunil maintained an air of indifference in his typically arrogant manner. He placed orders for tea and asked me in a blank voice how I was doing. I replied that I was fine.

After a spell of awkward silence, he said in a rather pedantic tone, "Let's not speak about the past. The past is dead and gone and will never come back again. Let's talk about the present! It is fresh and right before us here and now."

Without giving me a chance to respond, he continued. "This is my canteen—I mean, our canteen. I am a member of the local telephone exchange staff. I plug in and plug off the telephone lines to the console when people ask for telephone connections. This is what I do. This is my job." He laughed sardonically.

It was not pleasant news to me. He had been an excellent university student with so much potential. I felt sorry for him.

Suddenly and perhaps to change the topic, he said, "I'm in an amazing environment full of folks who wasted many springs of their lives due to the sheer necessity of keeping their bodies and souls together."

I looked at him curiously.

"You know what I mean? There are many women working with me who wasted so many springs of their lives that only left marks of time on their faces. They work in day and night shifts with headphones clamped to their ears in the drab atmosphere of the telephone exchange just because they had no better alternatives to earn a livelihood. Come; let me introduce you to some of my colleagues."

"Thanks," I replied, "but I think we could do that later."

"Why hesitate?" Sunil urged with an edge in his voice that I'd never heard before. "They are all decent women, mostly from middle-class Bengali families who had to flee for fear of being dishonored and victimized in their erstwhile homeland, now known as East Pakistan."

I realized his frustration and the reason why he transposed his own fate to others. I replied, "I would indeed be happy to meet them, but right now I think I would like to be with you. We have met after such a long time. I have so much to know from you and so much to tell you."

"I told you, I am not interested in the past," replied Sunil.

"Okay, then let's talk on any other topic you'd like to talk about."

"You are behaving like a typical middle-class bourgeoisie," Sunil sneered. "Are you married?"

"No," I said, somewhat taken aback by his blunt question. I, in turn, asked him, "How about you?"

"I don't believe in marriage," replied Sunil.

We brought from the stall counter two cups of tea and thin slices of cake.

After we had sat down again, Sunil asked, "Are you still staying with your parents?"

"No, not really. I look them up whenever I can go home," I answered.

"Then what is your problem? Why are you behaving so stiffly? You're a free man. Enjoy life a little!"

I didn't reply in so many words that it was not me but Sunil who was behaving eccentrically. I thought it best to let him burn off his frustration.

He said, "Look, life has many facets to choose from. If you choose seclusion, if you like to remain coiled up within your small cocoon of pride, you remain in the fool's paradise. You never know the real world. The world does not exist only for the small group of middle-class, highbrow literati. I now belong to the working class and I know the everyday affairs of the toiler's life.

"Besides, as you know, time does not wait for anyone. The moments that pass by do not come back again. I wanted to introduce you to the world I live in, the world that is not known to those who live in the ivory tower of so-called intelligentsia and think that they know everything about everything."

I could understand his frustration. At the same time, I couldn't appreciate his errant behavior. Sunil appeared so different now, so much changed. Nevertheless, I suppressed my disappointment and pleaded, "Sunil, we are meeting by chance, and after such a long time. Let's not waste time by playing on words and dodging in and out of things neither one of us wants to discuss. No more theories, please! Tell me what happened to you at college. Why did you leave your studies without telling anyone? And why are you here? I think I have a right to know all about you as your old friend."

"Oh, surely you are, but how do I start digging the past like an anteater digs the anthill? I am sorry; I don't believe in the past. Of all your questions, the only one that relates to my present state is how I came to be here. The simple answer to that question is that I was offered a job here, I accepted the offer, and so I am here." Sunil took a loud slurp of his tea and jabbed at his cake with a bit more force than necessary.

I really did not know what to do when he was behaving so obstinately. Both of us were quiet for a while. Sunil broke the silence and asked me rather hesitantly, "Would you like a drink? There's a place nearby. Let's go there. Shall we?"

He stood up. I understood that he wanted to nurse the effect of the hard drink he'd already had. Whether or not I agreed to go with him, I knew that he needed to go and that he would in any case go. I couldn't help asking him whether he was on duty.

"Oh, don't worry about my duty. We have no such problem. We work in a team."

Together we walked up to the nearby road junction. Right on the junction was the wine shop. We didn't enter the shop by the main entrance. Sunil led me through a narrow alley between the wine shop and the next block. I followed him without a word. We walked by the flank of a cement drain. Sunil slid into the shop through a door that was ajar. I followed him.

The room we entered was sort of a storeroom at the rear part of the shop. Inside it, there were cartons stacked up all over the place. Sunil made his familiar way through the gaps between the stacks, accurately leading me to an improvised arrangement, sort of a hideout within the labyrinth of cartons. There were two overturned packing boxes on either side with one in the center as substitutes for stools and a table.

"Sit here," said Sunil, and then he assured me, "Don't get upset; it's a safe place known to the police and the excise guys."

Gauhati, later Guwahati, was then a prohibited area under a state law, the Liquor Prohibition Act. Buying and selling alcoholic drinks were supposed to be strictly under license from the state, and no one could lawfully drink except as a medical necessity and under a permit. Violation of the law, however, was common. Licensed liquor dealers, like the one we had just entered through the back door, had their own ingenious ways of managing their businesses with apparent impunity.

Sunil appeared to be familiar with the shop owners. He asked me what I would like to have.

"May I have a beer?" I replied.

Sunil made a face, looked at me with disdain, and replied, "Beer, of all things!"

I nodded to confirm my choice. Sunil shrugged and went toward the front end of the shop, not visible from where I was sitting on one of the two upturned wooden boxes. He came back with a bottle of beer and a quart bottle of triple X rum. He put the bottle of beer before me on the inverted packing box and said, "I took a chilled beer from their cellar. They keep chilled beer for their important customers, and to others they sell beer that has been exposed to the sun. I am sorry, there's no glass; you have to drink from the bottle."

"That's okay. Thanks," I replied.

He opened the bottles and guzzled a large gulp of rum. His face contorted as raw alcohol burned its way down his throat. He took a second gulp, wiped his lips with the back of his hand, and then lit a cigarette. He sat on the wooden box opposite me, smoking the cigarette. After a while, he remembered that he hadn't offered me one. He took the pack from his pocket and held it out to me. I gestured that I didn't need one.

Now in a somewhat relaxed mood, Sunil asked me with a normal smile, "Do you remember our cigarette adventure in Queen Victoria Memorial Park?"

The scenario flashed in my mind and took me back to languid days long ago in our hometown. Sunil had managed to steal a matchbox and a single cigarette from his father's pack. Three of us, Sunil, Susanta, and I, tried to smoke the cigarette in the secrecy of the park. We took drags by rotation and coughed traumatically. It tasted bitter. For fear of being caught smelling of cigarette smoke, we thoroughly rinsed our mouths with water from a nearby municipal tap.

Both of us shared a hearty laugh recounting the memory. I felt relieved to find Sunil somewhat behaving normally. I drank some beer from the bottle. Sunil took another gulp of neat rum. Kicks of rum and the tang of tobacco smoke seemingly worked together to bring him back to a familiar mood. I felt better because we were able to talk and laugh like we were used to in our school days. Both of us were happy.

After a while, a well-fed specimen of a professional-looking man tapped on the wall of cartons in the smoke-filled nook. When both of us looked up, he whispered with a smile, "Hello, sirs. How're you doing?"

"We'll be leaving in a minute," replied Sunil. The man nodded and left.

Sunil lifted his bottle to his mouth and hinted at me to bottom up.

Silently and hurriedly, Sunil finished the contents of the entire bottle of rum, stubbed his cigarette against the cement floor, and dropped his bottle into an empty carton nearby. I followed suit and dropped my beer bottle in. As we came out from the place through the rear door, Sunil whispered his apologies to me.

"I'm sorry. Perhaps some important guys have come. Please don't mind. Actually, this is the understanding we have so that nobody lingers in that hidden alcove."

I was surprised at such a total change in Sunil, my talented friend. He must have been a regular customer in the shop; he must have been drinking heavily since morning every day, I thought. Anyhow, it was good that we could come out from the stuffy hole without being caught in the illegal act. I didn't know if Sunil had a permit. I had no permit.

The relatively fresh air outside was bracing. We rambled slowly and silently. I noticed that after tossing down his throat a full quart of neat rum and in quick drafts, Sunil was virtually somnambulating in broad daylight. I helped him to cross the main road. We began walking along the sidewalk of a quieter road with no purpose or destination in view.

I wanted to get away from the focal point of the intersection of roads and get to some inconspicuous place. I wanted to sit down and talk with my old friend who was so changed—now a thoroughly frustrated man. I walked very slowly, matching Sunil's unsteady gait.

To our right was the campus of Cotton College, founded in 1901 and named after the British chief commissioner Sir Henry Cotton. To our left was a confectioner's shop, a boutique with mannequins displaying clothes behind the plate-glass windows, and a store that was a combined pharmacy-bookstore, all in a row.

Following Sunil's faltering steps, we managed to pass the row of stores and reach a relatively quieter point near the municipal water tower, within a walled enclave. I could understand from his unsteady pace that the raw rum was causing havoc within him.

He was dragging his legs; I held him by his arm and asked him if he was okay.

Inarticulately, Sunil mumbled, "I am okay, yeah, and I am o-û-k-eh."

He didn't say anything else and abruptly sat down on some roadside masonry over a culvert, a few steps ahead of the municipal water tower. He pressed his stomach with both hands. From the look on his face, I could guess that he was suffering from a twitching stomach or a stomach cramp. He looked at me pathetically like a mute animal in pain, but he didn't want to give in. To hide his embarrassment, he babbled, "Please don't mind. I think I'll sit down for a few seconds. I'm all right."

I told him, "Please don't move; just sit down here. I'll be back in a moment."

Sunil nodded his head like an obedient child. I walked back and stepped into the pharmacy. I asked for some antacid tablets and a bottle of water. The man at the counter complied. I came back to Sunil, gave him two antacid tablets, and asked him to chew them, then drink from the water bottle.

Passively, Sunil took the antacid tablets and drank water from the bottle. He tried to thank me with a lump of emotion choking his throat. Both of us sat on the masonry for a while, holding hands. Perhaps Sunil felt the touch of care after a long time. He was overwhelmed with emotion intensified by alcohol. He was frantically quivering. After a while, he looked at me and murmured, "Sorry. Please don't mind."

Moments later, he again looked at me and muttered, "I never knew I had such a good friend even now!" Still under the spell of turbulent emotion, Sunil tried to smile to express his appreciation.

I patted him to reassure him. "It's okay, Sunil. Drink the water slowly; you will feel better."

Sunil drank some more water and tried to smile. Then, looking to me, he said with contrition, "My stomach was reeling. Suddenly I felt uneasy. Now I am okay. I am so sorry."

"Don't be silly, Sunil. You don't have to be so apologetic to me. If you're okay, I'm happy. You don't have to be so very formal with me. Aren't we old friends?"

Sunil's moist eyes glistened. He held my hand for support, stood up, lit another cigarette, and started walking, holding me by my shoulder. I restrained myself from telling him that smoking would cause more acidity in his stomach.

Still under the spell of alcohol-induced emotion, Sunil muttered, "You're really great." He seemed to regain his inveterate ego. Puffing out cigarette smoke, he asked me, "So you're a doctor now, huh? How could you learn about all those medicines? You were doing economics when we were at college, weren't you? I feel much better now. I don't know why I felt so bad. It never happened to me before."

Sunil was trying to find excuses to justify his collapse. I could understand how he must have been feeling. I was relieved that he felt better and was acting sensibly, although still under the influence of liquor. My only fear was that the police might take notice of us.

I realized that Sunil was deeply frustrated. His manner of speaking, his demeanor, and his drinking were all indicators of frustration. It was difficult for me to put together the image of the Sunil I had known in my childhood and in Calcutta, and Sunil as a telephone exchange operator, drunk during the day and in a public place. There must have been something somewhere that went grossly wrong with him, I thought. But I could not ask him anything because I didn't want him to feel offended. I felt sure that, due to some compelling circumstances, he had landed in such a plight and was not yet able to accept the situation. His frustration had definitely been intensified when he encountered me unexpectedly, because I was a reminder to him of who he once was. I felt very concerned about him.

Walking slowly and silently from near the wine store, we reached the point at which the road met the strand road, running parallel to the Brahmaputra. We crossed the road and reached the riverbank. Right before us stood the *Sukreswar* temple, a temple of Lord Shiva atop a small hillock, accessible by a steep flight of stairs. A few steps ahead and beyond a cemented patch of land were the broad and paved steps to the river.

The place was known as Sukreswar Ghat. People came here to take baths in the waters of the Brahmaputra to purify them before going to the temple. Devotees, men and women, carried holy water of the Brahmaputra in small pots to pour on the *Shiva Linga*, the phallic representation of the deity, to keep it constantly soaked in water. Men who had no other place to take a bath also came here because of the convenience of the cement steps leading to the river.

It was dry season. Near the spot we reached was the long and sandy riverside passage leading to the pier. From here, a private contractor's diesel-operated ferryboats regularly carried human beings, their baggage, bicycles, and even motor vehicles to North Guwahati on the other bank of the river. Many people commuted from the other bank to this bank every day to earn their living by the grace of Lord Sukreswar, who had been installed and worshipped here since some mythical time. It was believed that a sage named *Sukra* installed the lingam of Lord Shiva here, supposedly the largest Shiva Linga in the country.

In the midstream of the river stood *Bhasmachala*, a legendary island consisting of a small hill on which stood the epical temple of *Umananda Vairab*, another name for Lord Shiva. It is believed that Kama, the god of love, was burned to ashes on this island by Lord Shiva's curse. The island was woody with vegetation. A veiled thicket on the river island was the habitat of the hoolock gibbons, a species of howling arboreal apes. Their howling could be heard from the Guwahati Circuit House on the bank of the Brahmaputra.

We sat on the top step of the wide, shady staircase that led down to the brink of the river. The great river and the marble phallus of Lord Shiva were sacred to multitudes of men and women who pray to the lord under many different circumstances, seeking boons and seeking solace. Lord Sukreswar remained unmoved and eternally erect as the inexhaustible Brahmaputra provided water to the devotees who offered ablutions.

At that hour of the day, the ghat was deserted except for a solitary man standing in loin-deep water on a submerged step, rinsing his body with soap before taking a dip in waters on the next steps below him.

My engrossment with the setting was suddenly broken as Sunil blurted out, "I'm sorry if I have bothered you too much."

"Not at all," I replied, realizing his embarrassment. "It's nothing like that. Anyone might feel uncomfortable sometime or other. I guess you drank too fast and had some stomach acidity that caused the trouble. Are you feeling better now?"

"Thank you; now I am fine."

"How is your father doing?" I asked him to start a conversation.

"I have no father," replied Sunil.

"I am so sorry to know that you have lost your father. When did he pass away? What happened to him?" I asked anxiously.

Sunil gave an uneasy smile, sat in an upright position, and said cryptically, "Well, he isn't dead. He is very much alive. But he is not my father anymore."

"What do you mean, he is alive but he's not your father anymore?"

Sunil kept his upper lip stiff and repeated, "Yes, he is no more my father but he is very much alive. Maybe he is happier than he ever was before, and that's the truth about him."

"What do you mean?" Astounded, I asked him again.

"We have no relationship with one another, and we do not know anything about each other. I am on my own; there's no one I can claim as my father," said Sunil, trying to control his emotional outburst.

He lit another cigarette, and after a long puff, he released a cloud of smoke and looked to the sky. I didn't know what to say. A wise crow expostulated with a piercing call from the treetop. I looked to Sunil, eagerly waiting to know what had really happened between the father and the son. Sunil went on quietly making rings of cigarette smoke.

The man bathing on the steps had already left. The Brahmaputra reflected the strong glare of the midday sun over the wide surface of its flowing waters.

After a while, Sunil began, "You know, when I was studying in Calcutta, everything was all right. I was attending college, boarding in the hostel, taking food and snacks from the hostel kitchen and the cafeteria, all on credit as other students did, and paying the bills on the first week of the following month when the remittances came from home."

I nodded. Sunil went on, "When I was busy preparing for my exam, suddenly no more remittances came from home. I, naturally, felt worried. I thought my father was not well or that something had happened to him. I wrote letters to him; no reply came. Time passed, causing me more anxiety. I sent telegrams; no reply and no remittance came. I wrote letters to everyone I knew in the town, asking them to let me know how my father was doing, but nobody replied. Then I felt almost sure that he was no more.

"I decided to go home. The college and hostel authorities wouldn't allow me to leave, lest I escape without paying the fees. I was already wrecked by worries, and on top of that I felt humiliated, even insulted.

I could not write the exam or go home to find out what had gone wrong with my father.

"The college authorities wrote to my father at his home address, but no reply came. Finally, they expelled me from the college for not paying my bills and for my inability to provide them with any authentic explanation for my failure to pay. They, however, didn't do anything more to spoil my career and future prospects. They only asked me to leave the college and the hostel."

When Sunil paused to take a drag from his cigarette, I asked, "Why did you not tell me all these developments then and there in Calcutta? You knew I would have helped you."

Sunil replied with a counterquestion. "What would you have done if I had told you?"

"I would have done everything possible to help you to wriggle out of the situation. I could have written to my father to find out about your father. I could have helped you with some money, at least to pay part of the fees to keep things going."

"Those were the exact reasons why I didn't tell you anything," replied Sunil in his typical way. "In fact, I didn't tell you because I didn't like to be indebted to any of my friends. I always wanted my friends to be my friends, not my benefactors."

I had nothing to say. Perhaps he realized that his statement was too harsh. With a view to qualifying it, he said, "You might think that it was my ego. But just think rationally and put yourself in my situation. How could a student, who is dependent on his father, be the benefactor of another student, who too is dependent on his father? Besides, I was almost sure that my father was no more. So there was no question of trying to continue my studies without first finding out whether he was seriously ill or had already passed away. The situation was too much to stand."

I realized how overwhelmed Sunil must have been in a situation like that. I had nothing to say. I kept quiet. After a while, Sunil finished his cigarette and let out the last puff of smoke with a deep sigh.

"Anyhow, after being thrown out of the college, I went home. A hospital nurse paid for my travel expenses. She loved me and I loved her. Now we are not in touch with one another. I do not even know how she is doing."

"Who is she? You never told me about a nurse!"

"Well, do you remember when I was in Carmichael Medical College Hospital for surgery, and you came every evening to see me? I met her during my stay there. I named her Nightingale. She opened up before me a completely new vista of life. You might recall the story of Florence Nightingale; we read about her in school. Florence Nightingale was named 'Lady with the Lamp' by the wounded soldiers of the Crimean War. I named my nurse Nightingale because she was my lady with the lamp in Carmichael Hospital.

"She was a refugee girl from East Bengal who lost her only brother in communal riots in the wake of the partition. Her parents were dependent on her. I don't know anything more than that, but I used to crave her presence near my hospital bed. She was the most loving woman I had ever known. Her smile, her soft hand on my forehead, her words: everything about her was so special. I really don't know how to explain. I simply loved everything about her."

Sunil's face brightened as he spoke about the girl he loved. He recounted his love story as though he were talking to himself and not narrating to me. I didn't interrupt him. I knew it was best just to listen and let him talk.

"It was wonderful to be with her. Even after I was released from the hospital, I used to wait for her in the visitors' lobby. After her duty hours, she came down the flight of stairs from the second floor with a tired smile on her lips. I simply loved to listen to her and walk with her. Together we would walk up to the tramway stop, where she would get into the tram to go home. Sometimes I went with her up to the tram terminus at Tollygung and then escorted her to her home in a refugee colony."

Sunil turned his face to avoid the blowing wind while he lit another cigarette. He was lost in thought. After a while, he resumed.

"Nightingale wanted to pay my bills and dues. I dissuaded her. I told her that I must first find out what happened to my father. Since I was debarred from sitting the annual exam, I would have to start over from the beginning. I couldn't rejoin the college because the session was already over. So, if necessary, I thought I would drop out for a year or two and then resume my studies."

"You could have accepted her offer as a loan," I countered, "and paid her back later. You could have paid off the college fees and hostel dues with the loan and avoided the humiliation and the disaster. You loved each other, and there would have been nothing wrong in accepting her help to save the situation."

"How would I have paid her back as a student?" replied Sunil. "Besides, she already had a lot of expenses for her old mother, who had been suffering for a long time. In fact, the expenses for her mother's treatment were already too high for her to afford. Of course, I did borrow my passage from her and never repaid it. She does not know my address. I do not know how is she doing, or whether her ailing mother is dead or alive. I betrayed her like an ungrateful guy. I can't show my face to her again."

"But why did you not tell me anything at all? Maybe together we could have found out some a solution," I persisted.

"It's not that I didn't want to tell you about her. In fact, I had planned to tell you everything about her in Calcutta as the first person I would confide in. I thought I would do that after I had told her that I loved her, and after she reciprocated my feelings. But before I could tell her, I had to leave Calcutta."

Silence prevailed as Sunil mentally traveled back to Calcutta from Sukreswar Ghat. He smiled hesitantly, perhaps feeling shy for the surging bouts of emotion he could not control. I kept quiet to let him grow calm. After a while, he said, "I was telling you about my college. I'm sorry for the digression I made."

"It's okay; I understand. I'm extremely sorry that all this happened to you."

Sunil resumed, "Anyhow, I came home only to find my father a totally changed man. He was no more the lonely man drinking tea and smoking cigarettes. He had a new wife, and to my utter distress, I found him a drunkard, going to the gamblers' den. Can you imagine?

"Marrying for a second time was his personal choice; he had every right to do that. But the tragedy was that he lost his job, society discarded him, and he took to drinking and gambling with the despicable folks. He was ruined beyond restoration. And that was all that he could pull off during my absence from home. When I asked him why he didn't reply to my letters and telegrams and why he suddenly stopped sending remittances, he gave me no reason, no answer, and preferred to avoid me. Can you believe it?"

I felt astounded and at a loss for words. I could only shake my head in silent astonishment. Sunil said, "I felt real anger at his silence and for the devastation he had caused to my life and also to his own life. He could have told me about his marriage, about his inability to remit money, whatever the reasons. Don't you think his pointless silence was outrageous? He spoiled my career, he shattered my love, and he made me suffer all sorts of humiliation. And when I asked him about all those, he kept quiet. Could you excuse such a man, even if he was your father?"

"Your father was a nice person. How could he behave like that?" I interjected.

"In spite of everything, I stayed in the house for a couple of days, most of the time confining myself to my room—the particular room in the corner of the house where I used to study during my school days.

"I felt pity for the wretched old man," said Sunil. "He had no money, no status, no society, and apparently no love. I didn't know how to bring him back to the decent life he had lived as long as I was with him. Nothing really worked. He behaved in an impossible manner. He did not care to reply to my questions, just as he hadn't replied to my letters and telegrams. I found him a drunken man, heedless of everything around him.

"His so-called wife did not care for him. She would take her food on time and go to bed without bothering to wait for him. I kept waiting, starving night after night, hoping that he would come back to his senses and we would have our dinner together. I hoped that he would open up his mind to me, but nothing was possible. He would return home in a drunken state, speak to no one, take no food, and sleep like a log. He never bothered about my existence and never told me anything. I spent the rest of the nights crying like a child."

"What did his wife do? Who was she?"

Sunil was too emotional to be able to speak coherently. In a highly mawkish tone, he burst out, “Oh, she was a terrible woman. She looked upon me as an impostor, an unwanted entity. She never spoke to me, and apparently she had no relationship with my father either. She lived in her room, took her food, and didn’t care about anyone else.”

Just to console Sunil, I intervened to say, “Since he lost your mother soon after your birth, you were his darling child, his dream, his incentive to live. After you left for Calcutta, your father must have been feeling lonely. And that must be the reason why he married again. Perhaps after marriage, he thought that you wouldn’t like the idea of his marrying for the second time. He might have worried that you would find it difficult to accept a stepmother. I think something like that happened; some psychological problem changed your father. He was a fine person when I knew him. You could have taken the parenting role to tell your father that he had done nothing wrong by marrying for the second time,” I suggested softly.

“Fine,” replied a contentious Sunil, “but does that justify his getting drunk? Is that good enough reason for ditching me halfway through my studies? Does that justify his not speaking to me? Could that be an acceptable reason for concealing his marriage from me? Would you hold his brief on these points too? How would you justify his relationship with his second wife, who never cared for him? And above all, how could he lose his job?”

Sunil broke into sobs like a child. I felt baffled, not knowing what to tell him or how to soothe my afflicted friend. In that moment, it seemed as though there was no other soul in Sukreswar Ghat besides the two of us. The Brahmaputra was as unmindful as ever of human events and emotions.

I put a hand on Sunil’s back.

After a spell of silence, Sunil contained himself, wiped his eyes, and then asked me, “Do you remember Raghu?”

“I do, very much,” I replied. Raghu was his father’s personal attendant, provided by the bank. Raghu used to cook food and look after the father-and-son household in exchange for free food and shelter. He was technically an employee of the bank.

With tears still in his eyes, Sunil said, "After my father lost his job, Raghu no longer worked in the house. Once I met him by chance. He too was very sorry at the plight of my father. He told me in detail the story that wrecked my father's life. Raghu told me that she, the woman my father married, was a childless widow. Her husband was a wartime contractor. He maintained accounts in the bank in his and his wife's names. He was in a car crash and was killed instantly. After he died, his wife became the sole owner of the house and the bank accounts. She often came to the bank, and that is where she met my father.

"After I went away to Calcutta, she started inviting him to dinner. She drank hard drinks and introduced my father to drinks. That was how they became close to one another. It became a source of gossip in the town and then turned into a scandal. Because of her drinking habits and because she did not lead the conventional life of a Hindu widow, the social elite of the town rated her as a bad character, and my father's relationship with her as immoral. They threatened my father for flirting with the corrupt widow.

"Widow remarriage was legalized in the nineteenth century, as you know. Perhaps nothing would have happened to him if he had married her at that point. But my father did not care to marry her despite the mounting social criticism."

"Perhaps he thought that you wouldn't appreciate his marriage," I gently suggested, with a view to assuage Sunil's rage against his father.

"I don't know what was in his mind. He prolonged his affair and led a scandalous life, ignoring his social obligations even at the cost of his son's education and future."

Sunil was in a mood to pour out his accumulated anguish. He went on, "I learned from Raghu that the top dogs of the traditional society of the small town reported the matter to the head office of the bank. They demanded removal of such a delinquent manager. At that point, my father married the woman because he felt he had no other choice. The bank authorities transferred him to another station and asked him to move immediately. But his wife did not want to leave her property uncared for.

"At the same time, she was afraid of staying in the town to face the hostile society. She wanted to sell her house before leaving the town, and no buyer was immediately available. My father requested a stay of the transfer order for a later time, after his wife's house had sold.

"The bank considered its customers and their opinions more important than a branch manager. Thus, the bank authorities refused his request and asked him to move out to the new place of posting immediately or resign from the job.

"My father could not move due to his wife. He lost his job. Before and during his marriage, he spent whatever little money he had in buying gifts for his wife, and later in drinking and high-stakes gambling, hoping to get quick money. He had no moral courage to inform me about his marriage, losing his job, and having no money to remit to me. He preferred to hide the entire development from me. Perhaps he didn't know what to do, and so he plunged himself into alcohol as a way of escape."

"What about his wife's bank account and the property?" I asked. "He could have borrowed some money from her to finance your education, at least until your annual examination was over, to save you from the humiliation you had to face."

"I have no idea what that woman would or wouldn't do for my father, or even what my father's relationship really was with her even though he married her. Raghu told me that she had a lot of money and property left behind by her first husband. The same question disturbed Raghu and me. In fact, those were the most striking points that cast doubt about her sincerity and love for my father. Don't you think so?"

"I do," I replied steadfastly. "Perhaps she didn't like to stake her money in such a situation. Perhaps she thought that your father would waste her money in gambling. Perhaps she too wasted her money, and Raghu's impression was not correct. Everything sounded strange and incredible. How could the bank take such a drastic action against a senior manager? Your father should have taken the matter to the law court. He had a very good case, from all that you gathered from Raghu," I opined.

"Maybe you're right," said Sunil. "But the lawyers and the judges were also members of the same society. Besides, litigation is a time-consuming and expensive affair."

Slowly, Sunil resumed the story. "During my stay in my father's house, one evening there was a knock on my bedroom door. I opened the door and found my father's wife standing right at the door. I had never spoken to her before. She pretended to smile and asked me to join her for dinner. I closed the door right on her face. I really couldn't stand her. I never learned what her intention had been in asking me for dinner."

"I think that was a good opportunity," I uttered impulsively. "You should have accepted her invitation to dine together. She might have had many things to tell you. I think you missed the chance to know her part of the story. Perhaps she wanted to help you and ask for your help in reconciling their relationship and saving the situation."

"I couldn't stand the very sight of her. I hated her from the core of my heart. How could I accept her invitation? She was an evil person who misled my father and ruined him. I would have done anything other than join her for dinner and chat with her. I had already reached the limit of my patience."

I had nothing to say. After a while, Sunil said, "The next day, at the crack of the dawn, I left home. The old man was still sleeping. As I walked out with my bag in hand, his wife looked at me as though she would miss me."

The sting of sarcasm was in Sunil's tone. I still felt that Sunil had wasted his last chance to understand the situation, but it occurred to me that maybe his stepmother had behaved toward him in a manner that wasn't quite motherly, and he was trying to find a way to explain that.

I kept quiet. Sunil appeared lost in his recollections.

I still couldn't believe the story he had narrated. Again, I thought that except under compelling circumstances, Sunil would not have been a telephone exchange operator, but what he narrated was not a convincing story, either. Was he telling me a fake story? The thought flitted through my mind, but I doubted it because I knew Sunil so well.

The panorama of Sukleswar Ghat changed as the sun slid to the western sky, flooding the river and the sky with the spectrum of dazzling colors. The occasional sounds of loaded trucks whizzing by on the highway and splashes of flipping dolphins in the water interrupted the quietude. A gentle breeze was blowing in from the river, which somewhat soothed the melancholy mood set by Sunil's story.

I turned my eyes to a small fishing boat that a pair of fishermen were trying hard to scull by the fringe of the river to avoid the current in the mainstream. The overloaded ferryboat looked like a toy boat as it neared the opposite bank of the river. For a moment, I was absorbed in watching the scene on the wide waterscape of the Brahmaputra. I tumbled back to reality when Sunil broke the quietude with a question.

"Now tell me, did I do anything wrong? I have told you everything."

I wasn't sure how to answer him. I only said, "I really don't know, Sunil. I mean, I only feel sorry, extremely sorry, about the entire development. It was unfortunate. It was perhaps the worst time that all of you could have had."

I didn't know how Sunil took my answer to his question. Silence prevailed again. Then, in an effort to divert the topic, I asked him, "You didn't tell me how you landed up here."

Sunil lit up another cigarette, and after throwing out some smoke, replied, "Oh, that's another long story."

"Let's hear the story. It must be interesting!"

Sunil went on puffing out cigarette smoke and then suddenly went on. "I left home, left the town, with no purpose, no hope, and no destination in view. Like a drowning man catching at a straw, I took the job of an errand boy at a *dhaba*, a highway inn, where long-haul truckers stopped for rest and food. I learned how to clean pots and pans and learned how to make *tandoori roti*—flat bread baked in a clay oven. I learned how to cook spicy chicken and a few more items of food that truck drivers liked to eat. I also learned how to wash trucks, how to change truck tires, and such other odd jobs I needed to do. I shifted from one inn to another on the interstate highway, traveling free as an errand boy for the truck drivers. I did real hard work.

"In the process, I landed up in Lucknow, the historic seat of Mughal culture and the capital city of Uttar Pradesh. Lucknow is altogether different from Calcutta, as you know, and has its own distinct culture and language—*sui generis*, in a way."

With his usual stance of superiority, Sunil was back to his true form. He added, "If I may say, Lucknow represents the vestige of Mughal court etiquette, where Hindustani and Persian cultures melded into the unique fusion of euphonious Urdu."

I just smiled benignly by way of response.

"I was totally worn out. I wanted to get out of the nomadic life of moving from point to point in highway trucks. I wanted some respite; perhaps I needed some change. I decided to eschew my life as an errand boy for anything else that came handy," said Sunil.

"Lucknow's railway station was a railroad junction. Round the clock, the station bustled with activity. While working in the highway inns, I became acquainted with working-class life and quite a bit of the underworld life. I became used to the drudgery and deprivation suffered by the riffraff of civil society. It was a strange combination of utmost misery, cruelty, and the ubiquitous human urge to live. I experienced sights and situations I never would have believed had I not seen them with my own eyes.

"I realized that the underworld too has its own rules and ethics, its own criteria of justice organized in a strange blend of brutality and kindness. No one would understand the credo of the underworld if he had not been in the thick of it. It has masters and slaves, its own etiquette and protocol. It also has its own vocabulary and the secularity of the pariahs. It was not at all difficult for me to adapt to the platform dwellers' life." Sunil made a face.

The underlying pathos in his statement touched my heart. I felt terribly sorry to know the plight of my brilliant friend, who had so much potential. I couldn't look at his face. When I felt as though I couldn't bear to hear another word, Sunil came back with an impulsive stroke of amazement. He blurted out, "Can you believe that I became a shoeshine boy on the railway platform?"

"How could you be a shoeshine boy, of all things?" I exclaimed skeptically.

"Well, I already knew how to shine my own shoes, and working in the highway inns, I had earned enough to buy a couple of shoe brushes, some polishing wax, and a handy wooden box with a raised footrest, the kind that's commonly used by the shoeshine boys, as you must have seen. My rate was four *annas* for polishing a pair of shoes. Nonetheless, as a shoeshine boy, I earned more than what I had earned in wages working at the highway inns," Sunil said in a sarcastic tone.

"Astounding," I said.

"Initially, my tired hands ached due to constantly polishing shoes. I couldn't sleep without taking analgesic pills. But as I got used to the work, my hands no longer ached. It wasn't bad either, in terms of food and things. As a platform dweller, it was my rightful prerogative to spread my bed at a convenient point on the platform and sleep under the constantly swirling electric fan suspended from the high iron rafters of the asbestos roof of the historic *Charbagh* Railway Station. I was well known to the railway men, platform vendors, restaurant boys, railway police, and platform urchins and scamps, who had no more identity than their nicknames. I only had to pay six annas per night to sleep in a corner of the wide and crowded platform. Please do not ask me to whom I paid the rent."

I looked at him with amazed eyes as he explained, "Well, the underworld urchins and goons too are byproducts of so-called civilized society. Unlike the sophisticated tax dodgers of high society, all platform dwellers scrupulously paid their platform tolls, as was the custom. Nobody ever bothered to know who had how much share of the unofficial revenue. I can vouch that the custom was no less sacrosanct than the conventions of English common law."

I noted the ironic overtone in my friend's voice, and for no apparent reason both of us shared laughter.

Sunil continued, "I came to know one or two of those who wielded monarchical power over their serfs—bonded by the law of survival. There was no question about the legitimacy or the source of their power.

"An underworld supremo ruled over his domain until he was knocked out by a rival power. It was the law of natural selection and survival of the fittest that held sway in the underworld. Every platform dweller, and everyone who carried out his private profession in the railway station, ungrudgingly paid one day's earnings every week, called *hapta* or the weekly dues, when the toll collectors descended upon the platform. It was a closely controlled, totally peaceful affair. No one tried to evade the toll or raise a murmur of protest. Thus was the unquestioning obedience to the natural law of power. Understanding between all concerned in their respective spheres of rights and obligations was perfect. The underworld bosses could also decide with impunity what was right and what was wrong, and their judgments were invariably implemented without question."

He smiled. "I led a real proletariat life in a world totally unknown to the middle-class literati, who often theorize about underworld life and activities without having any knowledge of either. Of course, I too would have never known the realities of the underworld if I had not been a dweller in it. It was an astounding eye-opener for me when I realized that it's nothing more than basic human instinct that determines matters in both worlds.

"Had I not been acquainted with the affairs of the underworld, I never would have known that the high priests of equality, democracy, and social justice are also obligated to the underworld overlords. Without the latter's help and support, the former could not survive. The difference between the two arrangements is that while actions are direct and instantaneous in the underworld, those in the so-called civilized world are set to complicated procedures of codified law."

From the manner in which he spoke, I could guess that Sunil was coming out as the most sarcastic detractor of the world he had been derailed from by circumstances. Encouraging him to go on soliloquizing on the topic would only be adding fuel to fire. I wanted to dissipate the tremendous tension he was suffering from. I wanted him to go back to the platform story he had recounted in a lighter vein and tell some more of his adventures. I interrupted to say, "I really wonder why, of all things, you took to the profession of a shoeshine boy. You could have found something better to do, couldn't you?"

"I told you I had no more middle-class vanity. Besides, I had no qualification or experience of anything better than manual work," replied Sunil.

"How long did you do the shoeshine job?"

"Nine months and sixteen days, to be exact," replied Sunil with a smirk. After a thoughtful pause, he resumed in a reflective mood.

"There were two railway platforms in Lucknow. The main platform on the broad-gauge line was known as Charbagh Railway Station. Most times, I worked on that platform. Occasionally, I also worked on the meter-gauge platform. On the main platform, I met many unforgettable characters. One of them was the platform barber, Nassirbhai."

I looked to Sunil inquisitively, waiting to hear more.

"Nassirbhai was a guru, sort of a father figure to the platform dwellers. He was a *khandani hajam*, an aristocratic barber, who claimed a Persian bloodline. Bent with the weight of his age, he never shaved his beard, which was massive and immaculately gray. Standing six feet tall, Nassiruddin Khan, popularly known as Nassirbhai, was always clad in finely woven, embroidered *Lucknow chikan churidar-kamej*—a Lucknow-style pajama suit and a colorful waistcoat. He sported a pair of *nagra,* handmade leather shoes, and a Mughal-style *taqiyah* cap of Persian antiquity. He was not a platform dweller but invariably came to the platform at the first crowing of the cock at the dawn.

"Nassirbhai constantly chewed pure Lucknowi *paan* and spoke chaste Urdu in his courtier's accent. During the winter he carried a brass water pot, fixed to a handy carrying frame and placed on smoldering charcoal. A shave given by Nassirbhai with the foamy lather worked up with warm water from his brass pot, together with his incessant recital of Urdu couplets and the glories of old Lucknow, was indeed a royal treat for any traveler in Lucknow's railway station.

"Nassirbhai knew how to pamper his customers. He would address them in various Mughal terms such as *Sultan and Hoozoor* and approach them in such a manner that they would invariably yield their cheeks to him for a shave. Nassiruddin Khan earned more in baksheesh than he did in fees."

Sunil's storytelling was now flowing in a spontaneous manner. He went on, absorbed in his own recollections. "One winter morning, right at the break of the dawn, the Avadi-Tirhut mail from Assam arrived on the meter-gauge platform. Nassirbhai and I were waiting for customers. A middle-aged fellow alighted from a first-class compartment. The passenger entered the first-class waiting room. Probably he needed the restroom or wanted to wait until the morning fog cleared. Nassirbhai, holding his innovative gear for making warm water, winked at me, slowly pushed the swivel door, and entered the quiet waiting room. He tiptoed up to the couch on which the passenger was dozing.

"In his usual way, Nassirbhai bowed and greeted the passenger with a *kurnish*—a Mughal-style salutation. He respectfully submitted to the customer in figurative Urdu, using the third person as was customary in the Mughal court, '*Hoozoor*—Your Excellency, looks tired; Hoozoor must have traveled a long distance.'

"The passenger was taken aback. He looked with confused eyes at the bearded old man, and managed to say in broken Hindi that he had come from Assam. Nassirbhai in his expert manner said in Urdu, 'I rightly guessed that Hoozoor has traveled a long distance.' Then, in a flattering tone, he added, 'This *banda* (slave) would feel greatly honored if only he could have the privilege of giving Hoozoor a smooth and comfortable warm-water shave. Hoozoor may restfully relax and even go to sleep, as this banda gives Hoozoor the smoothest of smooth shave. Hoozoor will feel the comfort of the feather touch of my special razor that would glide over your blue-blooded cheeks.'"

"How amusing," I commented.

Sunil went on with a smile, "The baffled traveler yielded to Nassirbhai's pampering approach. Without giving the customer any chance to refuse him, Nassirbhai dipped his professional shaving brush into his pot of warm water and started stroking the passenger's chin to work up lather. Simultaneously, he began his narration of the lost glories of Lucknow. Before the passenger could agree or disagree to have a shave, Nassirbhai delivered his flowery elocution and completed the job. The dazed passenger gave him a few currency bills. Nassirbhai saluted his customer with another Mughal-style bow and exited the waiting room. Out of professional courtesy and genuine fellow feeling, Nassirbhai winked at me, signaling that it was a good chance to get into the waiting room and perform my job of shining the traveler's shoes."

Sunil took a puff of his cigarette. "I quietly entered the dimly lit room, in which the traveler had sunk back into slumber. I hesitated and thought I should not bother him. I was leaving the room silently, trying not to disturb him, but the traveler suddenly woke up and howled in English, 'Who is there?' I nervously said, 'Good morning, Sir. I thought I'd give your shoes a good shine. I'm sorry if I disturbed you.' The traveler sat up. I besought his pardon for the interruption. I turned to leave the waiting room, feeling sure that my urge to earn some extra tips would instantly land me in police custody."

I was dumbfounded. Sunil continued, "But to my surprise, the fellow said, 'Wait. You can surely have my shoes to shine. But before that, tell me, how you did learn to speak English, being a shoeshine boy on a railway platform? Did you go to school? Did you work with any Englishmen?'

"I felt relieved and replied, 'Well, sir, I know a little bit of only two languages, Bengali because it is my mother tongue, and English because it is the medium of education introduced by the British rulers of India. I know a little Indianized English.'

"'I see,' said the traveler, adding, 'everyone in Lucknow seems to speak in a very interesting manner!' The traveler switched on the bright light in the waiting room as a way to signify that he was interested in talking with me further.

"I submitted that it was impossible to know which traveler spoke which language. But most Indian travelers traveling by first class prefer to speak in English, the elite language. Therefore, I utilized my little knowledge of English in speaking to them. I added, 'Sir, if you're a nationalist, I beseech your pardon for speaking in English.'

"'That's okay,' the traveler said. 'I am surprised to hear a shoeshine boy speaking English; it is nothing more than that.' He gave me his shoes, and we chatted as I did my job. He asked me what school I had attended and up to what standard I had attained. I told him that I matriculated in the first division from a school in Assam and also got a couple of letters but could not prosecute my studies further to be a university graduate.

"After answering the traveler's questions, I worked on his shoes in silence, not wanting to explain my situation. After a while, he asked me, 'How about doing some government job?'

"'I wouldn't mind if I got one,' I replied.

"'May I ask you how much you earn as a shoeshine boy?' asked the traveler.

"'Barely enough to survive. I eat and sleep on the railway platform by the grace of the railway men, the railway police, and kind passengers like you.'

"The traveler laughed heartily as though I had said something very amusing. He repeated his comment that people in Lucknow spoke in an interesting manner.

"He said, 'Supposing you are offered a government job of one hundred and seventy-five rupees a month plus some allowances, free unfurnished accommodation, subsidized food in the cooperative canteen, and paid holidays, how would you like it?'

"'Sounds great,' I replied without really hoping to get a government job.

"In a serious tone, the traveler asked me if I had ever been convicted by any court of law. I said no, never. He then said, 'If you really like the idea, see me in my office in the first week of the next month.' He gave me his business card together with a five-rupee bill as tip.

"I raised my hand to my head, thankfully acknowledging his generosity. Looking at his card, I found that he was the deputy divisional manager of telecommunication, in charge of Assam Circle. Two weeks later, after a great deal of hesitation, I took a desperate chance to see him in his Guwahati office. Unlike typical bureaucrats, he granted me an instant interview.

"And to my surprise, I got the job."

12

In my third-year classes at college, Nirupama Sen was my classmate in the economics honors course. She was a simple girl with nothing special in her looks and manners. We knew each other just as we knew all other students in the class. Her deceased father had been a government employee in the Bengal secretariat during British rule. She was the youngest child of her parents. She lived with her widowed mother in her parental home in Park Circus, Calcutta. An introvert by nature, she was the most unassuming student in the class. Once, when she missed a class, she borrowed my class notes to make copies at home. She commuted by public buses to attend classes.

On a particular day, the teacher in the political science class took extra time in completing his lecture. He was discussing two Victorian-era English social reformers, Thomas Carlyle and John Ruskin, with reference to the French Revolution and its impact on contemporary English thought. It was the last class of the day.

By the time class ended, it was almost twilight. As we all came out of the classroom, Nirupama expressed her concern that she would not be able to catch a bus at that hour of the day, when offices close and buses are packed with the home-going crowd. She added that because of her anxiety about catching a bus, she could not concentrate on the interesting lecture we had just attended.

I listened and walked along with her as a matter of normal courtesy. As we approached the bus stop close to the college, she told me that she could not grasp how Ruskin was relevant in the context of the French Revolution. She said that Carlyle of course was a historian and was naturally concerned with the French Revolution.

"Ruskin was an art critic," I replied, "and later in life he wrote his ideas on reforming the English society of his time. Perhaps as a proponent of social reform, the philosophers of the French Revolution inspired him. I think that was how Ruskin featured in the lecture. I'll tell you if I find any more details on the point."

We reached the bus stop. The bus that came was jam-packed, with hardly a foothold anywhere. Some passengers were holding the door handle with their toes on the footboard, dangling like bats.

Those days in Calcutta, buses and trams had seats reserved for women commuters. Such reservation of seats, however, was of no help to Nirupama on that day, because the bus was already sardine-packed with homegoers of both sexes. She had to abandon the bus. As a matter of courtesy, I stood with her as she waited for the next bus.

The next bus on the route to Park Circus came some twenty minutes later. This bus too was similarly crammed with passengers. Poor Nirupama made a pathetic face and helplessly exclaimed, "Oh, it's so full! How will I go home? It's getting too late for me."

I realized her plight and said, "Let's call a taxicab for you."

"I can't go all alone in a taxicab in the evening. It's too risky for a woman; you wouldn't understand. Besides, a taxi would be too expensive," she replied.

Without any second thought, I raised my hand to call a taxicab. She looked at me with astounded eyes. The cab driver managed to pull up the car by the side of the congested road virtually jammed by all conceivable means of transportation, including rickshaws and pedestrians. He opened a rear door and asked us to get in quickly. I asked her to get in before she could utter a word. She looked at me and timidly got into the cab.

"Don't worry; I'll escort you home," I assured her.

She gave me a smile indicating her appreciation.

I sat next to her and asked the impatient cab driver to drive to Park Circus. The car started moving. I asked Nirupama to give road directions to the cabbie. She nodded and instructed the driver. We sat side by side in the rear seat like two strangers. She was sitting quietly with her hands on her lap; her books and handbag lay in the space between us, creating a sort of barrier.

I watched the traffic on the road, feeling unsure if I had done the right thing by offering to escort her. Winter evening smog blurred the roadside lights. Unruly Calcutta traffic and endless potholes made the taxi driver frequently honk and press the brake pedal with inevitable impacts on us. Nonetheless, we carefully avoided touching each other's bodies. We belonged to the English-educated, Bengali middle-class gentry of the time. We were too refined to be natural.

We reached Park Circus Square. From the Point of Don Bosco School, Nirupama guided the driver to her home, leading him deep inside along the Darga Road. The cabbie followed her directions until Nirupama asked him to stop at a particular point. The locality consisted of blocks of old brick-and-mortar houses, attesting to centuries of use and abuse. The cabbie managed to park his vehicle by the roadside. Nirupama opened her handbag and looked to the fare meter fixed to the car. I dissuaded her by putting my hand on her handbag and told her that I would go back by the same cab; she mustn't discharge the cab.

She looked at me curiously and asked in a tentative tone, "Won't you come up to my home?"

She got down from the cab near the entry to a shady lane. I thought that probably she felt insecure about going into the dark lane all alone. A sense of chivalry impelled me to help her. Instead of bidding her good night, I said, "I'll walk you home. Please wait."

With a thankful smile, she said, "Then let's release the cab; we have to walk down the lane. Why keep him waiting?" She stated all this in a practical manner. I paid the cabbie and he left.

I followed her through a badly lit, narrow lane. A rickshaw puller carrying a woman in a black *burka* passed us, tinkling his handheld bell. Walking silently, we reached the closed door of an old house. She rang the doorbell. An electric lamp inside the room lit up. A frail-looking old woman in a white sari opened the door. Before the old woman could say anything, Nirupama introduced me to her as her mother. She told her that the buses had been too crowded, and I was so nice as to escort her in a taxicab.

I greeted the old woman with folded hands. She returned my greeting. I turned around to leave. But the mother asked me to come on in. Hesitantly, I entered the house. She bolted the door and asked me to sit down. I sat on a sagging old couch in the front room. Nirupama excused herself and went farther into the house. Her old mother followed her.

I was sitting all alone, regretting my quick decision to enter. The living room was furnished with old furniture. On the pale, whitewashed walls, framed family photos and spiderwebs hung together. The room gave the immediate impression of age and lack of upkeep. It was a typical home of a disintegrating middle-class family. A lacquered bookcase with famous English and Bengali titles in timeworn dust jackets stood as the relic of contemporary Bengali middle-class culture.

My thoughts shifted from the old living room to the history of Park Circus, particularly when Calcutta was the British capital of India. Park Circus was created by the British administration as an extension of Park Street, running from the hub of Chawringhee Avenue up to the western part of the area. Lower-middle-class Anglo-Indians, English-educated government employees, and rich Muslim traders settled in the area. In the course of time, the area became home to famous mosques and Islamic shrines. After the partition of India, however, some of the Muslim inhabitants had left and migrated to Pakistan. Now it was a neglected area—a decaying township congested with houses upon houses.

After a while, the mother reappeared in the room. She spoke in a frail voice. "I so much appreciate your good sense in escorting Nirupama home. I was getting very worried when she was late. As you know, it is very risky for a young girl of her age to commute by bus, particularly after the sunset. I always tell her that if necessary, she should skip the last class so that she gets the bus home before the offices close for the day. But she doesn't realize how anxious I feel." The old woman gasped for breath after expressing her thoughts, as though she was exhausted after speaking so much at a stretch.

My discomfiture upon entering the house was somewhat lessened when she spoke to me, but I really didn't know what to tell her in reply. I could only say, "That's okay. It was nothing much that I did. She is my classmate. I thought I must escort her when it was getting dark and there was no room in the buses. I suggested that she should take a taxi, and said I would escort her because she was alone." After justifying my reasons, I asked, "May I go now?"

"Oh no, no. Niru (a nickname for Nirupama) is making tea for you. You must take a cup of tea at least. Please sit down. Niru told me how you helped her. It was so nice of you. God bless you."

Now we were sitting face-to-face. She took out a ten-rupee currency bill from the folds of her sari and extended it toward me, saying, "Please don't hesitate to take the taxi fare. You too are a student."

I politely refused the offer, following the customary etiquette. She went on insisting that she would feel very guilty if I did not take the money. When I didn't take the money despite her insistence, she put the currency bill on the table before me. Her hint that for a student to ride a taxi was wasteful spending made me all the more uncomfortable.

I stared at the old ceiling fan hung with spider-woven lacy designs. Time stood still as the old woman and I sat silently in the room. I didn't know how to keep the conversation going while waiting for Nirupama. In fact, I was keen to get out of the room and leave the old woman's company. I couldn't guess what she was thinking. Her thoroughly wrinkled face indicated that she was very old and possibly in frail health.

At last, Nirupama came back holding a plate of freshly fried *luchies*—fried flour dough—and other snacks. Her face glowed with a radiant smile of contentment. Now, both mother and daughter spoke to me as Nirupama and I ate, and her mother generously served us with more and more helpings.

After taking the high tea, I stood up to leave. Nirupama's mother thanked me once again and asked me to take the currency bill lying on the table. I took leave with another *namaskar* to Nirupama's mother. She returned the greeting and thanked me once again for escorting Nirupama. The ten-rupee bill remained in its place.

"Please do drop in whenever you can," added the mother out of courtesy. I, however, thought perhaps she didn't really mean what she said.

Nirupama gave me an affable smile and waved at me as I went out to the lane. I walked to reach the main road. For no reason, I felt a sense of triumph as I took the bus to my hostel.

We resumed attending classes as usual. There was no change in our relationship or manner except that I now felt a sense of familiarity with her.

* * *

The exciting time of election for the student union approached. My hostel mates, in their urge for solidarity, decided in a meeting to nominate their own candidates for all the positions in the student union. They nominated me to contest for the position of general secretary. They launched the election campaign.

For nearly a month before the election, the only topic for discussion was electoral rivalry and campaign strategies. As it turned out after the ballot voting, I was elected as the general secretary and my hostel mate, Guru Prasad Sen Gupta, was elected as the sports secretary. Thus, we held the most important portfolios.

The union, however, had a few other elected secretaries in other spheres of the union's activities. They were elected from among the day scholars of the college. I became the leader of the team by virtue of being the general secretary. Everyone, including Nirupama, congratulated me.

I felt a strange sense of importance and responsibility as the leader of the team. The election-time rivalry between groups of students no longer affected us. All of us desired, as members of a team, to excel in all our programs. We organized various events and occasions, including excursions, debates, dramas, and cricket matches.

Nirupama had to miss some classes because her mother was sick. When she returned, we began meeting in the College Street coffeehouses so I could help her catch up on what she had missed.

As our meetings became more and more frequent, I started addressing her as Niru instead of Nirupama. We chatted for a long time whenever we met, and our conversations transcended beyond the topic of classroom lectures. After the meetings, I invariably escorted her home in cabs. I went up to the front door of her home and carefully avoided entering the house. I never asked her, nor did she tell me, how her mother reacted to her late return from the college after the offices closed and the home-going crowd crammed into the buses.

On a Sunday morning, Niru managed to come out, and together we went to Dhakuria Lake in South Calcutta. Sitting on a bench by the lake, we enjoyed munching *garam muri*—freshly made popped rice seasoned with mustard and served in loose sheets of paper, a popular snack offered by vendors at Dhakuria Lake. A gust of wind blew the paper from Nirupama's hand. We enjoyed the fun of it. I hummed a line from *Rabindra Sangeet* in which the poet Rabindranath Tagore described the wild wind on a cloudy day. Nirupama joined me in singing. To my great delight, I discovered that she had a fine voice and she could sing *Rabindra Sangeet* perfectly.

The student union organized a train trip to Orissa during a long vacation. A host of students, boys and girls, and two young teachers joined the tour. Nirupama did not come. We had an exciting tour of Puri, the beach city, and many other places in Orissa, now pronounced as Odisha, full of magnificent stone sculptures adorning many temples all over the state.

I bought an exquisite hand-loomed stole as a souvenir. Soon after returning to Calcutta, I set out for Nirupama's place, carrying the stole in a gift packet. On the bus, I tried to envision the extent of her happiness at my surprise visit and her likely reaction to the gift that I would offer her.

I got down from the bus near the lane, walked fast to reach her home, and pushed the doorbell. Nirupama opened the door. She was surprised to see me appearing at her doorstep so suddenly, and in the evening. She, however, looked delighted to see me but scrupulously restrained her exuberance. She stood on the threshold for a moment and then exclaimed with a smile, "Hi! You have come back!"

I nodded happily.

After a pause, she asked, "How was the trip?"

"Good, but you know . . ."

Abruptly and before I could complete the sentence, she interrupted me, saying, "Please come on in."

I then realized that it was indiscreet on my part to visit her suddenly and at such an hour of the evening. I realized the cause of her hesitation. I tried to be as casual as I could, and instead of entering the house, I extended the packet to her without a word.

With surprise in her eyes, she asked, "What's in it?"

"Just a token, I mean, a small souvenir from Orissa for you."

As I made a move to leave, she said, "Please come on in. Don't go away like that."

I was happy and waited at the threshold, expecting her exultant delight when she saw what I had brought for her.

She opened the packet and cried out, "How beautiful! Oh, I love it." And immediately, she controlled herself and murmured, "But I cannot take it from you. What would I tell my mom?"

"Why? What's wrong about it? It's only a small souvenir," I said, imploring her.

She didn't reply but instead hurriedly folded the stole and put it back into the packet. To my chagrin, she offered the packet back to me, saying, "Sorry, I can't take it from you. My mother won't let me accept it."

Now I felt desperate, and a possessive tone permeated my voice. I blurted out, "I brought it all the way from Bhubaneswar only for you; you can't refuse it."

Just then, her mother entered the room from behind the partition door. Niru quickly put the packet under her armpit and covered it with her sari. Then she turned and went inside the house, leaving me to face her mother.

Surprised to find me on the doorstep, the old woman said, "Hello, how are you? Please come in. I was wondering who might ring the doorbell at this time. Didn't you go home during the vacation?"

I hated myself for the encounter with her, but I had to reply to her question because she was leading me into the living room. I could not suddenly leave.

"We went on an excursion to Orissa," I said stiffly. "Only today we returned from the trip."

I did not know whether to stay or leave. Hesitantly, I sat down as she took her seat. I was feeling extremely uncomfortable. Most casually, she asked me how the trip was, when the college would reopen, and such other common questions people ask when there is nothing else to talk about. Although she must have already known the date on which the college would reopen, I answered her questions, waiting for a chance to leave as soon as it was polite to do so.

Nirupama came back, holding a tray in her hand. She placed a cup of tea and a plate of crackers before me and sat on the couch. Her mother asked me with the customary courtesy to take the tea. I managed to gulp some tea and stood up, telling her that I was in a hurry because I had to go to my aunt's place in Tollygunj. I folded my hands in a *namaskar* to Nirupama's mother. She returned my greetings. I waved at Niru, came out to the lane, and walked at a quick pace toward the main road.

Vacation ended and the college reopened. We resumed attending classes. Every time I met Niru, I remembered the embarrassment I had felt when I went to her place with the stole. For the next few days, I could not speak to her or go out with her. A strange sense of humiliation haunted me. I didn't know how to ask her why she was so hesitant to accept the gift I had brought. In my heart of hearts, I yearned to meet her and tell her so many things I thought about when I wasn't with her. I was sure that she liked the gift I had given her, but she had restrained herself because of her conservative mother.

At last one day, Nirupama asked me, "You seem to be studying too hard. You look so serious nowadays."

"Not at all," I replied, trying to sound normal. "I am just attending classes. How about you?"

"The same; the course seems to be too much work and too hard. I don't know what will happen to me when the time comes for the final exam. I'm afraid I won't be able to prepare as well as you always do. You're so precise and to the point. Whenever I try to prepare an answer to a probable question, it turns out to be too lengthy and beside the point." She smirked as a way of laughing at herself. Perhaps she realized that I hoped for more warmth in her demeanor toward me.

"I know you're exaggerating," I commented with a smile, and then both of us laughed freely. Together we walked up to the bus stop.

I couldn't tell her anything more. I didn't ask her to come to the coffeehouse. I didn't call a cab. Her bus came; she got into the bus and left for home. We waved at each other.

Time passed too quickly, it seemed. We were nearing the end of the third academic year. Every year just before the onset of the winter, the student union organized and held the annual college social. It was always the last function of the year for the student union. The college social was a great occasion spread over several days. All the resources of the student union were pooled to organize the best possible annual event. Every general secretary and his team put forth their best effort to make the college social of their time the most outstanding function.

That year it was my turn. My friends and the officeholders discussed a number of ideas. Finally, we decided that we would have a three-day program in which students of our college and professional artists would take part. We hired the New Empire Theater as the auditorium for the social. We hired celebrated professional artists for the cultural show and paid advances to them.

The next important thing was to decide the scheduling for three days. We sat down in a meeting of all officeholders. We decided on the various events leading up to the concluding session, which would be a musical program composed, directed, and presented by students of the college.

My mate Ranjit Bhattacharya was a budding poet, and my friends already knew of my interest in music. In the next meeting, the union decided that Ranjit Bhattacharya and I would together compose a musical feature on the Indian seasons. We decided to compile the feature with selected stanzas of seasonal imagery from famous Sanskrit and Bengali poets, knit together with short commentaries and songs, especially *Rabindra Sangeet.*

With great diligence, we drafted the musical feature, weaving together our best selections of songs and poems. We also tried to write a great commentary to present the musical feature in the most attractive and interesting way.

Ranjit was to finalize the recitation part with suitable male and female voices, and I was to select artists who could render *Rabindra Sangeet* and had good voices. I already knew the students in the college who sang *Rabindra Sangeet.* On my invitation, most of them agreed to join the rehearsal.

I also knew that Nirupama had a wonderful voice for *Rabindra Sangeet.* I asked her to join. She felt shy and hesitated. She said that she had never before sung on a stage and before an audience. Nevertheless, because of my encouragement and persuasion, she too joined the team and managed to get her mother's permission to attend the rehearsal.

We finalized the selection of songs and verses for recitation and wrote the commentaries. Rehearsals began. Every artist tried to do his or her best. It took some two weeks to rehearse the musical feature. Every evening after the rehearsal, I escorted Nirupama home. We were entirely engrossed with the musical feature. Tunes of music and rhythms of poetry enchanted us and filled our beings, and we felt as though we'd been exalted to a higher plane. Nothing other than the musical feature and the ongoing rehearsals featured in our conversations as I escorted Nirupama home.

At last, the momentous day arrived. The musical feature went off better than expected. A packed audience gave us rousing applause. Our teachers and the principal of the college congratulated us, especially Ranjit and me as the event organizers.

My year's term of leadership in the student union ended with the college social. We had just one more year before we would be graduates of Calcutta University.

The fourth year is a year of intensive studying and preparing for the final examination. I consolidated my classroom notes and decided to cut back on every other thing to concentrate on my studies. But I had to attend my classes too.

Whenever I went to class, I met Niru. I felt tempted to be with her. In the hostel, my friends called me to join them in the canteen for the usual chitchat. I restrained myself from all these temptations and concentrated on my studies, but no one can study all the time. It was in my nature that whenever I felt like writing a poem or a lyric or composing a song, I couldn't resist. It was my own way of relaxation, which sometimes took quite a bit of my time. Nonetheless, I was determined to prepare for the exam as thoroughly as I could.

I met Nirupama once during the practice exam period. Afterward, the college was closed for a short time. Nirupama had once told me in a lighter vein that her mother thought that our free mixing might provoke criticism. I took it as a hint that her mother didn't like me to meet Niru and spend time with her. Again, I thought that perhaps her mother noticed that our relationship was taking a romantic turn. I felt encouraged.

On the reopening day of the college, we went to learn the practice exam results. Those allowed to sit for the final exam had their roll numbers hung on the notice board. Both of us got our roll numbers and the venues for the final exam, which were spread over various colleges in Calcutta. Students studying in a particular college were often required to write their exam papers at a different college. The notice board displayed the seat number and the venue for each candidate.

Good wishes from everyone, including my parents, my sisters Anita and Sunita, my brother Arun, my friends, my two aunts and their husbands in Calcutta, and my cousins, poured in. I sat for the final examination, which lasted for nearly two weeks with breaks on Sundays and holidays. It was a heavily programmed sequence of time. I had neither any urge nor any respite to think of anything else other than the exam.

After writing the last paper, I felt a sense of loss. An all-pervading feeling of void came over me because I knew this marked the end of an important period in my life. The thought that my friends and I would no longer be in the college and in the hostel overwhelmed me. Students residing in the college hostels would not come back whether or not they passed the exam. The colleges and hostels would remain closed until the examination results were published in about a month. A new batch of students would seek admission to the colleges and hostels. Those who passed the exam and became university graduates would take up some job or profession. Only a handful would go for postgraduate courses at the university. Hostelers and classmates would never again meet each other, except by chance.

Shadows of leave-taking created an overwhelming ambience. Many of my hostel mates had already left. Some were on a shopping spree before going home. The hostel was almost empty. I only found my friend Guruprasad putting his clothes into a suitcase. I asked him whether he was leaving. He replied that he was checking out from the hostel and going to Howrah station to catch whatever train was available to go to his hometown in Uttar Pradesh. We hugged each other, choking back our emotions, exchanged good wishes, and bade the most cordial good-bye to one another. Guru went down the stairs to take leave of the hostel warden.

I had not yet booked my ticket for home. The thought that I would have to leave Niru and go home disturbed me.

The sun was setting on the obscure horizon of Calcutta at the day's end. Like a spellbound being, I headed for Niru's place. I got down from the bus, walked up to the house, and pressed the doorbell. It was already dark.

Her mother opened the door and I stepped in quickly and rather desperately. With surprise in her eyes, she stood for a moment and then asked me to sit down. After another awkward moment of silence, she asked me if I was happy with my exam. Then she asked when I would go home.

I felt disconcerted and answered her questions as briefly as I could. I didn't care what the old woman might think or feel. I had come to meet Niru. I was determined to tell her my feelings about her, which I had never been able to express in words. I felt sure that Niru would reciprocate. Therefore, despite what seemed like her mother's unfeeling attitude, I endured her presence and replied to her questions.

At last, she said, "I'll tell Niru that you have come."

After a breathless wait, Nirupama came in. She looked unkempt and unmindful, as if she had just woken up from sleep and was still under the spell of slumber. I wondered what might have gone wrong with her. She gave me a cheerless smile and sat down on the couch rather stiffly. She did not look like the responsive Niru I had come to know and love. She looked blank.

Feeling anxious, I asked her, "Are you all right, Niru?"

As though still in a daze, she replied, "Oh, yes, I'm fine. I was just lazing. How are you?"

"Okay," I replied.

We sat speechless in the same room. She did not ask me anything more. I felt awkward, not knowing what to tell her. Impatiently, I blurted out, "Would you like to go out?"

She stood up in a spurt, and in a positive tone she replied, "I'll be ready in a moment!"

She went in, swaying the door curtains. Her definite reply encouraged me. I waited with great expectation. But she didn't come back in a moment. After a long and impatient wait, she reappeared wrapped in an ordinary sari, holding a bag in hand.

"Shall we go?" she asked me.

Together we stepped out into the shadowy lane. Niru carefully closed the door from outside. She looked back as she walked, then opened the bag in her hand. She took out the stole I had given her as a souvenir from Orissa and loosely wrapped it around her back and shoulders.

Encouraged by Niru's spontaneous response, I merrily exclaimed, "You look beautiful in this wrap. Let's go to the Esplanade."

"Thank you," she replied with a furtive smile and added, "I thought I must wear it today. How do I look?"

"Oh, you look terrific," I said appreciatively.

To my suggestion of going to the Esplanade, she said, "Let's not go to the Esplanade; it's too far. Let us stay somewhere near. I can't go to the Esplanade now."

I turned toward the main road by which I had come to her place so many times by bus and taxicab. But Niru continued to walk in the opposite direction along the lane. I wondered where she wanted to go by the dingy lane, whose ancient lampposts gave out more shadows than light. Nonetheless, I felt confident and happy to see her draped in the stole I presented her with a year before.

I was feeling brave, so I said, "Niru, I want to tell you something—"

Without giving me any chance to complete my sentence, she asked rather abruptly, "How was the exam? You must have done very well; I'm sure you did."

Walking side by side with her, I gained confidence to share my thoughts, especially after the compliment she had just given me. I wanted to make the evening intimate and share the feelings I had for her. I replied, "Let's forget about the exam. We have already had too much of it."

A rickshaw puller slowed down near us, hoping to give us a ride. Niru stopped the rickshaw and got into it. I followed her. She asked me to draw down the folded-up top. On the thin and hard seat, we sat so closely that I could feel the warmth of her body. With the top down, the seating space became more exclusive. I could smell the fragrance of her hair. I felt tempted to hold her in the privacy of the covered rickshaw.

But Nirupama sat rather stiffly, creating a sense of distance between us. She sat so rigidly that I didn't dare touch her. I didn't know how to behave in a situation like that. A strange sense of hesitation held me back from holding her hand.

Possibly, she guessed my feelings. She covered her shoulder and arms with the stole, implicitly creating a symbolic barrier of fabric between us. The rickshaw puller, habitually indifferent to his passengers' behaviors, pulled his human load steadfastly, ringing his handheld bell. The two-wheeled sleigh moved in its habitual way over the narrow lane of dents and cracks.

Our bodies tilted and touched, despite the fact that Niru was trying very hard to keep her distance from me. My traditional sense of decency prevented me from making any advances. I only dared to take her hand and stroke it gently.

She neither objected nor responded. I could not make out if she was expecting me to take the initiative or if she wanted to be reclusive. I was in a fix. Nirupama had a personality that would not yield to impatient overtures.

Time passed in silence as the rickshaw slowly moved to the end of the lane where it intersected with a road. The area was equally old but not inert like the shadowy lane. I couldn't make out what the area was by name. There were old blocks of buildings on both sides of the road.

Nirupama asked the rickshaw puller to stop. He lowered the stretched arms of his primitive transport. I helped Niru to get down, not yet knowing her plan. I paid the rickshaw puller, and then, standing together on the roadside, I impatiently asked her, "Are you all right, Niru? Please tell me if anything is wrong."

"I'm fine. Let's sit down somewhere, shall we?" She uttered the words in a serious tone.

"Sure," I replied, trying to sound unworried and casual as I walked with her by the side of the road, not knowing where to go. I was trying to figure out her intention. She seemed to know where she was going. Feeling edgy, I again asked her, "What's wrong, Niru? What happened? Please tell me."

She replied in a subdued tone, "Nothing."

I could feel that something was tormenting her that she was not telling me.

I was getting restive; I felt the urge to appease her, to hold her in my arms and comfort her. But we were on a city road in an ancient country and at a time when it was thought improper for a young man and woman even to hold hands in public. I was almost sure that she had had a fight with her mother, who must have objected to her going out with me in the darkness of the night.

But then why was she behaving so stiffly? Wouldn't she want to seek comfort with me now that we were out of the house?

We found a restaurant and entered it. We took a table in the farthest corner of the hall and sat down, asking for coffee. Niru took her time to control her surging emotion. I kept quiet, wondering what might be the problem.

It was an open restaurant with few customers and waiters. Niru, in her desperate effort to divert attention, slowly asked me, "Will you be joining the master's degree course in economics?"

I felt relieved at her question. I replied in a lighter vein, "Let me first of all get the results. I'm not yet a college graduate. How about you? What are you planning to do after graduation?"

She paused for a moment and then said quietly, "Whether I am a graduate or not, I'm not going for any more studies."

"Oh, Niru, what are you talking about? You must take up the next course in the university. Why should you back out?"

"Makes no difference," she whispered with a sigh.

I pressed her hand and implored her as kindly as I could, "Niru, you're not telling me what's wrong with you. I love you; I want you;

I want to know everything that troubles you. Niru, you're mine and only mine."

The words had flowed out with a life of their own. She lowered her face and drops of warm tears fell on my hand that still clasped hers. We kept quiet lest others see her shedding tears.

A waiter with inquisitive eyes came by with a tray in hand. He placed the coffeepot, cups, pot of cream, and sugar pots one by one—slowly, it seemed, in his urge to know what was going on with us. He waited for a while, perhaps expecting that we would order some snacks, and then left silently.

Nirupama wiped her tears. She slowly made coffee and poured sugar and cream in my cup. She already knew my taste. Then she filled her cup and stirred it without looking up at me. She appeared absorbed in thought. I took a sip from my cup, unable to decide how to take care of the unknown trouble Niru was suffering from.

Looking around with a furtive glance, as though to make sure no one could overhear, Niru leaned forward and whispered in a heavy tone, "My wedding date has been fixed."

"Oh no! Why? How could you . . ." I cried out impulsively, as everyone in the restaurant turned his or her eyes in our direction.

Both of us felt embarrassed at my exclamation. Jolted by the surge of emotion, I put my hand on Niru's and pressed it hard as I said in a distressed voice, "You never told me that are you getting wedded to someone!"

Nirupama avoided my question and tried to assume a serious face. She whispered, "Please don't misunderstand me. *Borda,* my eldest brother, fixed my marriage soon after I joined the third-year class. *Baudi*, my sister-in-law, knew the family and the groom. His name is Sudhangshu. He is an engineer in Jamshedpur. We would have been wedded soon after the marriage was settled, but my mother insisted that I should be allowed to complete my studies. Sudhangshu's father graciously agreed to wait until my final exam was over. Now that I have completed my exam, they have fixed a date in consultation with my mother and my brothers. After my marriage, my mother will live with my brother and sister-in-law at Jamshedpur."

She stated this like a soliloquy recited by rote on stage, but the realization of what this meant crashed down on my head. I was dumbfounded. Burning inside, I felt rejected and humiliated. I found it difficult to behave normally. The waiter brought the bill and I paid. As we walked out of the restaurant, I felt bitterly disgraced. I could only mutter, "How strange that you never told me you were already engaged."

She reacted sharply. "Believe me, I never loved anyone else. My wedding has been fixed with a groom who only came to see me formally with his father when I was in the third-year class. I know that his name is Sudhangshu, and I saw him for a moment when he came with his father. I don't know what sort of a person he is. I wanted to be a graduate, and my mother encouraged me."

"Stop it, Niru; stop it. Don't spoil your life. Why don't you tell them that you won't marry him and you want to go for higher studies? You're not a minor. Nobody can force you to marry. That's the law."

She did not reply to my point and asked me to call a rickshaw. I called a rickshaw from a nearby stand. We returned to her place in silence. Neither of us spoke until we were near the closed door of her house. She stopped the rickshaw a few yards before. She got down, neatly folded the stole, and put it back into the bag. I observed the caution she took in concealing my gift from her mother. I felt insignificant, and for the first time in my life, I realized that love cannot be claimed as a right.

Niru held my hand and whispered, "Please understand that if I resist the marriage at this stage, my old mother will be in trouble. She is old and sick as you know, and she will have to live the rest of her life with my brother and his wife. I cannot ditch her."

She hurried into the house and closed the door.

13

"She had the real fervor of a vivacious woman, sort of a glow that perked up everything around her. She had a delightful spirit that made her beautiful. You know what I mean?" I looked up from a book I was reading and glanced at the man sitting across from me on the train. I wanted to ask who he was describing but only nodded in silent participation. This heartened him to continue musing.

He exclaimed, "I really couldn't believe how such a thing could happen to her!"

"What happened?"

My abrupt question was like throwing a pebble into a quiet lake, but it had no effect on him. Absorbed in his thoughts, he went on, "It was a routine physical, the usual annual health check. A chest x-ray showed a small shadow on her left lung. Although she smoked, she had never suffered any ill effect from it, not even a cough. The spot detected in x-ray could have been just nothing. Nonetheless, her physician believed that she should go for a CT scan to have her lung checked more thoroughly.

"The scan showed that the shadow was a growth, and a biopsy confirmed that it was malignant. Thus, the diagnosis was that she was a case of non-small-cell lung cancer. Although not an aggressive form of carcinoma, it was carcinoma for sure.

"Naturally, she had to go through further tests. There was, however, no indication of cancer in her lymph nodes; only the small mass on one of the two lobes of her left lung was malignant. In view of the tests and scans, her oncologist and thoracic surgeon decided that she should have a video-assisted surgery to remove the small but malignant tumor."

I already knew that my narrator was a surgeon. We had made brief introductions when we first sat down after boarding the train, as we were the only two passengers in the two-berthed, first-class coupe of the Jammu-Tawi Express, but I have since forgotten his name. As he narrated the story, I, naturally, thought that he was referring to one of his cancer patients. The emotional undertone I detected in his speech, however, was unusual for a surgeon speaking about a patient. I felt curious about his relationship with her. However, I did not ask him, because it would have been inappropriate. I hardly understood the technical jargon he used in describing the case. I only knew that the woman had lung cancer. I thought it best to assume the role of a silent listener.

The surgeon continued, “You might have heard about Dr. Bragg, the well-known oncologist in pulmonary carcinoma?”

Although I never heard such a name, I nodded as a gesture of etiquette, and as a way to show empathy.

That was how we became friends within the short time we traveled together by train. Both of us had boarded the train at Jammu railway station. I was returning from Kashmir and he from the heights of the Himalayas. A pure Westerner in Indian kurta pajamas, he kept to a vegetarian diet and presumably lived an austere life.

From the prelude to his story, I could reasonably presume that we were heading toward a carcinogenic disaster. However, I said nothing and gave him an understanding glance to let him feel that I was paying full attention to his narrative. Immersed in his thoughts, he spoke nothing for the next few moments.

Clanking heavily, the train entered a long cantilever bridge that spanned a river. After crossing the bridge, we passed through cornfields on both sides of the track. Green cobs of corn wiggled in the wind. I turned my face from the window. In an effort to break the silence within the compartment, I reminded my copassenger, “Surgeon, you were telling me about a case.”

Roused from his engrossment, my narrator resumed his story. “Oh yes. Her doctors decided to surgically remove the tumor and hoped that malignant cells would not proliferate soon. She opposed the idea of having the surgical procedure. I soothed her and assured her of the efficacy of the procedure. At last, she consented to go for surgery.

"A renowned surgeon performed the surgery and removed the affected lobe of her left lung. The surgeon and the oncologist were sure that there was no likelihood in the immediate future of malignant cells spreading throughout her body. As usual, the oncologist advised that she must follow up the surgery with a few cycles of chemotherapy."

Another spell of suspense hovered as the coach swung from side to side with the rhythm of the speeding train. The surgeon continued, "But, you know, she was a strong-willed woman. She was aware of the various bad effects of chemotherapy, including hair loss. She refused to go for chemotherapy. She said that she would prefer to die of cancer rather than suffer the inevitable side effects of the treatment. Rose was a gorgeous woman with beautiful blonde hair. She never wanted to lose her hair and wear a wig. It was difficult to convince her that her hair would grow again within about six months after completing the treatment.

"After surgery, she went home, and in no time, it seemed, she was her natural self again. Against all medical advice, she felt confident that she wouldn't need chemotherapy."

Now I knew her name Rose. Although I could not ask him what his relationship with her was, I felt almost sure that she was his spouse.

"You know, we had everything that any couple could expect in life. Perhaps we had much more than we really needed. We were happy as ever. After the surgery, she religiously did breathing exercises to expand the remaining part of her left lung. She could breathe normally and had no problem with the oxygen level in her blood. She gave up smoking."

"Wonderful," I said, feeling relieved.

"For the time being our life was again full. We went out together and took short vacations. She was crazy about going places, and we traveled so much that we practically forgot that she had cancer."

I gave him an appreciative smile. He paused for a while, rearranged himself on the berth, and said, "In the ninth month after her surgery, we were planning a trip to Australia. Rose contacted her travel agent, and all preparations were complete. She was counting the days with excitement. Suddenly, one evening, she had a bout of wheezing and coughing as she had never had before. She had no fever and no other symptom. Her oncologist checked her and gave her some antibiotics and corticosteroid pills, and an inhaler to control the symptoms. Because of the history of malignant growth in her lung, he advised that she should have a PET scan, a kind of nuclear medicine imaging, for a more thorough checkup.

"Unfortunately, the result was positive. Traces of malignant cells were now found spreading in her lungs and respiratory organs."

"How sad," I said.

The surgeon did not react. It seemed that he had exhausted all his emotions through the ordeal he was describing, and now he just needed to talk about it with someone.

"The findings from the scan made her a totally changed person. She was no longer that lively woman she had always been. She looked unusually pensive. Whenever I tried to tell her that she would be fine again, she only gave me a vague smile. In fact, she hardly spoke. Now she meekly submitted to all tests and treatments her doctors prescribed. She behaved as if she had no more interest in life.

"Rose was being treated in the best cancer hospital in the city and was directly under the care of another well-known oncologist, Dr. Flaherty. A team of specialists looked after her. This time, in consultation with Dr. Bragg and other specialists, Dr. Flaherty decided to put her on a regimen of chemotherapy.

"Although everybody gave her hope, she appeared crestfallen. Whenever I tried to reassure her that she would be all right, she only gave me a vague smile. I told her by way of soothing her that she would be all right after the treatment and we would surely go to Australia for our next vacation. She responded with the same insipid smile without a word. Perhaps she had some premonition . . . some portent. I never knew."

I felt moved with compassion for the surgeon.

After heaving a sigh, he resumed, "Despite my professional preoccupation, I tried to be with her as much as possible. I brought her books, flowers, and whatever else she was fond of."

The surgeon gulped his emotion, and after a pause, he added, "Rose insisted that I should attend to my professional commitments instead of spending time with her in her hospital suite. But you know, I really loved her, and when she fell sick, I loved her all the more."

"I understand, Surgeon," I responded. "Knowing how much I love my wife, I understand completely how you must have felt."

My copassenger nodded his silent appreciation for my understanding, and then continued. "The first cycle of chemotherapy was completed, and Rose wasn't really scared or worried because there were not too many side effects. However, as you know, you cannot altogether avoid the side effects of chemotherapy. In the course of destroying the malignant cells, chemotherapy also destroys the immune cells in the body. The toxic effect of chemotherapy makes the patient tired and weak, besides being highly susceptible to other infections.

"Rose, however, had no such infection. She did not complain of weakness or anything else either. Whenever I asked her how she was feeling, she replied silently with her typical smile and a nod, indicating that she was doing fine.

"One day I had an important surgery. I hurriedly went to her hospital suite in the morning to spend a few moments with her before heading to my clinic. She gave me a lingering hug. I kissed her and then went to the door reluctantly. She waved repeatedly as I moved out. I looked back, and she gave me another smile.

"As usual, I went to my clinic and successfully performed a surgical procedure on one of my patients. The patient was still under the spell of anesthesia. I had to wait until the patient became stable. I gave the necessary instructions to the attending staff and came out of the operating theater.

"It was already afternoon. I thought I would have a sip of coffee and then go back to Rose's hospital suite to join her for lunch. Laura, my secretary, rushed in to tell me that there had been several telephone calls asking me to come to Rosemarie's hospital suite immediately. Anxiously, I asked her if Rose was all right. Laura fumbled rather clumsily, feigning ignorance of the situation. She did not answer my questions and only repeated that several telephone calls had come from the hospital.

"Laura was a smart secretary. She had worked with me for quite some time. I never expected such a vague response from her. Her blank, expressionless face on that afternoon worried me. I went straight to my car and drove to the hospital as fast as I could, stopping only at red lights as I jostled through the city's heavy traffic."

The surgeon turned his face toward the window. It was obvious that something serious had happened to his wife; she might have died before he could reach the hospital. I could sense that he was trying to control a surge of emotion. I felt for him and did not know what to tell him.

He contained his emotion, looked toward me, and said, "I didn't find her in her hospital suite. Instead, I encountered police officers who had taken charge of her suite. Police had taped off the area down on the street, too, which had given me an eerie sensation as I approached the hospital.

"I was informed that Rosemarie had wanted to sit on a lounge chair on the thirteenth-floor balcony overlooking the waterfront beyond the road. The nurse settled her on a chair, and then Rose asked for some coffee. The nurse went down to get her coffee. When Rose knew that she was completely alone, she jumped from the thirteenth-floor balcony of the hospital. According to police officers, she must have determined that there were openings in the glass panels of the long balcony, and she had managed to find one and jump out through it."

Overwhelmed by my copassenger's story, I could only utter, "I'm so sorry, Surgeon; I'm extremely sorry. I understand how difficult this must be for you to talk about."

The surgeon did not speak for a while and we rode along in silence, taking in the scenery whizzing past the windows of our berth. Then, in a flat tone of resignation, he said, "After her body was released by the coroner, together with a certificate of unnatural death, I gave Rose the most loving send-off I could." He breathed another sigh.

The train slowed down and stopped at a midway station. I looked through the window to relieve the depressing effect of my copassenger's story. I watched brisk activities on the platform for the couple of minutes the train stopped. The train moved again, slowly gaining speed and leaving behind the scenes of the railway station and the town.

In an effort to change the topic, I casually asked him, "Surgeon, you must have come to India on a sightseeing tour, yes?"

"Not really," he replied, attempting a smile. "After Rose left me in such a shocking manner, I lost all interest in life. You may be surprised, but that is the truth. I do not know why, but I started thinking about the mystery of life and death, of love and loss, and all that makes life a mere spell of *maya* or illusion as viewed by the Hindu philosophers. They described the ephemeral phenomena of life, so full of passion and ambition, as a state of pseudoreality, while truth is real and eternal is imperceptible—*Brahman.* You must have heard of the philosopher Sankara of ninth-century India, who viewed all empirical knowledge as *avidya* or ignorance, and asserted that *Brahma Vidya*, or the knowledge of *Brahman*, is the only and the ultimate knowledge.

"Brahman is also the Vedic Supreme Being, originally called *Purusa.* Swami Vivekananda later expounded the philosophy as the doctrine of Advaita Vedanta. I became interested in Hindu philosophy, and hence I came to India in search of *ananda*—bliss."

Before I could vocalize my astonishment at his knowledge of Hindu philosophy, the surgeon continued, "Upanishadic metaphor defines ananda as the ability to be with the infinite—the source of finite joy. One must therefore realize the infinite to comprehend joy. In fact, I came to India in search of a *rishi* who could teach me how to know the infinite and how to attain the state of bliss. I came prepared to perform all kinds of *tyaga, or renunciation of* earthly pleasures, if that would help me to attain ananda."

He gave me a placid smile. Until this point in our brief acquaintance, I had thought of him only as a bereaved man lamenting the loss of his beloved spouse. I felt astounded to hear him speaking on transcendental themes and referring to mystic thoughts from the Upanishads.

"Surgeon, you seem to know Sanskrit! How did you learn the ancient Indian language that very few people in this country know today? You must have studied Indian philosophy to know the spiritual concepts of India."

The surgeon ignored my appreciation and replied, "Learning a language is not much of a thing. Language, by itself, does not bring you the wisdom to be able to attain the state of pure bliss. Reading books only excites one to read more. I have tried to learn in my humble way, only to become aware that I need someone who knows much more than I do and can guide me on the path to bliss."

Now I looked at him in a different light. He appeared profound. Instantly he rose to an abstract level that was far above the experiences of everyday life.

"How did you come to this realization?" I asked in astonishment.

"I had always thought that so many people before me and in circumstances much harder than mine had done tough penance in their search for bliss. Others tried hard to know the ultimate truth through their empirical knowledge and experiments. In the end, all of them came back to the same point from which they began. The eternal question mark stood glaring all the same as they tried hard to find the answer.

"Perhaps that is the most frustrating aspect of human life—the breaking points of the human ego. I realized that sometimes when people are in difficult circumstances, they feel completely baffled and make drastic decisions—terrible decisions, such as the one Rose made to end her life. I didn't want to be like that. I refused to feel frustrated. I wanted to know the truth of life and death and to seek the path of bliss in a state of mind when nothing affects you—not birth or death, love or loss—nothing. Perhaps that is the state of pure bliss. You don't cease to live; you live a life free from worldly bondage."

I did not want to interrupt in his soliloquy. The surgeon paused and then said, "I haven't achieved anything.

"I've only realized that the search for ananda is itself a delightful pursuit. Every time I went to the colossal Himalayas, I had a sublime feeling, a feeling beyond description. It is like realizing the infinite, far beyond the world of ordinary perceptions—some explainable, some unexplainable. I don't seek the peace of death; I seek a state that is free from desires and yet full of delight.

"When I stand before the Himalayas, I feel that I am face-to-face with infinity. I wonder in awe at the snowcapped solemnity that merges with infinite space, the inestimable universe. I am searching for the one who can guide me to attain the state of pure ananda, the state of delight that is far beyond the apparent world."

Suddenly, I doubted his claim of seeking ananda. I suggested, "Surgeon, perhaps the word *ananda* literally connotes joy. The fact that we are alive and enjoying the pleasures of life is itself a matter of joy—and thus ananda."

"Yes," replied the surgeon, "your concept is known as the concept of divine grace. The facts that we are born and have all the gifts of life, the gifts of procreation and of salvation, are matters of divine grace. I am alive to all that and I have tasted the pleasures of life. I now want to taste the joy of *tyaga*, which is neither enjoyment of worldly life nor salvation. That is the state of ananda—the real taste of divine grace."

I do not like to enter into controversies with others, so I did not interrupt the surgeon. He said that he had come to India a few times and visited many Himalayan sites that Hindus visit on pilgrimage. He went to remote and difficult-to-reach altitudes of the Himalayas in search of sages who, he thought, knew the ultimate truth far beyond the reach of ordinary men with worldly knowledge.

He said, "It became my pursuit—my devotion, if I might say."

I could not resist asking him what he really meant by the search to attain ananda.

Calm and poised, he replied, "Well, I really don't know how to answer your question. Perhaps it is something that comes from within. It's a sort of realization that doesn't pertain to flesh and blood, touch and feel; something that can't be had through laboratory experiments and reading books and other such exercises."

He paused thoughtfully and then said, "In age after age, men have sought the knowledge of the ultimate reality, traveled through different paths and processes, and suffered immense penances. Nonetheless, the mystery remained unresolved. The most baffling aspect of the quest is that those who could know the unknown also became mysterious."

Now he gave me a natural smile.

After a while, I asked him about his trips to the Himalayas, and he replied again that he went in search of a sage. I asked him how he could believe that sages of the millennia-old Vedic-Upanishadic era lived today. The surgeon narrated the story that convinced him about the existence of sages.

He told me that once he went up to the Himalayan glacier at a point called *Gomukh*. Gomukh is an enormous cavern of melting snow from which the turbulent Bhagirathi River rushes down to the township of Gangotri and flows farther down to meet the Alakananda stream at Devprayag. He said that during his trip to Gomukh, he caught a fever and a cold. Trekking down the mountains in the frosty wind, he somehow reached the town of Gangotri.

Here, Hindu pilgrims gather to offer worship in the temple of the *Ganga*—the Ganges River, believed to be a deity. On the right bank of the river, pilgrims take dips into the flowing waters and offer oblations in a Shiva temple. The Bhagirathi is the first stream of the Ganges.

As the surgeon managed to trek down to Gangotri, he found an ascetic sitting in the lotus position inside a natural archway of rocks, a cave-like formation. Ritual burning of firewood brightened the cave. The ascetic was absorbed in deep meditation. Before him were an open book and a wood pencil for those who wanted to write their questions. The ascetic answered in writing. He would not speak because to remain *mauna*, mute, was a part of his penance.

The surgeon entered the cave heated and lighted by the fire and bowed his head down, as was customary in paying respect to an ascetic.

The surgeon told me, "The ascetic wrote in perfect English, *Please go back and take a dip into the holy waters of the Bhagirathi.* I wondered how the ascetic knew English. I wrote back that I was running a high fever. The ascetic replied, *That is precisely why you should take a dip*."

My copassenger said that an unexplainable urge prompted him. Like a spellbound being, he went back to the ice-cold waters of the fast-flowing Bhagirathi. In an unknown passion, he threw off his mountaineering jacket, his woolen clothes, his cap, and his boots and took not one but three dips into the stream. He said that immediately after he took the dips, he felt a great sense of relief, a sense of indescribable rejuvenation.

Feeling amazingly at ease, he came back to the ascetic and bowed down to pay his most sincere respects. Mouni Baba, the mute ascetic, extended his right hand over the surgeon's head to bless him silently and then wrote the following: *Henceforth, you will never have a fever. And remember that a diffident man can have neither bliss nor the knowledge of the ultimate truth.*

"Believe me," said the surgeon, "from that moment till today I have never had a fever or cold. Besides, it was obvious that the Mouni Baba, by his transcendental power, already knew my thoughts and my limitations. How would you explain that? Is it not miraculous? So I believe in his words. I believe, as he said, that a diffident man could have neither bliss nor knowledge of the ultimate. I do not want to be diffident; I have no hesitation in trusting the yogi. I believe that one can attain ananda."

I ventured to observe in a lighter vein, "It could be just a coincidence. One might be a healthy person and not get a fever or cold. Does that necessarily mean anything supernatural? You are a surgeon; you would know better."

"Yes, but how would you explain the instant disappearance of all symptoms of a severe Himalayan cold as soon as I took dips into the freezing cold waters? How could such a delightful sense of well-being refresh me? How could the sage know my thoughts? Aren't all these astounding, inexplicable aspects of the experience?"

"I suppose I have no ready explanation for that," I replied.

"To believe is a delightful experience, my friend," said the surgeon, "and to disbelieve is denying that experience to one's own self. I have no doubt that Mouni Baba was a great sage. Besides, it was impossible to know anything more about him because after writing his blessings, the baba asked me to leave him alone. Later, I went to that same cave and searched for him. I again went to Gangotri and trekked as far as possible in search of the baba, but I could not find him. I went to many other places in the Himalayas and asked many people. Nobody could tell me about the Mouni Baba. I think he was a real sage with great spiritual power. I am still in search of the exalted yogi. If he is in this world, he must be in the Himalayas only. I guess the baba has gone to a still-higher altitude to attain a higher level of enlightenment."

I countered him no more, as we were almost at our destination and I wanted to part on a positive note. The surgeon and I both commented that it had been fascinating meeting one another and having our lives touch in this unique way. Soon we took leave of each other at the New Delhi railway station.

* * *

Years later, memories of that conversation on the train came flooding back when my wife, Reba, and I went on a sightseeing tour to the Himalayan region of Uttar Pradesh, part of which is now in the new state of Uttarakhand. In Haridwar Circuit House, I met a crowd of Western and Indian tourists who were particularly interested in attending Swami Sadananda's talk on the Rig Veda. The swami was to deliver his address the next morning in his *ashram* on the Rishikesh Road, a few miles from Haridwar.

I had no idea about Swami Sadananda and his achievements. Nonetheless, Reba and I joined the team to attend the talk.

Haridwar was already a crowded place. We traveled from Haridwar on the mountainous Devprayag-Rishikash road that traverses the picturesque Himalayan landscape of Garhwal alongside the Alokananda stream of the Ganges. The ashram was located in a serene environment away from the tumult of the town. The refreshing sanctuary reminded me of the imagery of the ashrams of the ancient *rishis* (sages), where devoted disciples learned both pragmatic and spiritual knowledge from their respected gurus.

The swami's ashram combined the Gurukul tradition of ancient India with modern amenities, complete with a guesthouse and an auditorium. Shaven-headed disciples of the swami were engaged in their respective duties, including receiving the guests who attended the ashram to listen to the discourse of the swami. There were only a limited number of interested listeners present. Everyone knew that the swami would deliver his talk on the Rig Veda in English.

After we sat down in the auditorium, the swami appeared clad in ankle-length saffron attire with a matching turban covering his head. He was a tall, well-built man with a tuft of untrimmed, copper-gray beard. He returned the greetings of his audience and disciples, briefly wishing them peace and well-being. Without wasting time, he straightway began his introduction to the Rig Veda.

He said that gurus of the Upanishads consolidated, compiled, and interpreted the oral tradition of the metaphysical perceptions of the Rig Veda. That is precisely why the Upanishads are known as Vedanta or the end of the Vedas. The swami described the Rig Veda, which he said is believed to be world's first known cosmogony and perception of the Supreme Being. It perceives the ceaseless rhythm of creation, sustenance, and destruction as an eternal and all-pervading process.

He said that the Vedic rishis perceived the universe as infinite and eternal, a continuum of ceaseless sequences that never stop changing from life to death to life again. The changes are inevitable and sublime, and that is why the cosmos is never old and ever fresh. He added that later, the Upanishads taught that the greatest ananda for human beings is that we are able to perceive these changes and feel the glory of ever-flowing life. To comprehend the Rig Vedic perception, one must be able to accept that budding and shedding, birth and death, light and darkness, and many other apparent incongruities are part of the invariable cosmic process that includes every living being, every kernel of grain, and every chromosome. In this process, seasons change, and flowers bloom, wither, and shed their petals. Fruits grow, ripen, and decay. This endless, all-pervading process of change is irrevocable.

Nonetheless, there is no change in the force behind this continuous sequence of change. The Rig Veda names this changeless, imperceptible, and all-pervading Supreme Power as *Purusa*. Rishis of the Upanishads renamed Purusa as *Brahman*. Ancient Indian philosophers conceived the totality of the perceptible phenomena and imperceptible cause and causality of cosmic dynamism to be a single principle, which is termed Vedic Monism. Later in the ninth century AD, the philosopher Sankara introduced the philosophy of the Advaita Vedanta. Swami Vivekananda interpreted this philosophy to the Western world.

The crux of the philosophy is that the constantly changing cosmic phenomena are mere apparitions because they are fleeting. Brahman, the cause or the creator and the destroyer of every perceptible and imperceptible phenomenon, is constant, unchangeable, and indiscernible.

Simply knowing what is apparent, therefore, is not real knowledge. One must realize Brahman, the ultimate reality. *Brahma Vidiya*, or the realization and knowledge of Brahman, are the ultimate knowledge. This perception, said the swami, is the basic teaching of the Upanishads.

When the swami made this last statement, there were some whispers among the listeners. People wanted to ask questions. The swami raised his hand to stop them and resumed, unbothered.

He said that we must be conscious of this eternal process as we seek to understand the hymns of the Rig Veda. He reminded us that Vedic sages had searched their hearts and felt the existence of the Supreme Being. It is fascinating and reflective, said the swami, to follow the Rig Vedic sequence of the creation process. The swami said that he referred to the Upanishads because the Upanishads are the beginning of the entire body of post-Vedic literature, which, in the course of time, diversified into six Indian philosophies. Archeologists and historians have indeed discovered the traces of the lost civilization of the pre-Vedic Indus Valley Civilization of circa 3600–1200 BC. We, however, need not go into that in understanding the Rig Veda.

"In the hymns of creation—the *Nāsadīya Sūkta* in the Rig Veda—the sages perceived the cosmic situation before the creation process began. They described the state as one of absolute void when nothing existed: neither matter nor energy, neither space nor time. The sages chanted that neither nonbeing nor being was yet; there was neither space nor heavens afar. There was no water, bottomless and unfathomable, no death, and no immortality. There was no night, no day. In absolute emptiness, the One breathed. Beyond that nothing whatsoever was.

"Is it not a beautiful description of absolute void?" asked the swami.

There were murmurs of assent as those of us gathered around him tried to envisage the vastness of what he was describing.

He continued to explain that Vedic rishis, however, perceived the primordial and the eternal spirit, yet not named Purusa, as the absolute potency respiring in the atmosphere of absolute void. In the same set of hymns, they observed that existence was ingrained in nonexistence.

The rishis invoked their spiritual insight. They searched their hearts and perceived the darkness that swathed darkness as the world surged all over and the atmosphere was sheathed in pregnant propensity. Immense force of passion brought forth the One. Thereupon rose desire, charged with the primeval seed and force of power, as potency lay below and the spirit above. The rishis wondered from where creations come and where they go. The immense surge revealed the gods, who surely knew from where they came and where they go. Streams of creation have flowed ceaselessly ever since. Only the One who observed from the highest heaven knows.

When neither nonbeing nor being was yet and existence remained ingrained in nonexistence, Vedic sages perceived but did not yet conceive the absolute, Purusa—the primordial, all-pervading, infinite cosmic being that breathed in the atmosphere of absolute airlessness. Out of that absolute potency emerged the gods, and they worshipped their creator, Purusa. The Vedic rishis chanted hymns that made the Vedas.

They wondered from where duality crept up—darkness upon darkness or darkness concealing darkness. It all began with the primal desire to create when the seeds and the germs of the cosmic spirit rose. Sages who searched in their hearts discovered the kinship between existence and nonexistence.

Who knows whence the phenomena of the gods first came into being? What hymns, what chants did the deities sing to offer their adoration to their creator Purusa, the primal spirit? Who knows whence all deities offered their worship to their creator?

The swami explained that Vedic rishis named the spectrum of the amazing phenomena they perceived as gods and goddesses created by Purusa, the Supreme Being. They wondered in what hymns the gods and goddesses offer their adulation to their creator. The rishis chanted that only those versed in the recitals and the meter, those who knew the rites and the cosmic process, knew how the deities offer worship to their creator.

The Rig Veda contains the perceptions of seven godlike rishis led by the sage *Brahaspati,* or *Bramanaspati,* who knew the creation process. The sages are immortal and shine eternally as the bright stars in the *Saptarsimondāla*—the galaxy of seven stars, later called Ursa Major in the West. The "Hymn on Brahaspati" describes the immortal rishis as deities.

The next question was, who appeared as the first created phenomenon? Who emerged as the first wonderment—the first god created by Purusa to make all the marvels of gods and goddesses perceptible?

The Vedic rishis perceived the first cosmic phenomena, the first wonder, and the first god was made of vast grains of flaming gold. They chanted that in the beginning rose *Hiranyagarbha*, filled with grains of gold, born as the only lord of the created beings. He fixed and held the earth and heaven.

The swami added that Vedic cosmic being created Hiranyagarbha, the god of gold germs and the blazing source of light, heat, and life, when there was absolute darkness and nothing was visible. The moment Hiranyagarbha appeared as the first god created by Purusa, darkness disappeared. Hiranyagarbha's charioteer, *Aruna*, the dawn, drove him up in a chariot drawn by seven white stallions from the utmost East. Heaven's beautiful daughter, *Usas*, the goddess of the dawn, dressed in immaculate white, stood atop the snowcapped mountains to welcome Hiranyagarbha. The most delightful, dreamlike vision then overwhelmed the sky.

At the day's end when Hiranyagarbha bade adieu, Usas's exquisite sister, *Sandhyā*, the twilight, stood upon the western sphere clad in crimson attire to bid adieu to the god of blazing gold. Sandhyā's dazzling reflection swung on the ocean waves. The chariot slowly faded away. Sandhyā then changed into her dark and serene, star-studded robe and took everyone to the realm of *susupti*—the serenity of slumber.

Subsequently Hiranyagarbha, the powerful god made of flaming gold, was named *Savitar* and finally *Surya*, or the sun.

The swami narrated that as Hiranyagarbha cast the first spell of light, the Vedic rishis perceived many gods. They perceived *Agni,* the lord of fire; *Varuna,* lord of the sky; *Indra,* lord of heaven; *Soma,* lord of the sacred drink; *Yama,* the lord of death; and an endless manifestation of gods and goddesses that followed in an unceasing sequence of amazement. The spectacular phenomena of the cosmic universe transpired in the continuum of splendor.

Vedic sages chanted the rhythmic hymn of yet another quest: Who is the greatest grandeur? Who rules the vibrant world? Who ordains breath and slumber? Who is the lord of the beings?

The Vedic sages asked themselves, what god shall we adore with our oblation?

They realized that the entirety of the cosmic phenomena of the gods and goddesses are an amazing spectacle of constant change. They also realized that the existence of the all-pervading, eternal reality can only be felt, not perceived like the gamut of gods and goddesses.

The rishis of the Rig Veda did not assert in so many words that time is a constituent of the universe. They did not proclaim that space, time, and causality are fundamental to the entire observable universe. They did not speculate about the Big Bang theory. They did not elaborate on the huge, flaming golden ball. They did not chant quantum-relativistic models of subatomic physics or describe the interaction of electrons and positrons of the electromagnetic field. They only admired the eternal and infinite flow of the gold-germs that made it possible to perceive the amazing phenomena of the gods and goddesses.

The swami stated that Vedic rishis were the original poets of the ultimate wisdom. He averred that poets never elucidate their poems because elucidation is prosaic. The Upanishadic teachers later explained that even the gods could not pit themselves against Purusa. The entirety of reality is just one monistic whole when viewed from the angle of monistic metaphysics. Apparent diversity is nothing but the diverse perception of the endless plurality of the ever-changing phenomena caused by Purusa.

The wise realized the Brahman and thus could attain Brahman. They knew that the gods are only participants: regulated and regulating agents involved in the eternal dynamics of time and space that create innumerable phenomena of gods and goddesses.

Gods and goddesses—*devas* and *devis*—can never outshine their master, who leads them without being caught up in the cosmic process. It is in the continuance of the infinite and eternal process that the gods and goddesses symbolize the wonderment of their creator, their regulator—Purusa. The Vedic rishis were delighted only to admire the eternal harmony and splendor of the ever-changing phenomena of the universe.

In the Rig Veda, the rishis asked themselves as many as nine times, which god shall we adore?

Finally, they realized the ultimate reality and chanted the hymns:

> Purusa is all pervading, ingrained in perceptible and
> imperceptible existence,
> The Lord of Immortality as He manifests greater and still
> greater with every oblation we offer.

And thus,

> One alone exists.
> Sages call Him by various names.

The swami concluded his discourse by chanting a Sanskrit mantra, wishing blissful delight for all humankind on the earth.

Despite the changes brought by age, the Swami's voice, manner of speaking, and looks closely resembled the surgeon I had encountered on the train. I waited until the crowd of admirers thinned; I wanted to confirm if the surgeon in quest of ananda was now Swami Sadananda. But before I could ask him, he raised his hand and uttered in Sanskrit, "*Sarve amritasya putrah*," which means, "Every one of us is born out of the nectar."

14

In 1960, I was in Silchar, headquarters of undivided Cachar district of Assam bordering East Pakistan. It was little more than a decade since India was truncated into India and Pakistan as two independent nation-states. Bengali-speaking people thickly populated East Pakistan and the Cachar district of Assam.

On February 21, 1952, Pakistani authorities, functioning from West Pakistan, declared Urdu the official language of the far-flung territories of East and West Pakistan. Bengali-speaking people of East Pakistan, especially students of Dhaka University and Dhaka Medical College, came out in processions protesting against the imposition of Urdu on the Bengali-speaking people.

Pakistani security forces cracked down on the protesters, killing and injuring many. They arrested most of the activists, including important leaders of the Bengali language movement. That was the point when the Bangladesh liberation movement burgeoned, with Sheikh Mujibur Rahman as the most popular leader and the Awami League as the most popular political party in East Pakistan. February 21 has been declared by UNESCO as International Mother Language Day.

The developments in East Pakistan inspired the Bengali-speaking people of the Barak Valley (Cachar district) and Assamese-speaking people of the Brahmaputra valley to demand their respective languages as the official languages of the areas they inhabited. Earlier in 1950, *Assam Sahitya Sabha*—the Assam Literary Association—resolved that the Assamese language should be made the official language of Assam. The Assam Sahitya Sabha and other Assamese forums reiterated the demand from time to time. Assamese students decided to launch a language movement similar to the movement in East Pakistan.

The next stimulus to the demand for Assamese as the official language of the state came when in December 1952, Congress leader Potti Sriramalu died fasting in demand for a Telugu-speaking Andhra state. The death of Potti Sriramalu created a grave situation for the Madras Presidency, and Prime Minister Pandit Jawaharlal Nehru conceded to creation of Andhra state for Telugu-speaking people.

The question of the reorganization of states on a linguistic basis in India has a long history. British census commissioner G. A. Grierson, in a linguistic survey of India and the census of 1911, identified 179 languages and 544 dialects used by the people of British India. The Indian National Congress Party, in its Lucknow session held in 1917, resolved to carve a Telugu-speaking province out of the Madras Presidency.

In 1920, M. K. Gandhi, on his return from South Africa, took over leadership of Congress. He drafted a constitution and a manifesto for the party, which included creation of linguistic provinces in India.

In 1947, Congress passed a resolution to reorganize states in independent India based on the languages spoken by the majority of people in the states. On November 27, 1947, Prime Minister Pandit Jawaharlal Nehru declared in the constituent assembly that his government accepted in principle the creation of linguistic states.

In 1948, the constituent assembly appointed a commission to recommend the reorganization of states on a linguistic basis. S. K. Dhar headed the commission. The commission, however, reported that the creation of linguistic states in India would be counter to the greater interest of the nation. Instead, the commission recommended reorganization of states on other criteria, such as geographical contiguity, financial self-sufficiency, administrative convenience, and capacity for future development.

The creation of Andhra Pradesh had already set the trend for linguistic states. In 1953, Pandit Nehru appointed another commission, known as the States Reorganization Commission, headed by Justice Fazal Ali. The commission, in its report submitted in 1955, recommended that the language of the majority should be the criterion for fixing the boundaries of reorganized states. The Parliament of India accordingly passed the States Reorganization Act of 1956, providing that the language of the majority people in a state would be the official language of the state. The act thus legalized the principle that the language of the majority of people in a state shall be the official language of the state.

Assamese was the majority language in Assam, and Bengali was the language of the second-largest community in the state. Until the British reorganized areas of the adjacent provinces of Assam and Bengal, the two linguistic communities in Assam lived in peace and amity. The longstanding problem of Assamese-Bengali antipathy was the outcome of British political maneuvers.

Sylhet was originally a part of Dhaka district of the former East Bengal. In the process of reorganizing the territories, Sylhet became a district and center of higher education and commerce. Subsequently, the British administration in India incorporated Sylhet into the province of Assam, and it remained so until the referendum held in 1947. Bengali Hindus of Sylhet had the option either to immigrate to the Cachar district of Assam or remain in Sylhet in East Pakistan. Large numbers of Bengali-speaking Hindus of Sylhet immigrated. The Bengali-speaking Karimganj subdivision of Sylhet, however, remained appended to the Cachar district of Assam.

Thus, after the enactment of the language act, it became lawful for the Assamese people to declare Assamese as the official language of Assam, with sufficient safeguards for the Bengali-speaking community and other linguistic communities living in the state. Unfortunately, language riots began in Assam before the Assam Legislative Assembly, by a state law, could declare Assamese as the official language of the state.

Bengali-speaking students pursuing studies in Assam Engineering College, Assam Medical College, and various other educational institutions in Assam under the Guwahati University had to flee their hostels and boarding houses due to the uprising of 1959–60. The situation became further complicated when the Assam State Language Bill was introduced in the state's legislative assembly in 1960. The bill proposed Assamese as the only official language of the state for education and administration. The proposed legislation sought to compel those speaking languages other than Assamese, including the Bengali-speaking community and various hill tribes inhabiting Assam, to pursue their studies and carry out all official transactions in Assamese.

After the founding of the Guwahati University in 1948, schools and colleges in Assam naturally changed their affiliation from Calcutta University to Guwahati University. Bengali students, particularly in the Cachar district, were worried about their future. They were opposed to the imposition of Assamese as the medium of education. Tension grew up all over the district.

In the court campus at Silchar, an uncanny silence prevailed. No one spoke on the topic but everyone felt concerned. Outside the court in every meeting, whether in public places or on street corners, the only point discussed was the Assam Language Bill. A sense of suspicion and distrust grew up between the Assamese officials posted to Silchar and the Bengali community in Silchar. Students in the Cachar district were particularly concerned because the Assam Language Bill, if passed, would have a tremendous impact on their educations and futures. They sought to change the medium of education for the district from Assamese to Bengali.

Regardless of who were ancestrally from Sylhet or Cachar, it was true that Bengali and Bengali only was the principal language of the Cachar district, also known as the Barak Valley (as opposed to the Brahmaputra Valley). Tribal inhabitants of the North Cachar Hills, however, had their own dialect. Besides, Bisnupriya Manipuries and a handful of other tribes inhabiting the district spoke their own languages. Nevertheless, they all used Bengali for all official purposes and business transactions. Bengali was the language of the court, as well as the land revenue and land tenure system in the district.

Against the above backdrop, principal officials of the civil, revenue, and police administrations, and most other government officials, were Assamese from the Brahmaputra Valley posted to the Cachar district. All subordinate staff, including the police force, however, were comprised of local Bengali recruits. This was because, since the Assamese linguistic community was the majority of the state's population, there were a greater number of educated Assamese government officials than Bengali government officials.

Since independence, it had been the policy of the Assam government to introduce Assamese all over Assam to create a homogenous language and culture in the state. Assam had a colorful demography with many tribes of the hills and the plains, each with their own language and culture. The policy of introducing Assamese as the only language of the state was one of the causes of fragmentation of the state.

Riots in the Assam valley districts, beginning in 1959–60, not only terrorized Bengali students, but also scared Assamese officials posted to the Barak Valley for fear of possible retaliation. The district administration in Silchar promulgated prohibitory orders under the criminal procedure code, banning assembly of five or more persons, carrying of arms, and the staging of processions and rallies. The deputy commissioner and the superintendent of police asked for reinforcement of the local police force with officers and men from the Central Reserve Police battalions. Assamese officials in the district used armed police guards to protect themselves from probable retaliation by Bengali students. Rifle-wielding police guards stood alert at their residences and offices.

As a result, an artificial situation ensued that was disproportionate to the incident-free, nonviolent opposition of the activists to the Assam Language Bill. Armed police officers guarded the court and office complexes. Magistrates in police jeeps patrolled the streets of Silchar town, aggravating the situation further. Under the circumstances, local members of the staff at court and government offices, lawyers, and their clerks became suspects under the watchful eyes of the armed police. The mute faces of the local people reflected impressions of humiliation and resentment.

As I came to know the local elite, I discovered that most of the permanent residents of Silchar town were of Sylhet origin. They dominated the social scenario of the town. In their urge to prove allegiance to the state of Assam, they preferred Assamese government officials to Bengali officials. Perhaps their subdued feeling had its reflex in idolizing Assamese officials, which they never really meant to do.

The underlying truth was that by a fluke of political change, a large chunk of Bengali-speaking people from Sylhet became a minority community in the state of Assam. They realized that the dominant political power was with the Assamese majority. Politically conscious, educated members of the Bengali middle class deliberately lionized Assamese government officials to get their jobs done. But chronic ambivalence between the Assamese and the Bengalis of Assam had existed since the time of Assam premier Gopinath Bordoloi, who vehemently objected to appending a part of the Bengali-speaking Sylhet district to Assam.

Another conspicuous aspect was that indigenous Cachar Bengalis could not see eye-to-eye with the Sylhet Bengalis and vice versa. In the process, what transpired in Silchar civil society was an undercurrent of the tripartite division between the Sylhet Bengalis, Cachar Bengalis, and Assamese government officials, who administered the district according to the policy planned by their political bosses.

I paid a courtesy call to an honorable member of the *Lok Sabha*—the House of the People in the Parliament of India. He was an elderly, unassuming personality with confidence in his convictions. Earlier, he had been a member of the constituent assembly and an elected member of parliament in the first Indian parliamentary elections held in 1951. Since then, he had retained his seat in the Lok Sabha. He represented the scheduled caste constituency of the Karimganj subdivision of the Cachar district.

The old MP cordially received me and introduced me to his daughter, who did her master's degree in philosophy from the University of Delhi and was teaching in the local Guru Charan College.

In course of conversation with the old MP, the Assam State Language Bill introduced in the Assam Legislative Assembly came up for discussion. His daughter initiated the discussion and mentioned the growing discontent among the students in her college. The MP commented that the problem of ethnic identity, language, and culture had existed in India since British times as the most complicated issue affecting the vast multitude of Indian people.

He said, "You know, the people of my constituency have a distinct identity, culture, and language. They need to preserve their culture and language as a distinct community apart from the Bengalis from Sylhet. Indeed, they read and write in Bengali as I do, because there was no other language in the schools when we were students. The British introduced the Bengali language as the medium of instruction in Assam in 1837, soon after they established their rule in Assam as an extended part of the Bengal Presidency. But the people of my constituency, like so many other tribes, clans, and communities in Assam, continued to speak their own language that is their mother tongue. It is distinctly different from the language spoken by the Bengalis from Sylhet, who are now permanent residents of this district. Even if you call Cachar Bengali a dialect, it is clearly different from the dialect spoken by the Bengalis from Sylhet. People from Sylhet too do not speak standard Bengali. They speak a dialect of eastern Bengal."

The public leader took a sip of tea. "The original inhabitants of the Cachar district speak their own language, which is a local version of Assamese. Besides, we have the Manipuri people in our district who speak the *Bishnupriya* language, and some others speak *Meitei*. There are Nagas in the Cachar district. In addition, since the district is adjacent to the Lushai Hills, the Kashi and Jayantia Hills, and the North Cachar Hills, there are Khasi, Jayantia, Dimasa, Lushai, Hmar, Kuki, and other such languages too. In fact, in Assam there are numerous local languages spoken by many different tribes and clans. Nevertheless, the fact remains that the majority of the people in Assam speak, read, and write in the Assamese language. It is our national policy that the language of the majority community is the official language of the state. I am sure you know the provisions of the State Reorganization Act of 1956."

He looked at me. I nodded in affirmation.

Obviously, the MP was a Cachar Bengali. Nonetheless, the MP had been representing his constituency of the scheduled caste community in Karimganj, which was initially a part of the Bengali-speaking Sylhet district of East Bengal. He, however, claimed that the people of his constituency spoke a variant of the Assamese language, even though they had originally lived in the Bengali-speaking Sylhet district and did so until the partition of India.

The MP took another sip from his cup, gave me a smile, and then resumed. "Perhaps you know that according to the 1951 census, the growth of Assamese-speaking people in Assam was 150 percent. The census figure indeed appears fantastic, almost absurd in terms of natural growth. But that was, in fact, the revelation of the inevitable truth. It was the first census after independence. People felt free to declare their languages. So the indigenous people of the Cachar and Goalpara districts, and the Muslim inhabitants of Assam, especially those living in the Goalpara, Garo Hills, and Nowgong districts, could freely declare themselves as Assamese-speaking people.

"Of course, Bengali is the language of the second-largest community in Assam. Nevertheless, under the provisions of the State Reorganization Act, Assamese, being the language of the overwhelming majority of the people of the state, must be the official language of the state. Besides, the 1951 census has clearly established that the largest majority of the people in Assam desire Assamese as the official language of the state."

Looking toward his daughter, he said, "Well, there might be some teething trouble. Let's not forget that in the referendum held in July 1947, it was established that Assamese was the majority language of Assam. The option for Sylhet Hindus was either to migrate to Assam and accept Assamese as their language, or to remain in East Pakistan and retain Bengali as their language. Indeed, it is very hard, almost impossible, for the older generation to change their mother tongue, and perhaps no one would ask them to do so. Besides, the medium of education and administration is not always the mother tongue. English was never the mother tongue of Indians, but they had to accept it and learn it because it was the language of education and administration during British rule. The young generation should have no difficulty in learning Assamese, which has the same script as Bengali. They must accept Assamese as the medium of education and administration."

The MP's daughter blurted out, "But in our district, Bengali is the language of the majority. It has always been the medium of education. We all studied in Bengali when we were in school. If Assamese were suddenly imposed on the Bengali-speaking people of our district, people would naturally resist. No one other than the Assamese officials posted to this district and members of their families speak Assamese. For their children, there is a separate school. I'm sure students would vehemently resist if Assamese were imposed as the medium of education in the Cachar district."

The MP replied with an indulgent smile, "Historically, the original inhabitants of the Barak Valley spoke their own language from the time the valley was ruled by the king of Cachar. Raja Gobind Chandra, the last king of Cachar, was assassinated by some conspirators on April 24, 1830, at a place called Haritikar. The British administration took over the kingdom on the grounds that the king died intestate, without any apparent heir. On June 30, 1830, T. Fisher, an officer of the British army, was appointed in charge of revenue collection and administration of the Cachar kingdom. In 1833, the headquarters of the kingdom were shifted to Dudpatli and then to Silchar. The plains of the former Cachar kingdom were formally annexed to the British dominion in August 1832 by a proclamation of the governor general in council, and the area was placed under the administration of a superintendent."

He continued, "It was only natural that the people here assimilated many words and expressions of the Bengali language rather than Assamese because of their everyday dealings with their immediate neighbors, the people of Sylhet. The North Cachar and Mikir Hills stood between the Barak River Valley and the Brahmaputra Valley, thus facilitating contact between the people of Cachar and Sylhet. The other historical factor is that in 1874, Assam, including the Barak Valley, was made a part of the Bengal Presidency with Bengali as the official language."

Looking to me, he continued, "If you look carefully, you will find that there are many things in common between the Bengali-speaking people of Cachar and the people of the Brahmaputra Valley in terms of both language and culture. During British rule, Bengalis dominated the whole of eastern India, including Assam. They swallowed up the language and culture of the original inhabitants of the extra-large Bengal Presidency as an inevitable sociological and historical process.

"Now, after independence, the situation has changed, and people of every state in India are seeking to adopt the language of the majority as the official language of their state. The demand not only reflects the popular will but is also in consonance with national policy and the law. The Barak Valley is now a part of Assam for all practical purposes, and the people here must choose Assamese as the official language. This is the import of the States Reorganization Act enacted by the Parliament as the law of the land," concluded the MP.

* * *

Shops in Silchar drew shutters down in protest against the language bill as was introduced in the Assam Legislative Assembly. Students in schools and colleges went on strike. District administration had already banned meetings and processions under provisions of the criminal procedure code. The deputy commissioner of the district set up a round-the-clock control room in his residential office. Executive magistrates were on duty in rotation all twenty-four hours. Armed police in open trucks and executive magistrates in jeeps patrolled the town and the nearby areas. As a precautionary measure, almost all student leaders were put under arrest. The entire town looked like a seized territory. Lawyers stopped attending the courts. Sheepishly, office staff went to their offices and remained in their seats until their duty hours ended. They could neither afford to lose their jobs nor to annoy the students—their children, brothers, and sisters.

Senior police and paramilitary officials brought to the Cachar district on special duty thronged the Circuit House and other available accommodations. Tension mounted. Suddenly and for no ostensible reason, in the middle of the night distant slogans of Hindu-Muslim riot disturbed the tranquility of the sleeping town. The slogans came from two distinct areas of the town. Flames of faraway fires flickered against the night sky.

During this period, the Assam government declared that Assamese would be the only medium of education all over Assam. The order provided that in Bengali-speaking areas of the state, students must take a two-year course in the Assamese language to facilitate learning in Assamese.

On May 19, 1960, right at the break of the dawn, a few young students, quietly and one by one, managed to enter Silchar railway station. They sat on the railway tracks, picketing against the movement of trains to and from Silchar. That was how they planned to protest peacefully from six a.m. to six p.m. against the imposition of the Assamese language.

Rifle-wielding policemen from a special police battalion stood guard in the railway station. Executive magistrates were put on duty in rotation in the stationmaster's office. They were to give on-the-spot orders as and when necessary. From morning until three p.m., the first magistrate was on duty. According to him, the students squatted peacefully. They did not shout slogans nor did they do anything else to aggravate the situation. The magistrate said that he had nothing to do except take tea with the stationmaster and chat.

At three p.m., a senior magistrate relieved him. Soon after he took over, the booming sound of gunshots was heard from the station area. Simultaneously, truckloads of armed police rushed to patrol the town. The magistrate on duty reported that suddenly the students became violent, and police had to open fire on them, terminating the lives of eleven students.

Another story was that the magistrate on duty reported by phone to the deputy commissioner's control room that the situation in the station had gone out of control. A deputy inspector general of police (DIG) was resting at the Circuit House. He was asked by the control room to rush to the railway station.

There was a brick wall with an arched gate separating the roadside and the railway station, in an area called Tarapur in Silchar. Reportedly, even before alighting from his jeep, the DIG shouted, "Fire!" and police opened fire. Ironically, the DIG concerned was a Bengali officer.

Whatever the truth, the entire town was overwhelmed with grief at the sudden loss of eleven young lives. Next morning, people in a silent mourning procession, under strict police guard, removed the eleven dead bodies and took them to the cremation ground for last rites.

Next day, there was neither a lawyer nor a litigant present in the district judge's court at Silchar. The judge sat on his seat on the dais, and the only other persons present from his office were his bench assistant and a peon. Outside the courtroom were police officers and policemen on duty.

The court had always been a public place open to all. The prohibitory order barred five or more persons from moving or gathering at one place. But the order could not prohibit an individual from entering the courtroom. One by one, a batch of students entered the courtroom, led by a girl student of the local Guru Charan College. Under the law, police couldn't arrest a person within a courtroom unless ordered to do so by the presiding judge. The students entering the courtroom hadn't committed any offence for which the district judge could proclaim an order of punishment.

The girl who led the students in was the daughter of a retired magistrate, ancestrally from Sylhet and permanently settled in Silchar. Her brother was then a serving magistrate in the Assam cadre. In the circumstances, the district judge thought it proper to quietly flee the courtroom by a rear door to his retiring chamber. The magistrate's sister ascended the dais and sat on the judge's vacant chair. She presided over a mock trial, with other students acting as the prosecuting and defending lawyers. At the conclusion of the mock trial, she pronounced a death sentence on the chief minister of Assam for committing the cold-blooded murder of eleven students.

After the students laid down their lives for their mother tongue in Silchar, the government of Assam appointed an inquiry commission with Justice Gopalji Mehrotra as the head to inquire into the police shooting on May 19, 1960, at Silchar, and also into the language riots in Goreswar and certain other places in the Assam valley. The report never saw the light of the day. The government of Assam, however, made Bengali a medium of education and official transactions in the Barak Valley.

Subsequently, the Cachar district split into three political and administrative districts: Cachar, Karimganj, and Hailakandi.

15

Reba enchanted everyone and entranced me as she presented the colorful *Laiharaoba*—dance of the gods, a well-known form of Manipuri dancing. I was one of the inconspicuous student-organizers of the music conference organized by the Indian People's Theatre Association and held in Guwahati, the principal city of Assam state in India.

It was a most gorgeous and elegant dance in which she was the cynosure. As one of the backstage managers of the conference, I only admired her as an intriguingly charming maiden, who in her own right won a three-year research scholarship of the Sangeet Natak Academy—the music and dance academy of India, a central government institution. She opted for the dance academy at Imphal, capital city of Manipur state. Her résumé and photo were published in the Indian media. At home, my mother, while glancing through a newspaper, commented within my hearing, "Look at the photo of this pretty girl. I wish I could have a daughter-in-law like her."

A couple of years later, I encountered her again at Silchar, the district headquarters of the Cachar district. It was an unexpected coincidence and a delightful surprise. In fact, I came to the local music school to pay a courtesy call to the principal of the school, as a matter of usual protocol. As I approached the school, the droning of a tambura, strains of a violin, beats of *mridang* drum, and tinkling of *nupur* (anklets) filled the air with melody and rhythm, instantly rousing my urge to join the artistes. I entered the school, justifying to myself that I had only come to pay a courtesy call.

I stepped inside and entered the main hall. A sundry group of artistes of different ages and sexes was sitting on a rug spread over the permanent stage in the hall. As I entered, the music stopped abruptly, and all eyes were on the stranger.

The principal, a woman in her forties, came forward with a broad smile. We greeted each other with namaskars. I had made an appointment with her, and she knew that I would be visiting her school on that evening. The woman said in her local accent, "Welcome to my school; I already know about you." She added in a flattering tone, "I also know that you sing *Rabindra Sangeet* very well. It's my pleasure to receive you in my school."

Her high-flown words embarrassed me. I didn't know how to reply to her overture.

A spark of thrill electrified me as I spotted the dancer, who had captivated me at the music conference. She was standing at the center of the floor, her eyes filled with intriguing curiosity. Next to her were the old dance guru and a few young girls. The guru held a Manipuri mridang drum suspended from his neck by a piece of cloth. Later, I came to know that he was her original guru before she stood first in an all-India dance competition held under the auspices of the Sangeet Natak Academy and earned the scholarship.

The principal introduced me to the guru first, who was for some time in the poet Rabindranath Tagore's resort, Santiniketan. He belonged to the Visnupriya sect of Manipur, and coached his students in the Visnupriya style of Manipuri dancing.

I greeted the guru with a namaskar. He reciprocated my greeting and, raising his hands toward the sky, vocalized in broken Bengali, "In this way and by His grace, I have spent my life floating in the pure delight of dancing as my worship to Him." The guru wore a Vaishnavite *tilak*—a sectarian mark, painted on his forehead with sandalwood paste.

He pointed to the dancer and said in an overwhelming tone, "She is our pride; she has brought so much glory to us."

She bashfully lowered her face.

The principal also introduced her with superlative acclamation as the most outstanding student of her school. Seemingly embarrassed, the dancer blushed and returned my namaskar. On that evening, she wore an ordinary sari, her braided hair tied with a ribbon. She wore no makeup.

Still, she looked terrific with her stunningly lyrical grace. Her artistic bearing had an air of creative pain that heightened her exquisiteness.

For a moment I did not know what to say or how to behave normally in the situation. The principal's declamatory introduction helped me overcome my sudden stiffness. In a while, I recovered my ability to behave normally.

One by one, the principal introduced me to everyone present. All of them were learning singing, playing on musical instruments, or dancing, except for a middle-aged, betel-chewing woman wrapped in a handwoven Manipuri skirt, who escorted the guru to the school.

The principal introduced me to a young girl who, she said, sang *Rabindra Sangeet.* After some formal conversation, the dance guru and his assistant excused themselves and left for home. After they left, the principal proposed a session of songs. The girl who sang *Rabindra Sangeet* compliantly began the session. I could not ignore the principal's request to sing. I joined in.

On that evening in the music school, I did not know how she and my other listeners took my renderings of *Rabindra Sangeet*, but my initial dithering and hesitation was no more as I poured myself into the songs. When I was done, my eyes met the dancer's eyes. She lowered her face. I felt a strange feeling of victory.

My intense feeling was interrupted as the principal and other listeners applauded. The dancer only murmured, "You sing so well."

"Oh, no," I replied, overwhelmed with a sense of triumph. Perhaps I had been singing only to her.

After a cup of tea with the principal and others, I came out of the music school and walked back to the State Circuit House, where I was temporarily put up. The principal extended an open invitation to me to visit the school at any time I liked.

I had to maintain my official face in a town, where many people already knew me. I shifted from the Circuit House to my residence and visited the music school in the evenings, once in a week or a fortnight, so that my visits did not become too conspicuous.

On an October evening, while taking a walk on the road near the music school, I found the dancer all alone in the front veranda of the school. I walked up to her and greeted her. After the usual exchange of courtesy and common words, I took the liberty to ask her, "Do you remember that we first met in backstage during the music conference, when you came to perform your dance numbers?"

"Oh yes, I do," she replied with an engaging smile. Then she asked me, "How do you find your new job? Isn't it altogether different from your interests?"

"You're absolutely right. It is completely different from my interests. When I am in court, I feel as if I am on a different planet, not in the world I knew. In court I have to deal with human beings accused of all sorts of deviant behavior and practicing lawyers interpreting the evidence and the law. I deal with characters and scenarios that are in absolute contrast to normal life. Nonetheless, it is an interesting and engaging job in a strictly formal environment."

As I spoke about the court atmosphere, I suddenly realized that I was putting my impressions about the law court to an artiste. She could not be expected to be interested in the matters of a law court. I apologized with, "I'm sorry; I think I bored you with matters of the law court."

"Oh, no. It's interesting; something that I never knew. It must be a very complicated and very serious job. A lot of brainwork, isn't it?"

I was not sure if her comment was sincere or sarcastic. I did not reply. Silence prevailed for a few moments. She said in a thoughtful tone, "When I came to know that you'd joined the judiciary, I found it difficult to believe."

"I didn't like the profession of an attorney-at-law or practicing as a shadow of my father. I wanted a change. When I was offered the job in the judiciary, I accepted it. It all happened in fast sequence, and in the process I landed up in this particular district headquarters. In this country, there are very few choices—as you know," I replied.

She kept quiet. I already knew that the town to which I had come on posting was her hometown. Her words made me happy to think that she not only remembered me but also kept track of my life and activities. I dared to mention, "Somehow, I had a feeling that you won't forget me."

Suddenly, she became conscious that she had broached a very personal point that pampered my ego. She changed the topic and asked me, "By the way, are you still writing poems?"

"Not really," I replied. "Since my world now has no place for poetry or music, I come to the music school whenever I can escape. I come here to forget the dealings of the court, at least for a while, and to meet you to enliven my spirit."

She blushed at my compliments and, perhaps, realized my hint. Her face changed. Lest she propose to go away, I asked her whether she was further cultivating her dancing and what her latest find was in her research on lost folk dances. She replied, "Actually, I have no recent find, and there is nothing that I am working on now."

She made a gesture to move. I asked her, "When is your next program, and where will it be staged?"

She replied, "Well, I'm not a professional dancer. From my childhood, I loved to dance. I learned dancing just because I liked to dance. When I got the scholarship, it encouraged me. I joined the academy; I went to Manipur to learn more and more from the authentic sources—my gurus, who live in remote villages in Manipur. I recovered a few lost folk forms of my home district. I also learned a little bit of the ethnic and folk dances of various regions, including near-obsolete folk dances. I learned a little of the creative dances of Santiniketan of the poet Rabindranath Tagore. I had the privilege of acquainting the famous choreographer and dancer Udaysankar with Bou Nautch, a folk form. Whenever I was invited by the organizers and connoisseurs of art and culture, I performed. I tried my best to present whatever little I knew in the authentic styles I learned from my gurus. And now I'm here, as you know, because I cannot take dance as my profession. You know the social constraints on women."

She gave me a smile. She appeared serious and emotional when she told me her story. I felt embarrassed and regretted unknowingly touching the most sensitive chord of her heart.

I had to say something to lighten the situation. I said, "You're so talented, so special. You must do something to keep it up and to establish yourself as a famous dancer, nationally and internationally."

She replied in a poignant tone, "I'm only a student of dancing, living in a remote corner of a tradition-bound country. If I take to dancing as my profession, I will have to live outside of the society I was born and brought up in. The performing arts as a profession are of a different world altogether. People in our society like to enjoy performances but do not like to respect the artistes. I am sure you understand what I mean."

"I do, I do very much understand," I sympathetically replied.

She continued, "If I become a dance teacher, I'll have to live the austere and socially insignificant life that most artists and art teachers in our society do. My mother, who earlier encouraged me to learn dancing, now insists that I must get married. She does not realize that if I am wedded to a government officer or a professional, I will have to be a housewife. That will mean giving a complete go-by to many years of hard labor in learning dance. I am in a fix. I really don't know what I should do.

"So I have stopped thinking. I enjoy sharing with others whatever little I know. I come to the school to stay in touch with dancing—just to sustain my spirit."

I felt for her, but I couldn't take her into my arms to soothe her. Only a spontaneous sense of empathy connected us; something like mutual compassion that at once brought us emotionally close to one another. At least, I liked to think so.

I was moving to step inside the school when she said, "Today's session is over. I am going home."

I turned around and, somewhat awkwardly, said, "Sorry if I have delayed you."

"Oh no, not in the least" she replied. "I just have to go home."

We came out together from the school premises and went down to the street. We walked side by side toward her home. I didn't know if it would be proper to take leave of her or to walk with her. She broke the silence and asked me, "Are you still in the Circuit House?"

I felt relieved and replied, "No. I have just shifted to the residence."

"Oh, really? My home too is on that road." She appeared happy.

"Nice to know that we are neighbors," I replied with expectations.

The emotional ambience that had clouded the atmosphere melted away as we changed the topic. We resumed normal conversation. We walked together for some time, and then she pointed out to an old house within a low, fenced compound. A wooden gate in a passage led to the house, and an oleander plant was by the side of the gate.

"This is my home. Won't you come in and meet my mother?" she asked me.

"Oh sure. It would be my pleasure," I replied. "I have seen the house many times while passing by this road. I didn't know, however, that this is your home."

She opened the gate and showed me in. I followed her up to the veranda in front of the house. She pushed the doorbell. Her mother opened the door. The old lady in a white sari looked surprised to find a stranger accompanying her daughter.

She introduced me to her mother, and I greeted her with a namaskar. The mother reciprocated my greeting, and we entered the living room. There was an old sofa set. Walls were filled with framed needlework and family photos. Inside a glass armoire were displayed collections of cups and trophies, presumably won by her in the many dancing competitions and demonstrations she had participated in since her childhood. An enlarged photograph of her father wearing a Western outfit was conspicuous in the room. His large eyes and well-groomed mustache had an undeniable effect. He had been a British-era magistrate and died a premature death while on a tour.

Her mother gently asked me to sit down. She spoke cordially with the refinement of a cultured middle-class mother. She asked me the usual questions about my home, parents, brothers, and sisters, as was the customary etiquette. She made tea and offered it to me. We had it together. My friend's youngest brother joined us. I spent about half an hour and then took leave of them. I was happy to think that I had made the acquaintance with a nice family.

I entered through the guarded gate of my official residence, walked on the driveway, went up to the front veranda, and then entered my residential office. I switched on the light and sat down on my chair behind the desk in my residence office. The law books and leather-bound journals in the glass armoire looked like a simulated wall built with sacrosanct printed words. The stationery on the table and the stack of papers emitted a stale odor. The locked drawers contained case records, including old and pale sheets of paper, recorded statements of witnesses, and other legal documents that would determine the destiny of the litigants and criminals. My office had a depressing ambience.

I left the office and entered my bedroom. I switched on the light and turned on the record player. The melodious strokes of Yehudi Menuhin's violin filled the room. I hurled myself into the cushioned lap of the couch. I turned off the light to let the soft moonlight penetrate through the open window. Music worked well to revive me from the gloomy environment of loneliness. She appeared in my thoughts, sustaining the stream of my dream sequence as I enjoyed the serene strains of the violin.

* * *

For some time, I had been toying with the idea of writing a ballet based on a folklore with my own lyrics and music. In fact, I had already prepared a sketch of the scenarios and sequences of the musical drama. I also wrote a few lyrics. Now, I thought, I must complete the entire thing so that it could be produced in flesh and blood. I thought of asking her to do the choreography for the dances and play the role of the heroine of the drama.

I started writing the scenarios, the lyrics, and the music, burning the midnight oil. Within a few days I completed the draft and gave it to her. I asked her to choreograph and also to tell me where and how she would like changes in the lyrics and music. She said she would go through the script overnight and give me her feedback.

The next day, she unquestioningly approved my draft sequences and music. The principal of the music school decided to start rehearsals in her school and invite all available dancers and musicians to join. Only the proposed heroine of my work was too modest. I had to convince her that she and she only would be able to grasp my ideas and interpret my thoughts in dance. I told her that it was my first venture to compose the script of a dance drama, and she must agree to play the principal role.

With reassurances from the dance guru and the principal, she took the responsibilities to both choreograph the dances and act as the heroine. I finalized the lyrics and the music, and the rehearsals began. I had an excuse to visit the music school every evening.

After rehearsals, we would walk together to her home. Sometimes I escorted her rather late in the evening. Her dance- and music-loving mother did not mind even when she returned late. Winter had already set in and I remember the black overcoat she sported, walking to her home on dewy evenings. I now had her permission to call by her first name, Reba. She became an inseparable part of my existence. At my request, she secretly gave me one of her photos.

Among many things I tried in my life, I also tried painting. I had all the gadgets for painting. I took out my painting gear. I fixed a canvas on the easel in my bedroom and put her photograph upright against the backrest of a chair as the model. In the privacy of my bedroom, I tried to paint her portrait with my little knowledge of painting. Working meticulously on successive nights, I gave the final touches to the piece, thinking I had painted a great portrait.

The night broke into a sunlit Sunday morning. I put the piece aside to dry and told my orderly, Nimai, to be very careful so that the work was not spoiled in any way.

Nimai always wore a serious expression. For the first time, he turned up his lips in an impish smile and slipped out of the place.

Suddenly, like a providential vision, I saw Reba from my window, walking on the road all alone, holding an open Burmese umbrella. Enthused, I asked Nimai to run to her and tell her that I wanted her to come in for a moment to have a look at something. Nimai obediently ran to the street. It was a quiet morning with hardly any traffic. I could observe from my window that Nimai reached out to her and presumably gave her my message.

She stood for a moment, spoke something to Nimai, and resumed her walk. To my discontent, Nimai turned to come back. Moments later, I saw her turning around and hurriedly walking toward my house. I came out to welcome her. She looked this way and that and hesitantly sneaked through the gate. Overwhelmed with joy, I received her as warmly as I could. She entered the living room and, in a voice full of concern, whispered, "I'm not supposed to visit you. Aren't you a solitary bachelor?" She posed as if to censure me and then added, "If anyone sees me entering your house, it will be a scandal. Tell me quickly what you want me to see. I must go away immediately."

I was too excited to bother about anyone watching and possible scandal. I replied, "Don't worry about all that. We aren't doing anything wrong! Just come on in."

I led her to my bedroom and showed her the portrait I had carefully painted. She looked at the piece with amazement. Her face flushed. She didn't say whether she liked it or not. She only exclaimed, "How could you do it?"

"I used the photo you gave me as the model," I replied.

"You're too daring. What would people think of us if they saw this?"

"They would only know the truth—that we are in love," I said.

"As though . . ." she said bashfully and moved to go out. I took her in my arms and kissed her. She responded, and we were wrapped in each other's arms for an overwhelming moment.

Suddenly, she broke off and hurried out through the open door. I stood immobile, deluged in delight. I don't know how long I lay on the lounging couch, feeling the ecstasy of taking her into my arms and kissing her.

Next evening she didn't attend the rehearsal. When I asked the principal, she replied that Reba had reported that she was unwell and regretted her inability to attend rehearsal on that day.

My first reaction was to go to her place and inquire about her. But, on second thought, I decided not to go. One may not feel well and may not attend the rehearsal for a day. I mustn't bother her, I thought.

But the situation was not that simple. The next evening, Nimai knocked at my bedroom door. He, in his usual submissive tone, said that he had been returning from the market when her mother called him and gave him a small envelope, asking him to deliver it to me.

I opened it. There was a chit with a one-line message. Reba's mother asked me to see her immediately. I wondered why she called me so urgently and by a chit. Could it be regarding her daughter's visit to my place? I thought that it must be for something serious.

I hurriedly put on a jacket and went to her place. I pushed the doorbell. The door opened. The mother asked me to come in. I went in, and she slammed the door behind me. She asked me to take a seat. We sat down face-to-face. Reba was nowhere near us.

Without a prelude, she began in a serious undertone, "Although we are supposed to be living in a progressive society, there is no dearth of orthodox people and their emissaries. I got a report that you called my daughter to your place, and when I asked her, she confirmed it. With all humility, I must tell you that you might be a powerful entity in your courtroom, but you have no right to call my daughter to your residence."

Then, in an irate tone, she said, "To us, you're a bachelor of unknown origin. How dare you call my maiden daughter to your place? This could lead to a scandal. Her reputation would be ruined. Nothing would touch you. You would merrily go away on transfer, but no respectable groom would ever marry her. You have done the worst possible harm to her."

Her words struck me like the touches of a branding iron. I felt terribly insulted. But I could not behave impertinently with the mother. After she paused, exasperated, I replied as soberly as I could, "I didn't call her with any bad intention. I think you're taking it too seriously. I only wanted her to see something that was in my house. I'm sure she would bear me out."

"People in the town would not bother about your intentions. They would only think that you, a bachelor, called my daughter, Reba to your place and she was with you for some time in your residence. May I know what was the invaluable exhibit for which you had to call Reba to your place?" Her question was loaded with sarcasm.

"Nothing to be concerned about," I replied. "I tried to paint a portrait. I asked Nimai to call her to come and have a look at it, and that's all."

"If you were interested to show it to her, you could have brought it to my house."

"Indeed I could have, but the paints were not dry enough to take the piece out. It was just a coincidence that she was going by, and I felt like calling her."

"Whose portrait did you paint?" she asked me in a relatively sober tone.

"I'm not a painter; I only tried to paint her portrait after her photo," I replied awkwardly.

"Where did you get her photo?" was her next question.

"She gave it to me," I replied.

The mother sternly commanded, "Return the photo right now. You won't meet her again. If people see her portrait in your place, it would be too bad. You can't do that!" She appeared infuriated.

Her statement and the manner in which she behaved crossed the limit of my tolerance. I retorted, "I'm sorry. I can't return the photo, and I can't promise that I won't meet her unless she tells me not to do so. Would you please call her? I want to know from her."

"She won't see you anymore," replied the mother.

"I would like to hear it from her in her own words. Would you please call her?" I desperately repeated.

She replied with a firm no.

Insulted and humiliated, I left her place. She slammed the door behind me. I could hear the sound of the bolt locking the door with more than the required force.

Next evening, lying flat on my bed, I could not find answers to my most natural questions. Why had she allowed her mother to insult me that way? Why had she never come out and supported me? She was an adult woman, fully aware of whatever she was doing. Had she played a devious role? Was she flirting with me just for the heck of it? Nonetheless, her love for me appeared true. I felt miserable about the whole thing.

I didn't know how to show my face to Nimai, to the principal, and to so many others who already knew about our relationship. They would not know that she suddenly ditched me, that her mother had treated me so shabbily. It was too much. I could not bear the insult. And yet there was nothing that I could do about it.

Someone rang the doorbell. A flash of hope kindled in me. *Could it be she?* I wondered, but I could not move. I heard Nimai open the door. I eagerly waited.

Nimai came back to tell me the name of an elderly lawyer, who ostensibly had come to pay me a social call. That was the worst thing that could have happened at such a time, I thought. Nevertheless, I had to come out to receive him in my office room. I greeted him and asked him to come in and take a seat.

The bald-headed, feeble man walked in, leaning on the cane he gripped in his skinny hand. I helped him to take his seat. He asked me about my well-being and about my parents, because he somehow knew my father. He was a respectable man, one of the oldest surviving members of the district bar association. Originally from East Bengal and permanently settled in the town, he did not practice anymore, but attended the bar library every day and without fail. He was a protagonist of the purported superiority of the caste Hindu community. He was also known for his curt way of speaking.

As he entered my house, I felt sure that he had come with some purpose in view. From the very first day I met him, I never liked the man. I was apprehensive that he might tell me something about my relationship with Reba. I decided to confront him if he spoke about my relationship with her and tell him that I didn't care about what he or anyone else might think. But again I wondered how I could do that when she didn't support me when her mother behaved so badly with me. She had let me down before everyone.

My visitor was a veteran lawyer; he didn't say anything directly. He began, "I thought I would come personally to see how you have settled down in the lonely residence. Since I know your father and the family, I thought it my duty to look you up. Does Nimai cook your food all right? If not, I can find a good cook for you; there are a few in the town, I know. Any one of them would love to work for you."

"Thank you for the inquiry. Nimai cooks very well, and I don't need to change him," I replied. "How is your health now?"

"Okay," he replied. "I am too old to have fine health. I have been used to dragging on with my bad leg. I go to court out of so many years of habit, although I do not appear nowadays. While going home, I dropped by the fish market, as is also my old habit. I rarely come out for social calls. Today, I thought it was my duty to look you up." He attempted a smile as though he obliged me by stating his daily activities.

"So nice of you," I replied.

Nimai brought tea and a plate of cookies and placed them before the visitor on a table.

"Good to see you settled down all alone. You're doing very well in the court. The lawyers are full of appreciation for your work and ability. Your parents must have been looking for a good bride for you to marry so that you could make a home in the true sense of the term. No house is a home without a wife." He was meddling in my personal affairs. He again attempted a smile. After a few seconds, he said, "Only a girl from a high-caste family matching your caste and status could make a good wife for you. You know what I mean?"

"Thank you, but I don't think I must marry yet," I replied.

He ignored my reply with a cynical smirk. "There are many girls all around. But there are only one or two well-groomed, high-caste, eligible girls I know and could recommend. You must be careful not to get entrapped by a local girl. Most of them are unsuitable for you. They are not eligible; they don't belong to our caste. You come from a high-caste family. You must also be conscious about your own status. I hope you understand."

He exposed his dentures in an imitation of a smile. Abruptly he stood up, grasped his cane, and limped his way out, taking leave of me by raising a hand. He had come in his ancient car driven by an old chauffeur, who escorted him to the car and helped him get into it. The two drove away.

I felt terribly insulted, my ears burning. But I could neither say anything nor get up from my seat. It was too much to stand the unsolicited advice, a virtual reprimand, from the cynical old man. I felt like lifting him up and throwing him out of the house. But I had to control myself.

After the elderly lawyer conveyed his caustic message to me, I felt disgusted with the situation. I decided to submit my resignation and go away.

Just then, Nimai gave me a sealed letter. It was from Reba. She profusely apologized to me for her mother's behavior and subtly tendered her love to me. She mentioned that her mother has restrained her from meeting me and from attending the rehearsal at the music school.

The message complicated the situation further. I didn't know what to do. I was disgusted with the town's caste-ridden, compartmentalized society. I really didn't know what to do.

Days passed. Mechanically, I went to court and came back to the residence. I could neither tell anyone about my trouble nor bear it all alone. It was a hard and dull time. The only news I gathered from my trusted orderly Nimai was that her elder brother, a Burma Oil Company engineer posted to the oil town of Digboi, had come with his wife and a toddler child to see his mother and sister. He left for his place of work after a couple of days.

Nimai gave me a verbal message that Reba's mother had asked me to see her. I deliberately delayed. Eventually one evening, I went to her place. I pushed the doorbell. The door opened and the mother appeared. She asked me gently to come in. I entered and inquired if she had asked me to see her. She affirmed that she had and asked me to sit down. She closed the door and went farther into the house. Reba was nowhere nearby.

"I'm sorry to keep you waiting," the mother apologized in an impassive tone as she came back and placed a cup of tea before me. She sat down on a couch opposite me, holding her cup of tea in hand.

Without any prologue, she went straight to business. She said, "I'm sorry for being rude to you the other day. I wanted to meet you so that our relationship could be normalized. I have no intention of interfering in your personal life, and I expect you to do the same thing. My daughter likes to attend the music school. She is now a grown-up girl, and I cannot restrain her from attending the school or from going to her friends or anywhere else she might like to. I called you to tell you that both of you must behave in such a manner that no more scandal is spread. The best thing would be if you don't meet."

"I really don't understand what you mean to say. You know that Reba and I were preparing to stage a dance drama for which the principal of the music school has already made every arrangement. Rehearsals were going on when suddenly you stopped her from attending. If there is any scandal, it is due to the sudden interruption of the rehearsals. I don't think I am responsible for that. I also don't understand how, if we don't meet each other, we can thereby normalize our relationship," I retorted.

She avoided my points. In a serious but polite manner, she said, "In our society, free mixing of young men and young women is not looked upon as normal, unless it ends in marriage. In your case, marriage is impossible, even if you think of marrying my daughter. You and we belong to two different communities. There cannot be any matrimonial alliance between us. The elders in my community have already expressed their disapproval of your free mixing.

"I'm a widowed mother. I have gone through much stress and press of time. I am left with my last duties to perform: to get my daughter married to a suitable groom of our community and to get my youngest son educated. I don't want to get entangled with any more problems. I hope you understand."

"I appreciate your point," I replied, adding, "I would only like to know from her that she too does not want to meet me anymore. Then I'll never again meet her."

Despite my polite statement, the old woman got irritated. She stressed, "I'm her mother. I have every right to make decisions on her behalf. I know what is good for her and what is not. I think you are encroaching upon our family affairs. You're no one to decide matters involving my daughter and me. I already told you that the elders of our community do not approve the way you were behaving. We have to live within the society we belong to. You're an outsider here."

"Excuse me for asking you, but aren't you Indian? You're using expressions like *outsider* and *community*. What does all this mean? Does it mean caste? We are not living in a primitive community dictated by village elders. I don't understand what you mean by the elders of the community. I want to have a talk with your daughter. Would you please call her?"

She smirked, avoiding my request to call her daughter, and sarcastically responded, "You may be a progressive man. You may not believe in caste and community. But we live in a society, and we must obey the tradition and the rules of that society. And that is precisely why you too must behave as a social being in an organized society. If you want to live beyond the society, you must find your own place."

After a few moments, she continued, "Look, we belong to a *sampradaya*—a sect, which I was referring to as our community. We are the original inhabitants of this district. We don't believe in the caste system. But we have matrimonial alliances only with the other members of our sampradaya. We do not even discriminate on grounds of language or cultural orientation as long as one is of our community.

"But you don't belong to our community. Elders of our community have objected to your mixing so freely with my daughter when you are not eligible to marry her. I cannot do anything about it. I only suggest that we forget about whatever has happened and whatever gossip was spread. You live your life and let my daughter and I live our lives."

I couldn't resist any more. I asserted, "Under the law, you cannot prevent us from meeting and even getting married if we like. So-called elders of your sampradaya cannot do anything at all. This is an obsolete and clannish view of life, opposed to the law of the land."

She listened to my statement and said, "Marriage is a permanent relationship, a happy occasion. You may ask your father. I am sure he too would never accept an alliance between your community and ours. I have done many things on my own for the good of my children. If your father agrees to my daughter's marriage with you and assures me of his cooperation, come what may, I'll stand by you. But I must hear it from him, not from you."

She stood up. I got the hint and walked to the door. She opened the door. I suppressed my annoyance and exited. She slammed the door behind me.

I came back to my residence and decided to write to my father to teach her a lesson. I knew that he loved me dearly, and as a highly educated man, he surely would not believe in caste and community. I wanted to lay my father's reply before Reba's mother. I wrote a detailed letter to my father and asked for his views.

My father replied to my letter by return post. He asked no questions about whatever had happened. He said that if the girl's mother was really keen on having an alliance with our family, the proposal must come from her. He cautioned me that I must not take any initiative in the matter. Finally, as a special favor, he granted me the liberty to ask the girl's mother to write to him and give the details he needed.

I went to Reba's mother, showed my father's reply, and told her that if she liked, she could write a letter to my father with the details he wanted.

On that day, Reba was present in the living room with her mother. But she did not make any comment. Her mother said that she would give it serious thought. I gave her my father's postal address.

A few days later, the mother called me again to her place. She said nothing and quietly gave me the letter she had received from my father. My father had written a two-line letter, rejecting her proposal outright.

I felt extremely humiliated at the reply my father had given. I apologized to her and expressed my regret for asking her to write a letter to my father. From her face, I could make out that she was terribly annoyed. But she suppressed her anger and told me, "I had already told you that an alliance between your family and our family was impossible. Just because you wanted me to write, I sent the formal proposal. This is how your father, in his arrogant vanity, responded. He did not even consider the proposal. Pardon me for telling you, but the caste Hindu community is far more bigoted than others."

She smirked and tore the letter in clear contempt, concluding, "Let's call it a day. I hope you won't tread this path anymore."

Reba ran inside the house, holding back a stormy outburst. Sad and humiliated, I left the house. The door closed behind me with a thud.

* * *

The superintendent in my office informed me that he had gotten a message that the chief justice was coming to the town on a surprise visit. He added that he had been in service for a long time and had never had any chief justice of the high court come on a surprise visit. I felt disturbed, though the chief justice had been personally known to me since before I joined the judiciary, because both of us were interested in literature. Nonetheless, I had a feeling that he made the secret plan because of my affair. I was puzzled, however. It was a very personal affair and had nothing to do with the business of the court.

Anyhow, the chief justice came and was duly received in the Circuit House with a police guard of honor, from which he took the salute. We met in private in his Circuit House suite.

Without any prelude, he blurted out in a suppressed voice, "What are all these reports I'm getting about you? You seem to have fascinated my old friend's daughter with your poems and songs. Is that true? She is a very good girl. Are you flirting with her? What is the idea? I've come all this way only for this."

I never expected such a question from the chief justice. I replied, "We came to know each other at the local music school. She choreographed a dance drama I wrote, and the principal decided to stage the drama. We were having rehearsals. I once attempted to paint her portrait. She came to my house for a moment to have a look at the portrait. Her mother objected and prohibited her from meeting me. The rehearsals came to a sudden stop. That is all that happened."

"But I have gotten many reports from different quarters that you have been involved in a scandal that has undermined the prestige of the judiciary. A very senior lawyer wrote to the high court to immediately transfer you in the interest of the reputation of the judiciary. To transfer you from here to another place is matter of a moment. But because it involved you and my friend's daughter, I thought I must personally come and find out what really is the matter. I could have asked you to come to Gauhati and see me, but I wanted to hear both sides before coming to a conclusion," said the chief justice.

He took a sip from the glass of water placed on the table before him.

After a moment, he asked me rather seriously, "How would you describe your relationship with her?"

"I love her. I want to marry her. I have already told her mother. But she raised the question of caste bar and the objection of the elders of her community. She said the elders of her community would not approve of marriage between us. I wrote to my father, and he too is opposed to the alliance. We want to be partners in life, and that is how I would define my relationship with her. I'm sure she would bear me out. You will appreciate, sir, that this is entirely a personal matter. Anonymous reports or a senior lawyer's letter should not have any bearing in a matter that is exclusively personal. It has nothing to do with the affairs of the court."

I dared to reply in a resolute manner. I thought I would challenge the chief justice if he thought he could meddle in my personal affairs merely because I was now his subordinate. I could resign, go away, and marry her in a court marriage. I didn't care.

To my surprise, the chief looked relaxed. He said with a smile, "I didn't rely on the letter and reports. That is precisely why I have come personally—to know from you and from her. I belong to the same community to which she and her mother belong. If you promise to marry her and take care of her all through her life, I will stand by you, and nobody will be able to create any problem for you. I will write to your father. I will convince him. But I have come to find out whether you are serious and she too is willing to marry you."

He smiled and then said, "I appreciate your choice. She is an accomplished girl, an acclaimed student of classical dancing. Her father was a good friend of mine, and when he was no more, I felt I must ensure that she was not deceived by anyone. After giving it the most serious thought, you should decide to marry her."

"I've already given the most serious thought to the matter," I replied.

"Then come with me." He stood up.

Both of us got into his car. He dismissed the police pilot and the police escort and asked me to lead the chauffeur to her mother's place.

When we reached the house, the chief justice got out and walked to the veranda in front of the house. I pushed the doorbell. The mother was very happy to receive him. Reba and her younger brother touched his feet to give him due regard as their father's friend. He seemed to be familiar with everyone.

He asked me to sit down and went farther inside the house, together with the mother and the daughter. They conferred for nearly an hour. It was a very long wait for me.

Finally he came out, followed by Reba and her mother. He took her hand and put it on my hand and declared, "Your marriage is settled. Are you happy?"

Her mother winked at Reba, hinting that she must bow down and touch the chief justice's feet. We both bowed down and touched his feet. He lifted us and said, "Let you two be blessed with lifelong happiness."

We also bowed down and touched her mother's feet as was customary. She felt shy and said, "Oh, you needn't touch my feet. You have all my blessings."

Looking to her mother, the chief said, "Let me know when you fix the date of wedding."

To me he said, "I'll write to your father telling him that I have united you in a marriage with full responsibility. If he refuses to accept you after your marriage, just come and stay with me in my house. I'll give you a private suite."

I thanked him. Reba looked overwhelmed with happiness; her eyes were moist with emotion. I accompanied the chief back to the Circuit House. On the way, he gave me some advice and told me about her father and the family.

* * *

The next sequence of events followed quickly. Her mother fixed a date for our wedding. I informed my father, and no reply came from him. According to her wishes, we were wedded in a ritual Hindu wedding in her brother's bungalow in Digboy. Of the greetings telegrams, one was from the chief justice and another from my father. My father's telegram contained just two words: "Blessings, Father."

Immediately after the wedding, we boarded the train to a hill station to go away on a vacation. We went neither to my parents' place nor to the chief justice's place.

It was only after our first child was born that my brother came to my place and took the three of us to my paternal home. As we alighted from the car, my mother took the child into her lap, and we bowed down to show our respect to my parents. My sister joined us. My mother thus had the pretty daughter-in-law she had once desired upon viewing her photo in the newspaper.

16

In 1971, the Government of India Ministry of Home Affairs asked me by a wireless message if I was willing to join the proposed centrally (federally) administered union territory government of Mizoram as one of four secretaries to the new government. Mizoram was then a terrorist-affected area, with the Mizo National Front and the Mizo National Army demanding sovereignty and secession from India. Earlier the area had been known as the autonomous Lushai Hills district of Assam. Immediately before it became a union territory, it was administered by a chief commissioner, aided and advised by the autonomous district council.

Most of my friends and relations advised me not to go to a terrorist-affected area. But my wife and I were interested in accepting the offer as an unusual experience. Mizoram was a picturesque area of rolling hills and valleys, inhabited by a colorful people of Tibeto-Burmese origin who spoke their own language, observed their distinct tradition and culture, and professed Christianity.

I accepted the offer on a five-year deputation term and joined the new government in 1972 as secretary to the government in the law, judicial, legislative assembly, and local administration departments.

As secretary, I was in overall charge of elections, supervision, finance, and development of the autonomous regions inhabited by the Pawi, Lakher, and Chakma tribes. Under the Sixth Schedule to the Constitution of India, all three tribes inhabiting southern Mizoram had autonomous district councils. The Lakher or Mara tribe, however, had a district council as far back as 1945, with Saiha as the headquarters, before India was independent and the Constitution of India came into force. The Pawi or Lai tribe established their autonomous district council in 1953, with Lawngtlai as their headquarters. The Chakmas got their district council only in 1972, with headquarters at Chawngte. The Chakmas were a Bengali-speaking tribe. They renamed Chawngte "Kamalanagar."

All necessary preparations to hold elections to the autonomous district councils were complete. The director of local administration and his staff, with the help of the administrative officers (AOs) posted deep into the remote areas, were responsible for organizing and holding elections through secret ballots. The AOs concerned attended training classes held in Aizawal, capital of Mizoram, and were provided with printed instructions and guidelines.

On the day prior to the date fixed for the election, the finance secretary, Pu Lalkhama (later chief secretary of Mizoram and one of the signatories of the Mizoram Accord of 1986), gave me a sealed letter addressed to me and written by the deputy commissioner (DC) of the Lunglei district, who was the chief electoral officer for the district council elections. The DC had given the letter to Lalkhama two days before. Unfortunately, the finance secretary forgot to give it to me immediately upon his arrival in Aizawal from Lunglei.

The young DC wrote that he had information that in thirty remote polling stations, the names and symbols of the candidates seeking election were not displayed in "conspicuous places" in the polling booths. This was in violation of a mandatory provision of the election law. The elections in question were due in the remote areas of the Chimtuipui district in the Kaladan River valley adjoining Burma (Myanmar). The DC mentioned that, the matter being highly confidential, he thought it appropriate to let me know by a letter, which the finance secretary had kindly agreed to carry. He sought my instructions to remedy the lapses so that the election could be held in accordance with the law.

Perhaps he forgot that he was the chief electoral officer, and it was his duty to make sure that no flaw existed in respect of the legal requirements for the electoral procedure. There was also a director of the local administration department, with a hierarchy of staff, who was responsible for supervising the electoral process. As secretary of local administration, my job was to advise the lieutenant governor in matters pertaining to planning and policy decisions relating to the autonomous district councils.

Lunglei was the nearest town to Saiha, headquarters of the Pawi and Lakher district councils. Chawngte or Kamalanagar at the northeastern corner, on the bank of the Tuichawng River, was the headquarters of the Chakma District Council. At that time, these remote areas were difficult to access by surface for want of jeep-worthy roads. Lunglei was the most convenient town, accessible by jeep via a winding, hilly road. It took at least twelve hours to reach Lungeli from Aizawal by a jeep.

In the circumstances, it appeared impossible to do anything overnight to correct the error reported by the DC in his letter. Polling was to commence the following morning, and the election was sure to be invalidated for noncompliance with the mandatory provisions. There couldn't have been a more frustrating news at a time when the government of India was trying hard to introduce the political process in the terrorist-ridden border area.

I really didn't know what to do in this situation and within such a short time. I went to S. P. Mukherjee, the first lieutenant governor (LG) of Mizoram, in his residential office called *Rajniwas* on top of a small hillock in Aizawal.

After an exchange of courtesies, I quietly showed him the letter from the DC of Lunglei. By nature jittery, Mukherjee was totally upset. His immediate reaction was a vehement rage. He dictated to his stenographer a devastating note against DC.

Next, he accused me and questioned why I had not followed up on matters to ensure that everything was in order. Why had I waited until the last moment, he demanded to know.

I could have replied that I had done everything possible. In fact, I had done more than my duty as a secretary. But I didn't like to argue with him at that moment. I kept quiet.

The LG soliloquized in bitter regret that he wouldn't be able to show his face to the secretary of the department of home affairs if the election failed.

Meanwhile, his stenographer printed the note he had dictated. He had a copy made to send to the deputy secretary of the Ministry of

Home Affairs in Delhi. Mukherjee signed the note and the copy and gave the file to me. The LG, however, neither said anything nor wrote anything against the finance secretary, who had forgotten to hand over such an important letter immediately upon his return to Aizawal. He also mentioned nothing against the director of local administration.

In this situation, I was equally disturbed. I could have censured the director of local administration, but that wouldn't have set the matter right. Distressed, I took leave of Mr. Mukherjee and impulsively asked my chauffeur to take me to the brigade headquarters of the Indian Army, at a point called Zemabok, near Aizawal, to try to get a helicopter to rush to Lunglei.

Brigadier Wadke was then commanding the Indian Army brigade in Mizoram. He was sipping gin and lime before lunch. I told him the entire story and asked him to help me get to Lunglei immediately.

Nonchalantly, the brigadier said, "Have a drink. Let's see what we can do."

He asked the brigade major to contact the air force base at Jorhat in Assam and find out if any chopper (helicopter in army language) was available to take me to Lunglei. Before the brigade major came back with the reply from the air force base, the rumbling sound of a helicopter was audible.

The brigadier asked me to take physical charge of the chopper as soon as it landed on the helipad in Aizawal and ask the pilots to take me to Lunglei. He added that he would ask the air force base to issue the necessary commands to the pilots. He also assured me that he would instruct the army commander at Lunglei to render all possible help to me.

He asked one of his junior officers, a lieutenant, to accompany me to the helipad. He instructed the officer accompanying me to ask the helicopter pilots to take me to Lunglei and to tell the pilots that the brigade headquarters would be contacting the air force base for the issuance of the necessary commands. The brigadier regretted that he had no control over air force pilots.

At the helipad, I found the helicopter had just landed, and two pilots of huge stature were standing near the aircraft. They looked tired and impatient in their soiled dungarees. After my accompanying lieutenant greeted them and gave them my identity, I exchanged greetings with them and said that I had to fly to Lunglei on urgent official business. I sought their help and sneaked into the helicopter through its open door before the pilots could tell me anything in reply.

The lieutenant accompanying me explained to them the urgency and the instructions of the brigadier. The pilots flatly refused the lieutenant's request and said that for the last four days, they had been running rescue operations. They were too tired, and they needed to go back to their base for rest.

I then intervened to say that I was already in the aircraft. If they flew me to Lunglei, I would ensure that they get the necessary command from the air force base, and I would try my best to make them comfortable at Lunglei. On the contrary if they didn't comply with my request, they might fly me anywhere, but they would have to bear the consequences.

I don't know what they thought of my ultimatum. They grumbled that civilian officers are impossible people. However, they took off and flew toward Lunglei. I thanked them for helping me. I was so much preoccupied with the situation that I even forgot to ask the brigadier or the lieutenant to inform my wife that I was proceeding to Lunglei for urgent business and she shouldn't worry about me.

After some time, we landed on the Lunglei helipad. The DC had gotten the information from the army that I was on my way to Lunglei. He was present at the helipad to receive me and asked me to come to his residence for dinner. I, in turn, asked him to take me to the Indian Army camp at Lunglei.

When we reached the camp, Colonel Multani, who was the officer commanding the Nineteenth. Punjab Regiment in Lunglei welcomed us. The Indian Army was fabulously hospitable. Besides, the brigadier had already instructed the colonel to help me. I asked Col. Multani to look after the two pilots and explained that they had been on duty for four days at a stretch. He deputed an officer to look after them.

After introductions with Col. Multani's officers, they placed a huge map of the area on the table and identified with colored pinheads all thirty points where, according to the DC, the names and symbols of the candidates seeking election were not displayed. They said that of the thirty points, twenty-five points had army posts that were readily accessible by the radio relay (RR) system.

The colonel asked me to dictate to his stenographer detailed instructions for the AOs about what to do and how to do it. He said that he would relay the instructions to his posts, and the officers in the posts would immediately send instructions to the AOs concerned. For places where there were no army posts, he told me that he would ask the nearest army posts to send runners with the message for the AOs of those areas, with instructions to get the mistakes rectified before dawn.

In the message, I asked the AOs concerned that if they had lost the printed names and election symbols of the candidates sent to them from Aizawal, they should type the names of the candidates in bold letters. They should draw the individual candidates' election symbols with pen, colored pencils, or crayons, whatever was available, and affix those to some conspicuous points near the polling booths immediately and during the night.

Nothing better could be done within the night. Our effort was to somehow comply with the provisions of the election law.

By nine that night, the entire exercise was complete. I then asked the colonel to connect me to the LG on the RR system. I told the LG that I was in the army camp at Lunglei and told him the manner in which we had tried to solve the problem. He was happy with our plan and asked me, with a note of surprise, how I had reached Lunglei so quickly. I replied that I would tell him the full story on my return to Aizawal. I added that it was all because of the help rendered by the army commanders in Aizawal and Lunglei.

The LG was fairly satisfied. He also thanked Col. Multani. I asked him to call my wife and tell her that I was safe and comfortable in the army camp at Lunglei.

Next morning the elections were held, and fortunately no protest was made by any of the candidates seeking election.

A couple of years later, the particular officer who had been DC of Lunglei during these elections was posted to Aizawal as a joint secretary to the Government of Mizoram. I showed him the note dictated by S. P. Mukherjee, which would have seriously damaged his career. I told him that I did not forward the copy to the deputy secretary of the Ministry of Home Affairs in Delhi, because the elections were somehow held and there was no objection raised by anyone. The nonplussed officer profusely thanked me. We shook hands.

During the initial phase of setting up a new government in the terrorist-stricken, isolated, hilly terrain, everyone had many new experiences, everyone made mistakes, and everyone faced difficulties in communication as part of their efforts to build up the infrastructure of the nascent administration. Nonetheless, everyone helped one another. Occasionally, civilian officials had to ask the help of the army and find out ingenious ways to get the jobs done.

Since 1952, the area now known as Mizoram had been a part of Assam and administered as the autonomous district of Lushai Hills. Manipur, Burma (Myanmar), and East Pakistan (Bangladesh) bordered the district.

Historically, various warlike tribes of Tibeto-Mongoloid origin, ruled by the chieftains of the clans, inhabited the variegated terrain of rolling hills and river valleys. In the course of time, somehow, the tribes came to be known by the common name Mizo, and they spoke a common language known as the Mizo language. The word *Mizoram* literally means "the land of the highlanders."

The majority of Mizos professed Christianity, except the Chakma tribe living on the southern tip of Mizoram bordering the Chittagong hill tracts of Bangladesh. The Chakmas professed Hinduism and Buddhism. They spoke a strain of the Bengali language akin to the dialect spoken by the people of the Chittagong hill tracts. There were Chakmas in Myanmar, Tripura, and Bangladesh as minority communities.

Originally known as Kukis, the various headhunting clans of the Lushai tribe migrated from the Chhinlungsan or Shinlung area of the Yalung River valley of China. They first settled in the Shan state of Burma and then moved to the Kabaw River valley of northern Burma. Thereafter, they migrated to Khampat in the Chin Hills in the Chin state of northwest Burma. The area extended up to Manipur state and to the Lushai Hills in India's northeast.

By the middle of the sixteenth century, their migration was complete. The Lushais were the last of the Mizo tribes to migrate to India. Tribal raids and retaliatory expeditions marked their history in the eighteenth and nineteenth centuries.

Some accounts hold that the Shan tribes had already settled in their state around the fifth century, and the Mizos came to Shan state from Chhinlung. The Mizos and the Shans fought with one another, and the Mizos established themselves and prospered for nearly three hundred years. Thereafter, they moved again to the Kabaw River valley, and during the eighth century, they migrated to the Lushai Hills area.

During their settlement in the Kabaw River valley of Burma (Myanmar), the Mizos interacted with the Burmese. The two tribes and their cultures influenced each other in respect of their dialect, dress, and customs. Traditionally, Mizo women wore a knee-length skirt called the *puan chei* and a top called the *kawi chei*, woven on domestic loin-looms using flying shuttles. The dress is somewhat like the Burmese *longyi*.

Culturally, Mizos are akin to the Burmese. They built their villages and named them after their respective clans. These villages were so scattered in the hilly terrain that it was not possible for one Mizo clan to keep in touch with another. A chief ruled his clan, following the customs of the clan. These chiefs were despotic and wielded absolute power.

In 1838, the British East India Company assumed governance of the area. After their coming into the region, the British often had clashes with the tribesmen. Under the Bengal Eastern Frontier Regulation of 1873, the British isolated the entire hill area of the sub-Himalayan terrain of northeast India, including the Lushai Hills. Section 2 of the regulation empowered the company to prescribe and alter the line of demarcation from time to time by notification. The regulation prohibited any person living outside the line to move into or live within the regulated areas.

The government of independent India also adopted the regulation, then commonly known as the Inner Line Regulation. People from the rest of India still needed a permit to visit or live for a period in Mizoram.

The first prime minister of independent India, Pandit Jawaharlal Nehru, thought it proper to protect the faith, language, and culture of the hill tribes of northeast India from the influence of Hindu gurus and Islamic mullahs. Nehru appointed Oxford-educated

Christian-missionary-turned-anthropologist Verrier Elwin as the advisor for tribal affairs in northeast India. Earlier, Elwin had worked with Gandhi and adopted Hinduism. He married a woman of the Gond tribe of central India, acquired Indian citizenship, and settled down in Shillong in northeast India.

The British annexed the northern and southern regions of the Lushai Hills in 1895. They amalgamated the two parts of the Lushai Hills district of Assam by a proclamation in 1898. Aizawal town, at an altitude of 1,132 meters above sea level, was the district headquarters. The Frontier Tract Regulation enacted in 1880 enabled the British East India Company to isolate certain frontier tracts of Assam, in the words of the regulation, "*inhabited or frequented by barbarous or semi-civilized tribes.*"

The British wanted to bring the tribes under control by use of force. They segregated the tribes from the mainstream of life in India. With a view to pacify the tribes, they introduced Christianity in the hills. They recruited the frontier constabulary from among the hill tribes of northeast India because of their familiarity with the hilly terrain and the hard life in the remote areas.

All kinds of facilities and free access to the area were granted to the Christian missionaries. They were encouraged to open government-aided schools in the hills. The British administration granted a franchise to the British Baptist Mission to operate in the Lushai Hills and in the Naga Hills. The mission first set up their post in the Mizo hills in 1836. Some twelve years later, the revival movement began against mass conversion to Christianity. Waves upon waves of revival movements swept the land until the entire Mizo community had abandoned its original animistic faith for the new religion, Christianity, by the end of the Second World War.

Christian missionaries established the first primary school in Aizawal in 1898 and the first high school in 1944. In the process, starting from a literacy rate of 0.9 percent in the 1901 census, Mizoram achieved a literacy rate of 88.49 percent in the 2001 census. According to the 2011 census, Mizoram's literacy rate was 91.58 percent, second only to Kerala with 93.4 percent. The census also reported that Mizoram was the only state in India that has no homeless people. Besides English, Mizos read and write in their own language in Roman script.

Despite Western influence, Mizos have retained many of their own traditions in terms of language, culture, and way of life. It is interesting to note that E. Lewis Mendus, one of the pioneer Christian missionaries to the Lushai Hills, observed in his book *Christianity in North East India: Historical Perspective* that in the process of converting the pagans to Christianity, Christianity had been paganized in the Mizo hills.

During my tenure in Mizoram, the young Mizo research officer Pu Punte suddenly died a natural death at home. When we got the sad news, my wife, Reba, and I went to pay our condolences to the deceased's wife. Mourners already filled the house. Mizo drums were beaten in a traditional rhythm, and everyone was served with tea, called *thingpui* in the Mizo language.

But the deceased's wife was not to be seen anywhere. On inquiry, we learned that, following the Mizo custom, she was immediately taken to a relation's house. The relative would feed her and take care of her. We realized that the original custom was to notify the villagers by the beating of drums that death had occurred in a particular house. At once, the entire village gathered to offer solace and support to the bereaved family. Following tradition, the relations and neighbors took the deceased's grieving wife out to feed her and console her. This was but one of many ways that Mizos, notwithstanding Westernization, had retained their old customs.

Armed Central Reserve Police Force (CRPF) sentries guarded the Mizo ministers and high officials. They also moved with armed escorts and bodyguards everywhere, making the situation embarrassing and uncomfortable for them and for the people they represented and served.

Members of the Mizo National Front (MNF) volunteers consisted of young Mizo boys who left their parents and families to join the rebels in their camps in jungles close to international boundaries. In a situation such as that, it was impossible to know who among the Mizos supported the insurgents and who was loyal to the government of India. It was somewhat like Mao Tse-Tung's well-known aphorism that insurgents are like fish that thrive in the sea of the people.

The British administration started the process of consolidating the tribal populated areas of Assam in 1919. Under the Government of India Act of 1919, they declared the Lushai Hills, and some other hill areas of Assam, as *backward tracts*. Under the Government of India Act of 1935, they declared the tribal areas of Assam, including the Lushai Hills district, as *excluded areas.*

In fact, during British rule, and along with the spread of Christianity and English education, Mizos underwent tremendous social and cultural change. The British administration and Western Christian missionaries, however, did not interfere with the social customs of the Mizo tribes despotically ruled by the chieftains.

Along with the spread of literacy, Mizos became politically conscious and demanded the abolition of chieftainship. Their aspiration was not only to remove chieftainship, but also to consolidate the Mizo-inhabited areas scattered all over the adjoining areas. In the process, their aspirations developed into the urge for independence for the land of the Mizos. They demanded greater Mizoram.

Indian political parties at that time hardly had any existence in the Lushai Hills. On April 9, 1946, a political party known as the Mizo Common People's Union came into being. The party demanded abolition of chieftainship, known as the *Tal* system. The party also aspired to consolidate the Mizo-inhabited areas scattered in adjacent states, including those in eastern Bengal, and achieve autonomy for the Mizo people.

In 1947, India became independent and the partition of the nation isolated the Mizo-inhabited areas that fell into East Pakistan. The Mizo-inhabited areas of the Jampui Hills likewise fell into the princely state of Tripura. Thus, the division of the country frustrated the party's objective of consolidating the Mizo-inhabited areas to form a separate Mizo state.

The Mizo Common People's Union changed its name to Mizo Union, and the party contested the general election in 1952 with a manifesto of abolition of chieftainship, consolidation of Mizo-inhabited areas, and autonomy for the Lushai Hills district. Mizo Union, as a political party, won a majority in the election.

The party was successful in abolishing chieftainship. The popular institution of village councils was substituted for chieftainship in the Lushai Hills. Under the Mizoram Administration of Justice Rules 1953, every village having at least sixty houses could constitute an elected village council. Village councils to some extent fulfilled Mizo Union's demand for autonomy. Under the Government of India Act of 1935, the Lushai Hills district was already an excluded area, beyond the administration of the province of Assam. The creation of village councils further isolated the hills from Assam and the rest of India in matters of local administration.

The slash and burn method of rice cultivation, called *jhum* cultivation, practiced on the hilly terrain was inadequate to meet the requirement of rice for the people. Mizos thus suffered from scarcity of food. Many parts of the Lushai Hills were inaccessible by road. After India gained independence, the constituent assembly appointed a committee called the North East Frontier Tribal and Excluded Areas Committee. Assam chief minister Gopinath Bordoloi was the chairman of the committee. The committee recommended incorporation of the Lushai Hills under Article 244(2) of the Sixth Schedule to the Indian constitution. The recommendation of the Bardoloi Committee was accepted. Lushai Hills thus became an autonomous district. The autonomous district council of Lushai Hills came into existence in 1952.

Pawis, Lakhers, and Chakmas were distinct ethnic tribes other than the Mizos. They inhabited the Chimtuipui district on the Kaladan River valley in the southern part of the Lushai Hills. In 1953, regional councils were created under the Sixth Schedule of the Constitution of India for the Pawi, Lakher, and Chakma communities.

Earlier, on the eve of Indian independence, the constituent assembly set up an advisory committee to deal with matters relating to the minorities and the tribes in India. A subcommittee under the above committee was presided over by Assam chief minister Gopinath Bordoloi to advise the constituent assembly about the tribal areas in northeastern India. The Mizo Union Party submitted their old demand in a memorandum to the Bordoloi subcommittee, seeking consolidation of the Mizo-inhabited areas in India's northeast and in Burma.

Concurrently, a new political party called the United Mizo Freedom Organization (UMFO) demanded that the Lushai Hills join Burma.

In 1954, the Mizo Union Party once again came before the State Reorganization Commission (SRC) and raised the claim for consolidating the Mizo-inhabited areas of northeast India. The recommendations of the SRC, however, disappointed the Mizo leaders.

The tribal leaders of northeastern India met in a conference in Aizawal in 1955, and a new political party called the Eastern India Tribal Union (EITU) came into existence. The party demanded a separate state for the tribal people of northeast India. Mizo Union split, and a breakaway faction of the party joined the EITU. The UMFO too joined the EITU.

The tribes of northeast India are so diverse in their ethnicity, languages, and cultures that no such state of the tribes only of northeast India was a feasible proposition. Nonetheless, this sequence of events established the fact that the Mizos, like the Nagas, had been demanding autonomy and statehood throughout the stages of their political history.

During 1958–59, a devastating famine occurred in the Lushai Hills district. The famine was known in Mizo language as *mautam*—bamboo death. The famine occurred due to the flowering of bamboo plants, which multiplied the rat population. Rats destroyed the rice, thereby causing the famine. The famine had a distressing effect on the people of the Lushai Hills district. The Assam government, by dropping bags of rice from private contractors' airplanes, could hardly bring adequate relief to the famine-stricken people of the hills.

Several nongovernmental voluntary organizations (NGOs) came forward to render help to ameliorate the situation. They particularly extended famine relief by carrying bags of rice to remote areas inaccessible by vehicular transport. Earlier in 1955, the Mizo Cultural Society was formed with Pu Laldenga as the secretary. The cultural society was renamed Mautam Front in 1960. The Front united the voluntary famine relief organizations and demanded relief as a matter of human rights, thereby attracting the attention of the political leaders of Assam and India.

In September 1960, the Front changed its name to Mizo National Famine Front (MNFF). The MNFF became a popular organization. Scores of Mizo young men and women joined the Front to carry bags of rice dropped from airplanes to the famine-stricken people in remote areas. Food dropping by private contractors was insufficient, as mentioned earlier. The famine and inadequate response for relief by the Assam government exasperated the Mizos.

In 1960, introduction of the Assam Language Bill in the Assam Legislative Assembly caused further discontent among the Mizo people. When the Assam State Language Bill was passed in 1961, declaring Assamese the only official language all over Assam, including the Lushai Hills district, the MNFF changed its name to Mizo National Front (MNF). The Front demanded secession from India. They took to armed insurgency in their demand for the independence of Mizoram.

Available records indicate that MNF was born as a political party on October 22, 1961, under the leadership of Pu Landenga. The objective of the party was to attain sovereign, independent statehood of greater Mizoram for the Mizo community scattered over areas of northeastern India, East Pakistan, and Burma. Large-scale disturbances broke out from February 28, 1966. The demand reverberated in other tribal areas of northeast India.

The Assam government and the government of India looked upon the insurgency as an uprising aided by bordering foreign powers. It was treason and guerrilla warfare against the government of India. Large-scale repression was perpetrated to curb the violent disorder in the Lushai Hills. The government deployed the Indian Army and Air Force to quell the insurgency and destroy rebels' hideouts.

For the first time in independent India, the Indian Air Force bombarded Indian citizens in Aizawal and other areas in the Mizo hills with incendiary bombs. They also strafed the people from fighter jets. These actions by the army and air force, instead of suppressing the movement, hardened the attitude of the insurgents. The MNF claimed establishment of a parallel underground government with its own army, called the Mizo National Army (MNA). It was now obvious that bordering foreign powers were aiding the insurgents.

In 1967, the government outlawed the MNF. Mizo villages were grouped and regrouped by the roadsides for easy accessibility by army personnel to identify the insurgents suspected of hiding in the villages. The strategy was adopted following the model of the British army's strategy of counterinsurgency operation in Malaysia and the US Army's operations in South Vietnam.

Grouping and regrouping of villages isolated family members from one another, enraging the Mizos generally. It has even been alleged that in some cases of grouping the villages, Mizo parents were grouped in one village and their adolescent children were grouped in another, thereby disrupting and disintegrating families. A general discontent grew up in Mizoram against the Indian Army and Indian administration.

Nonetheless, leaders of the Lushai Hills District Council and the church leaders realized that it would be absurd to support a claim for independence from India. In this context, I recall my meeting with one of the church leaders, Reverend Zairema, who did not support the demand for independence from India.

Finally, the saner segment of the Mizos resolved to claim separation from Assam and statehood within India. A delegation met Prime Minister Indira Gandhi, demanding full-fledged statehood for Mizoram. After talks, a deal was struck. Mizo leaders, other than those of the MNF, conceded to the status of a union territory with a promise to upgrade to a full-fledged state in time. Thus, the Union Territory of Mizoram came into being on January 21, 1972, under the North-East Areas (Reorganization) Act of 1971 and the Government of Union Territories (Amendment) Act of 1971.

However, acts of insurgency and the parallel underground government of the MNF continued. The area had been declared a regulated area under the British-made Inner Line Regulation of 1873. Besides, the Armed Forces (Special Power) Act of 1958 granted extraordinary powers to the security forces engaged in counterinsurgency operations.

After the liberation of East Pakistan and creation of Bangladesh, the situation changed for the MNF insurgents operating from the international border areas. The Mizo Union Party too gained political advantage. The party held the majority in the general election, winning twenty-one out of thirty seats in the newly created legislative assembly. The Indian National Congress Party won six seats, besides three nominated members allied to the Mizo Union Party. There were two members of the parliament, one for the Rajya Sabha and the other for the Lok Sabha. The Mizoram Council of Ministers was headed by Pu Lawrence Chal Chhunga as the first chief minister, to aid and advise the lieutenant governor functioning on behalf of the president of India.

Nonetheless, the underground insurgency continued under the banner of the MNF. The government of India poured in the highest per capita outlay in plan and nonplan sectors for accelerated development of Mizoram. On my invitation E. F. N. Rebairo, chief of the government of India's Town and Country Planning Organization (TCPO), visited Aizawal to assess the needs of town and country planning in Mizoram.

In this context, I recount my subsequent visit to the Planning Commission of India in a delegation from Mizoram. The members in the delegation represented various departments of the Mizoram government with their respective plans and projects for discussion and sanction by the commission. My mission was to get the plans of the local administration department approved by the Planning Commission of India. This necessarily included town and country planning in Mizoram.

As I stepped into the office room of E. F. N. Rebairo, he showed me a large map of Mizoram that hung on the wall in his office room. He told me that Mizoram was always in his mind, and he would help us build Mizoram in whatever way possible.

That evening, he was to catch the nine o'clock train to his hometown in Goa, together with his family. He was going on leave. He invited me to a homely dinner in his place. I was feeling hesitant because my going to his place for dinner would interrupt his wife's last-moment preparations before taking the night train. But he insisted, and I had to join him for dinner.

He brought out a bottle of French wine and said that he had been waiting a long time to open this particular bottle of wine only when a very special friend came to his house for dinner. I had a homely Goanese dinner with Rebairo and his wife. After dinner, I saw them off to New Delhi Railway Station.

When I joined the new government at Aizawal, besides the superintendent's (later deputy commissioner) residence on a hilltop, the Aizawal Club, the superintendent's office complex, the district council office, and the assistant superintendent's bungalow down the hillside, there were only a few government-owned hutments for the subordinate officers and staff of the superintendent. Aizawal, with a population of 228,280, was a fairly congested town dotted with typically constructed private residences built on the hills and terraces, invariably with an open tank to collect rainwater.

The superintendent's residence, now named *Rajniwas*, was built in the early nineteenth century, during the time of British superintendent Lt. Col. J. Shakespeare. S. P. Mukherjee, first lieutenant governor of the Union Territory of Mizoram, was the occupant of Rajniwas. R. M. Agarwal, first chief secretary, occupied the assistant superintendent's bungalow down the slope.

The erstwhile district council's office complex, with some hurried modifications and extensions, was the makeshift secretariat. The superintendent's office continued to be the deputy commissioner's office.

I was allotted a vacant rice storehouse for my residence, just below Rajniwas on the slope of the hill. Thanks to the engineers and architects of the Mizoram Public Works Department (PWD), the storehouse was converted in no time into a habitable bungalow. They made partitions with wooden battens and plywood sheets to create separate rooms and outfitted a kitchen and bathrooms. They also fixed the finest available curtains and electric lamps and furnished the rooms.

Mizoram had heavy concentrations of army and paramilitary forces, including the Border Security Force (BSF), engaged in building roads and bridges to connect the remote areas in the hills and valleys. The Assam Rifles was the oldest security force in Mizoram, and, for that matter, in all tribal areas of India's northeast, raised more than a century before to protect the borders of the region close to Burma (Myanmar). In addition, the rifle-toting CRPF was everywhere in Mizoram, signifying that insurgency and counterinsurgency initiatives hung heavy over the seemingly peaceful milieu of picturesque hills and valleys that were officially ruled by a democratically elected government.

The rhythm of life of the colorful people of the classless, free society of the Mizos, however, did not change due to the presence of the security forces. Neither did the rare and beautiful orchids cease to bloom on high trees, especially in *Phawngpui*—the blue hills area of the Saiha district in the Kolodyne Valley. In spite of the insurgency, Mizoram had its own charm.

Along with the spread of education, Christianity, and a Western lifestyle, old customs like *zawlbuk,* or bachelors' dormitories, died a natural death. In fact, Mizos lived a free life, uninhibited by too many social restrictions. They retained their customs, like the one called *nula rim* or courting the sweetheart. It was a common sight in the evening to find young boys jangling Spanish guitars and singing to their girlfriends at the doorsteps of domestic houses. The original custom was that if the girl conceived during courtship, the boy must marry her or pay a compensation of forty rupees or a *mithun*. Now codified, Mizo Customary Law governed such customs. Nonetheless, nula rim remained common. At the end of the courtship, if the couple decided to marry, the boy had to pay a bride's price. He could pay the bride's price by installments; the principal installment was called *manpui.* Now that Mizos were Christian, weddings were generally held in the church, the bride and the groom being dressed in modern Western attire. Sometimes, the bride was dressed in traditional Mizo costume and the boy in Western clothing. A custom retained was that the bride presented the groom with a rug, called *puandum,* for use as a shroud for wrapping his dead body at his time of burial.

Women had equal status with men, even though men took the leading roles in social and political matters. Educated women were employed in the secretariat and other government offices in all positions. They worked both at home and outside. Mizo women in handwoven, colorful wraparound *pawns* (skirts) ran shops and stores and managed small trades and businesses. As homemakers, they did the household chores, raised children, and also made *zoo*—rice beer.

Mizoram had a classless society. During my tenure, I saw Chief Minister Lawrence Chal Chhunga's wife selling domestic fowls in the open market and the chief minister sharing a drink with an office peon in his residence.

After an elected government took office, the peace-loving people of Mizoram were much relieved. Nonetheless, the old rift between the MNF and the Mizo Union Party that formed government was as wide as before. The birth of Bangladesh substantially reduced foreign support for the rebels. Rebel leader Pu Laldenga hinted at having dialogue with the government of India, but the Indian authorities showed no interest. He put his deputy Pu Biakchhunga in charge of the MNF, and after visiting China, he went to the Arakan Division of Burma and then to Islamabad in Pakistan. Reportedly, the Pakistani authorities reluctantly provided him with asylum but did not offer any military support.

The lieutenant governor of Mizoram, S. P. Mukherjee, was a career civilian. Nonetheless, he worked in close collaboration with an Ati Vishisht Seva Medal (a rare honor) winner, Brigadier General Visva Nath Sharma (later chief of the army staff), who was then general officer commander-in-chief of the eastern command. They did quite a lot of welfare activities in Mizoram in their effort to convince the Mizos that they were genuinely interested in ameliorating the grievances of the Mizos and in bringing peace and development to the hilly terrain.

On the one hand, the civil administration and the army's mission was to cease hostilities between the civil government and the underground Mizo National Front (MNF). On the other hand, their policy was to undertake many welfare and developmental activities for the benefit of the people of Mizoram, to inculcate the Mizo people with the conviction that the government of India and the Indian Army were genuinely interested in the welfare of the Mizos.

To what extent their approach was appreciated by the rebel Mizos at that time is another question. A series of political dialogues between the elected leaders of the Mizo Union, the Indian National Congress Party, and the government of India took place. Besides the offer of amnesty, the MNF rebels upon surrender would receive lucrative dividends of cash and rehabilitation facilities within Mizo civil society. At least one important leader of the MNF surrendered.

Nonetheless, suddenly, the MNF issued a quit Mizoram notice, asking all foreigners (meaning non-Mizos) to quit Mizoram or face death.

On March 10, 1974, MNF insurgents ambushed S. P. Mukhrjee while he was traveling in a thoroughly secured motorcade on Silchar-Aizawal Road. He sustained an injury to his thigh. Surgeons in the army hospital in Aizawal extracted the bullet. Mukherjee left for his home in Calcutta and from there resigned from his position.

S. K. Chhibber succeeded Mukherjee as the lieutenant governor of Mizoram. While S. P. Mukherjee came from a traditional Bengali family and was a career civilian officer, Bakshi S. K. Chhibber was of Mohyal heritage from Punjab and came from an army background. He adopted an altogether different strategy for Mizoram.

I recall a very interesting event soon after Mr. Chhibber took office. *Chapchar Kut*, or the spring festival, is an important festival of the Mizos. Traditionally, in Aizawal, the festival was publicly celebrated in the Assam Rifles' parade ground. The celebration was conducted with cultural programs and feasts.

The Assam Rifles' parade ground, in the heart of the town, was like a stadium with graduated rows of seats. Besides the local crowd, ministers, and all government officials and their wives, including the lieutenant governor and his wife, attended the festival on invitation.

In that particular year, Pu Harangaia, then president of the ruling Mizo Union Party, presided over the ceremonies. Local artists performed colorful dances and music. At the end of the cultural show, the president of the function asked my wife, Reba, to distribute the prizes to the best performers. Reba was popular among the Mizos because she not only learned the Mizo language, but she also set up a loin loom at home and wove a Mizo puan.

Nonetheless, it was totally out of protocol to ask a secretary's wife to distribute prizes when the LG and his wife were present. Reba, naturally, felt very embarrassed and asked the president of the function to invite Mrs. Chhibber to distribute the prizes. But the president stuck to his point. He said that Reba was the only non-Mizo woman present who had learned the Mizo language and even sported a Mizo puan that she herself had woven. He added that as a token of appreciation, he was inviting her to distribute the prizes.

On the president's insistence, Reba had to distribute the prizes in the presence of Mr. and Mrs. Chhibber. The incident displayed the frankness and simplicity of the Mizos, in sharp contrast to the sophisticated intelligentsia of the Indian plains.

* * *

January 12, 1975, was a Sunday. In the morning, Chief Secretary R. M. Agrawal, Inspector General of the Police, G. S. Arya, and Deputy Inspector General of Police L. B. Sewa were in my place. It was a casual get-together. Mr. Arya was a Sanskrit scholar during his student life. We were enjoying his recitation from memory of Sanskrit verses of the fifth-century poet Kalidasa's lyrical poem "*Meghaduutam*—the Cloud Messenger." Although most others at the soiree hardly had much knowledge of Sanskrit prosody, everyone appreciated his rhythmic recitation.

In the course of conversation, *Paus Sankranti*, also known as *Maker Sankranti* or *Uttarayan*, a Hindu festival celebrated on the last day of Bengali month *Paush*, came up. Traditionally, during Paus Sankranti in most Hindu households, various dishes and sweets are made, and relations and friends are invited to share and to celebrate the day. Paus Sankranti fell on the following day.

L. B. Sewa and his wife were vastly interested in celebrating the occasion, but it was difficult to do so in a place like Aizawal. Sewa assured the womenfolk that he would send an officer to the nearby Bengali town, Silchar, to get coconut and other items needed for making sweets. He asked them to make a list of things they would like to have. It was decided that the celebration would be at my place, and Reba and Mrs. Sewa would play the hostesses. The Sunday morning get-together ended happily with a homely lunch. We all expected to meet the next evening to celebrate.

Next morning, January 13, 1975, everyone as usual attended his or her respective offices. From my secretariat office, I went to the improvised office suite of Pu Nikhuma, the minister in charge of the local administration department. The minister's office was located on top of a small hillock overlooking the road below. Both of us were to leave for Delhi the next week on government business. We were discussing development projects for the towns and villages of Mizoram that we prepared to place before the Planning Commission of India.

All of a sudden, booms of gunfire resonated. I went to the open window. Looking through it, I saw that CRPF men deployed on security duty were blowing whistles and hurrying to take positions. I sensed that something had gone wrong somewhere. As I hastened to get out of the minister's room, I found the chief secretary trying to run. Everyone was following him. He was shouting to the sentries *"Gher dalo! Gher dalo!"* in Hindi, meaning "Cordon off the area!"

I followed the chief secretary running toward the inspector general's office nearby. As we entered the office, we were aghast to find the inspector general, his deputy, and a superintendent of police, K. Panchapagesan, dead on their chairs, their heads tilting down, the carpet below soaked in blood.

Later we heard from eyewitnesses to the ghastly incident that four MNF men, all in police uniforms, approached the gate, driving a government jeep with a Mizoram government number plate. The sentries opened the gate, believing they were letting in four police officers on duty. The insurgents entered the inspector general's room where the other two were in conference with him. The infiltrators fired their handguns at point-blank range. In the frightfully confused situation, the assassins left by the same jeep in which they had come.

Paus Sankranti thus turned into a most miserable day.

Later, in the course of the investigation, it came to light that MNA Captain Lalhleia and three others were the assassins. A locally recruited young typist in the inspector general's office, a woman, was one of the suspects involved in the plot, and the assassins used a government jeep stolen from the fleet belonging to the directorate of the local administration department.

Retired Brigadier of the Indian Army G. S. Randhawa succeeded G. S. Arya as the inspector general of police. Surendra Nath of the Indian Police Service replaced Chief Secretary R. M. Agrawal of the Indian Administrative Service. (Much later, Surendra Nath took over as governor of Punjab and died in an air crash.) Brigadier Randhawa hand-picked police officers and officers from paramilitary organizations to set up his team.

Lt. Governor S. K. Chhibber and Inspector General G. S. Randhawa introduced a new strategy of counterinsurgency operations. Chief Secretary Surendra Nath was very adept in collecting intelligence from within and beyond the office. The policy adopted was to send surrendered MNF activists with arms to MNF and MNA hideouts in the jungles close to international boundaries. They could easily masquerade as members of the MNF and MNA and eventually assault the rebels or plant explosives in their camps. These pseudorebels slew a substantial number of insurgents, thereby breaking their morale.

They also informed the security forces of the exact locations and other information about the camps of insurgents in the jungles, enabling the security forces to launch attacks of their own. This method of operation was crowned with tremendous success. The insurgents were utterly flustered.

Disillusioned MNF emissaries now approached Chief Minister Pu Chal Chhunga for negotiation. Two large groups of the rebels surrendered and ceremonially laid down their arms. Ministers and civilian officials, in addition to army officials, attended the surrender ceremonies held in the brigade headquarters in Zemabok.

Since 1961, Pu Lalthanhawla had been the secretary of the underground MNF. He was arrested and put into Silchar jail. After his release in 1967, he joined the Indian National Congress Party. In 1973, he was elected president of the Mizoram Pradesh Congress Committee (MPCC). A political process was thus reintroduced to bring the MNF over ground.

Mrs. Purabi Mukherjee, secretary of the West Bengal Congress Committee, visited Aizawal to consolidate the organizational structure of the Congress Party in Mizoram. In 1974, the Mizo Union merged with Congress. The merger, in a way, crushed the backbone of the MNF.

In 1975, two large groups of Mizo insurgents ceremonially surrendered their arms. MNF leader Pu Laldenga met in Geneva with a representative of the research and analysis wing of the government of India of a reconciliation. However, the meeting was abortive. In the same year, Pu Laldenga visited Delhi with no effect. Thus, the counterinsurgency efforts advanced with a two-pronged approach—political and martial.

* * *

On a quiet evening in Aizawal in 1974, a CRPF lance commander who was on surveillance duty around my residence knocked at the door and gave me a business card, informing me that a visitor wanted to meet me. I looked at the card and found that it was for an Indian Army retired brigadier, Thenphunga Sailo, decorated with the AVSM (Distinguished Service Medal). According to my intelligence reports, Brigadier Sailo's son was an active member of the MNF and was in an MNF camp in the jungles on the border.

That evening, Brigadier Sailo told me that after his retirement from the Indian Army, he had a premonition that he must go back to his homeland, Mizoram, and work to relieve the sufferings of the people. He thought it proper to call on all important public leaders and government officials and introduce himself to them. He said that he came to Mizoram to seek everyone's help and cooperation in his mission to establish peace.

He sounded very unusual and somewhat enigmatic. I wondered what kind of help and cooperation he expected from government officials. He said that, as a soldier, he knew the mind-set of the security forces, and as a Mizo, he knew the woes and aspirations of the people. He appeared a shrewd man with a very modest bearing.

Within a few days, Brigadier Sailo launched his Human Rights Committee, fighting for the cause of Mizo civilians caught between insurgency and counterinsurgency. Two years later, at the initiative of the rival political parties, and ostensibly based on an intelligence report, the brigadier was detained under the infamous Maintenance of Internal Security Act (MISA), although for a short period.

As the law secretary of Mizoram, I was a member of the MISA Review Board, the other two members being the chief minister and the chief secretary of Mizoram. The decision to detain the retired brigadier was on the basis of majority decision.

In 1977, Brigadier Thenphunga Sailo became chief minister of Mizoram after winning the general election, and took over on June 2, 1978. His ministry lasted for a short period, to November 1978. After a spell of president's rule, Brigadier Sailo again won the election and took over as the chief minister. This time he was in power from May 8, 1979, to May 4, 1984. Mizoram Congress President Pu Lalthanhawla was the opposition leader.

Meanwhile, several political changes took place in Mizoram. The Mizo Union Party merged with the Indian National Congress Party. In 1984, positions changed when Congress swept a thumping majority in the election; Pu Lalthanhawla became chief minister and Brigadier Sailo opposition leader.

In February 1985, Pu Laldenga met Prime Minister Rajiv Gandhi. Meanwhile, MNF gave up its insurgency and surfaced as a political party. On June 30, 1986, the Mizoram Accord was signed between Pu Laldenga, Union Home Secretary R. D. Pradhan, and Mizoram Chief Secretary Lalkhama. Mizoram became a full-fledged state.

The MNF as a political party led by Pu Laldenga won the majority votes in the next election. Pu Lalthanhawla relinquished his position in favor of MNF leader Pu Laldenga, but defections toppled Laldenga from the position. He was not in good health and passed away in 1990. Pu Zoramthanga, earlier secretary of the MNF, took over as the chief minister of Mizoram from December 1990 until December 1998.

Brigadier Thenphunga Sailo was awarded the National Award of Padma Shree for social work. Congress won a majority in the next election, and Pu Lalthanhawla again took over as the chief minister from 2008.

After 1976, I was no longer in Mizoram, but I kept track of events and developments as one of the pioneer officials in shaping the infrastructure of the government in the insurgency-stricken, beautiful, hilly terrain at the southeastern end of India. I had many friends in Mizoram I never forgot.